"These guys don't seem to have missed a thing when it comes to how to make a digital movie for peanuts. It's a helpful and funny guide for beginners and professionals alike."
—**Jonathan Demme**
Academy-Award, winning director of
Silence of the Lambs

"Gaspard and Newton are the undisputed champs of straight talk when it comes to moviemaking. With their easy-to-digest brand of humor and common sense, they once again cut through the jargon and empower visual artists by showing them how to think outside the box."
—**Timothy Rhys**
Publisher and Editor
MovieMaker Magazine &
MovieMaker.com

"Strong, smart, funny advice for independent filmmakers from people who've gone through the process more than once - and lived to tell about it."
—**Peter Tolan**
Screenwriter
The Larry Sanders Show
Analyze This
My Fellow Americans

"A collection of informal yarns from the authors, the book is a humorous approach to ultra-low-budget, guerilla digital moviemaking... *Digital Filmmaking 101* will certainly give a taste of what is in store for those who choose low-budget moviemaking as a career."
—**Glen Berry**
Moviemaker Magazine

MICHAEL WIESE PRODUCTIONS
www mwp com

Since 1981, Michael Wiese Productions has been dedicated to providing novice and seasoned filmmakers with vital information on all aspects of filmmaking and videomaking. We have published more than 50 books, used in over 500 film schools worldwide.

Our authors are successful industry professionals — they believe that the more knowledge and experience they share with others, the more high-quality films will be made. That's why they spend countless hours writing about the hard stuff: budgeting, financing, directing, marketing, and distribution. Many of our authors, including myself, are often invited to conduct filmmaking seminars around the world.

We truly hope that our publications, seminars, and consulting services will empower you to create enduring films that will last for generations to come.

We're here to help. Let us hear from you.

Sincerely,

Michael Wiese
Publisher, Filmmaker

DIGITAL

FILMMAKING 101

DALE NEWTON & JOHN GASPARD

Published by Michael Wiese Productions
11288 Ventura Blvd., Suite 621
Sutdio City, CA 91604
tel. (818) 379-8799
fax (818) 986-3408
mw@mwp.com
www.mwp.com

Cover Design: Alexander Arkadin
Book Layout: Gina Mansfield

Printed by McNaughton & Gunn, Inc., Saline, Michigan
Manufactured in the United States of America

ISBN 0-941188-33-7

Library of Congress Cataloging-in-Publication Data

Newton and Gaspard, Dale and John
    Digital filmmaking 101 / by Dale Newton and John Gaspard
        p. cm.
        ISBN 0-941188-33-7
        1. Motion pictures--Production and direction. 2. Digital video.
        3. Low budget motion pictures. I. Gaspard, John, 1958- II. Title.

PN1995.9.P7 N47 2001
791.43'0232--dc21   00-068563
                                                                CIP

TABLE OF CONTENTS

ACKNOWLEDGEMENTS

We always knew that filmmaking was a collaborative art, but we had no idea that a crowd was required to write a book as well. There are many people to thank for their help and support in putting this book together:

Randy Adamsick (Minnesota Film Board), Robin Alper, Bruce V. Assardo, James Babcock, Soodabeh Babcock, Jeff Baustert, William Bayer, Tom Belanger, Daniel J. Berks, Jill Black, Michael Brillantes, Jeff Butcher, Julie Chang, Ruth Charny, Al Cohn, Daniel Curran, Wade Danielson, Michael de Avila, Victoria Eide, Heidi Ehalt, Beth Gilleland, Richard Glatzer, Trent Harris, Walter Hart, Julie Hartley, Jess Hill, Jay Horan, Jennifer Howe, Rachel Katz, Janusz Kaminski, Sean King, Ted King, Seth Kittay, Marc Kramer, Michael Paul Levin, Tom Lieberman, Steve Lustgarten, Jane Minton (IFP North), Steve Molton, Peter Moore, Eric Mueller, Nicola Muoio, Liza Nagle, Jerry Nelson, Roger Nygard, Andrew Peterson, Daniel Polsfuss, Dave Reynolds, Tim Rhys (*MovieMaker* magazine), Deb Rose, Richard Seres, Donna Smith, Nelle Stokes, Eric Tretbar, Mark Tusk, Thomas Vitale, Cynthia Widlund, and Amelia Oriani (for her excellent poofreading).

Special thanks to Kathy, Jenny, and Holly for their infinite patience, and to all the actors and crews who have made our movies possible.

INTRODUCTION

Now you've done it.

You opened this book because you want to make a movie... if only you knew how... if only you had enough money. Well, your life just got complicated — because we wrote this book to tell you how to make your feature-length movie a reality and how to do it on an ultra-low budget. You hold in your hands a guide to making your dream come true. Now what do you do?

It's up to you, but let us tell you about the path we chose that led us to writing this book about digital filmmaking. It might help you decide.

An earlier edition of this book, *Persistence of Vision: An Impractical Guide to Producing a Feature Film for Under $30,000*, passed along everything

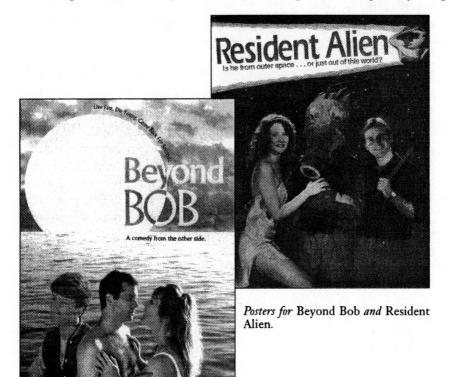

Posters for Beyond Bob *and* Resident Alien.

we learned from doing two independent low-budget feature films. The films were *Resident Alien* and *Beyond Bob*, a science-fiction comedy romance and a romantic-comedy ghost story, respectively. Of course, there were trials and tribulations in making them, as well as some the best fun we've had in our lives. We love film. We're products of the home-movie boom in the 1950s. Well, actually by-products because, in the true spirit of independent filmmakers, we each started filmmaking using 8mm cameras that were cast-offs from our uncles. There's nothing like the excitement of looking at the film after it comes back from the processor or splicing together a scene out of your shots or realizing you're part of a 100-year chain linking back to the Lumière brothers' first movies. Like most filmmakers, between films we also tried out film's electronic cousin, videotape. We even found jobs working with video. But our first love was always film.

It's a measure of the magnitude of the digital revolution that when we were planning to embark on *Grown Men*, our third feature-length movie together, it quickly became clear that we would shoot it on digital video. We also realized that we might never shoot film again, at least not when we were putting up the money.

There have been signs for a half dozen years that a revolution was in the making. The advent of low-cost nonlinear editing systems and inexpensive, high-quality formats like Hi8 and S-VHS changed how filmmakers edited and how documentary filmmakers shot. When digital video formats entered the arena with broadcast quality and price tags that were within the reach of filmmakers' personal finances, the revolution burst onto the streets. The movie products from these new tools have proven good enough to be transferred to film stock for theater presentation, and good enough for cable television and home video, which are the most common distribution routes for low-budget, independent movies.

Now, far be it from us to suggest that film is dead. It's a well-loved format that is deeply embedded in our perceptions of what cinematic storytelling is, and it's survived virtually unchanged for over 100 years. As moviegoers, when we see the look of a film, we've been visually trained to settle back and fall into the story being told. Film's not going away anytime soon, but on the other hand, independent filmmaking won't ever be the same again. Digital filmmaking further loosens the budget shackles on movie production, and lightweight, moderately priced, flexible equipment creates new opportunities for those of us working on the fringes of the movie world.

Also, the Internet and the continual invention of new ways to communicate with it promise to revolutionize the second half of the moviemaking process — getting your movie to an audience. The gates of distribution in theaters have long been guarded by the large corporations that run the Hollywood movie machine. Only a small percentage of little movies were ever granted permission to pass into distribution. Using the Internet, independent filmmakers — such as the makers of *The Blair Witch Project* — are already starting to find their audiences without Hollywood's help and may soon be able to deliver their movies directly to their audiences.

All of these changes have turned the two of us into digital filmmakers. The quality of the digital format and its low cost fit our possible audiences and our budgets. And this book tells you everything we've learned about making digital movies. As we write this book, digital filmmaking means shooting on one of the digital videotape formats, but video-disk camcorders are already on the horizon, and undoubtedly, other developments won't be far behind. What we won't be talking about are shooting and editing on motion-picture film. So if that's your plan, get a copy of the earlier film edition of this book. If a digital movie is your goal, don't worry that you're missing good stuff from that earlier book. In this digital edition, we've kept the parts that are universal to movie storytelling and the parts that tell you how to turn the chaos of a movie production into an actual finished movie. Of course, we've also included fresh examples, updated information, and new insights on digital movie production.

The one disadvantage to the fast pace of change in digital production is that this book started to be outdated the moment it was published. The technology is changing faster than software developers change Porsches. Then again, every book on digital filmmaking is going to be behind the times before it reaches the bookstore shelf. But if you're an independent moviemaker (the polite way of saying "mostly impoverished moviemaker"), that's not all bad. Outdated technology is cheap, and it still does the job.

And, even though the technology changes, the techniques for doing a professional-looking movie on a shoe-string budget apply whether you're making it on digital videotape, a video disk, or the latest and greatest technology.

These low-budget production techniques served us well. We used them when we shot our first two feature films in four weekends each. *Resident Alien* was described as "the best low-budget independent project ever to come out of the area" by a big-city newspaper critic in Minnesota, which was high praise given the large number of independent films done in the metropolitan area where we live. *Beyond Bob* received a bronze award at an international film festival up against other films with budgets close to a million dollars. Studio executives and distributors who saw the films guessed that they had casts from New York or Los Angeles and had budgets in the million-dollar range. In truth, the casts were all from the talented pool of actors in our area, and our budgets were 30 times less.

Our techniques put all of your tiny budget up on the screen where it helps to tell your story. With our first digital feature, *Grown Men*, we used these methods along with new digital techniques that saved us a bundle in production and postproduction costs, so we could dedicate our efforts to getting a great story on the screen, rather than raising funds and searching for deals on lab work. If digital video had been available, we could have shot a half dozen feature films for the cost of our first two 16mm movies. Because independent movies are financially risky, it's important to keep your budget low to reduce the financial stress of the production, letting you spend more time doing what you love — making your movie.

What this book won't do is spend a lot of time on movie history and theory. There are lots of good books on those topics; some are listed in our bibliography. We're here to help you get your project finished, so expect nuts-and-bolts, down-to-brass-tacks, practical advice on how to take your movie from a nagging idea in a corner of your brain to the glowing screen in front of your audience. The new digital-video tools can do great things, but owning a hammer doesn't mean you know how to build a house. We'll tell you what you need to know in order to put these new tools to use creating a professional-quality production. But that doesn't mean it will be easy. Some people will tell you that making your own movie is impossible. We've heard that, and so have lots of other moviemakers. What makes independent movies happen is a fierce persistence of vision — a complete unwillingness to give up even when all signs and reason say you should. Be sure you have a bunch of this persistence stored up in your closet, in the attic, and under the basement steps before you start. You'll need all you can get your hands on.

Besides a little bit of money and a lot of persistence, you'll need a strong vision and some creativity. If you've got these ingredients, we'll be happy to be your guides in putting them all together into a movie. We realize that the readers of this book may have a wide range of experience and knowledge, so we've tried to balance our presentation so we don't talk down to people who've done a lot of film and video work and so we don't confuse those just starting out. Undoubtedly, we'll fail sometimes. So if you find yourself patronized or perplexed, please accept our apologies in advance.

Well, have you decided to take a shot at that dream of making your own feature-length movie? If so, hop on board for a wild ride.

THE DREAM
(Taking a Leap)

Everything we're about to tell you is wrong.

Really? Well, no. Not really.

However, a healthy dose of skepticism will help sustain you on the long journey that lies before you — making an ultra-low-budget movie requires breaking lots of rules. Sometimes all the rules. Even the rules we've laid out in this book.

However, if nothing else, the rules in this book can act as a good starting point and touchstone for you as you make your way through the pre-production, production and postproduction processes.

And how, you impatiently ask, do you start on this amazing, frustrating, and often exhilarating journey?

With a dream.

🎥🎥🎥

They used to call moviemaking a "silver addiction," referring to the old days when silver salts were used to create film stocks. Although you won't need film stock to make your movie, you will need that addiction. And it better be a strong one. It has to be, because often the dream of making your movie is all that carries you over the long days/weeks/months/years that it takes to go from idea to finished product. Since you're reading this book, odds are that you already have at least the beginnings of a dream. You have:

• A story you're dying to tell, or
• A character you'd love to see developed, or
• An idea or issue you're burning to explore.

The next step is to look at that dream with a cold, realistic eye: Is it a reasonable dream? Can you produce it with few resources? While there's certainly no absolute answer, there is a ballpark that you should at least try to play in if you're going to work at this level.

For example, is your story idea a historical costume drama, involving large crowd scenes and multiple, historically accurate locations? If so, then keep dreaming.

Or is your idea a small, contemporary dramatic (or romance, comedy, suspense, horror, farce, mystery, melodrama, science fiction) story that can take place in just a few locations with a handful of characters? Great. Now you're in the ballpark.

Once you've defined your dream, you're ready to take the next important step. Start telling people that you're going to make a movie. It doesn't matter where. At a cocktail party, after church, on a bus, or at the office water cooler. It also doesn't really matter who. Your parents. Your significant other. Your coworkers. Your dentist.

It only matters that you say it. And that you say it out loud: "I'm going to make a movie."

Why do you have to say it, say it out loud, and say it to someone else? Two reasons: The first is that, since this is a statement most people aren't used to hearing, you're bound to get some interested responses. Responses along the lines of, "What's it about?" "Where are you getting the money?" and "Great. Can I help?"

While all these questions are valid and important, it's the last one that you're really listening for, because once you've got the dream, the next step is to get other people excited about it. You need other people excited about your project because there's virtually no way you can do it alone.

The second reason you should tell people that you're going to make a movie — saying it often and out loud — is because it begins to make your dream real. Just saying it isn't going to make it happen, of course — but it does put your pride on the line. You're more likely to push forward if your friends start asking, "Whatever happened to that movie thing you were going to do?"

2

It also makes the idea more concrete, and it raises other questions that you have to start thinking about. When will you start shooting? Where will the equipment come from? How will you fund it? Who's going to be in it? When is it going to be done? How are you going to edit it? The following chapters will provide you with the means to answer those questions. But nobody's going to ask the questions until you make the statement. Out loud.

"I'm going to make a movie." (Congratulations. You've just taken the first step.)

🎥🎥🎥

Making a feature-length movie, even for someone who's done it before, is a daunting process. For someone who's never done it, it can be downright overwhelming. Take solace that it isn't one long process, but instead a series of discrete and attainable steps. Each step leads logically to the next.

You also don't have to navigate these unfamiliar waters without charts. Others have done this before, or at least something similar. The model for making a digital feature is very similar to making any type of feature-length project, whether it's a low-budget Roger Corman-style masterpiece or a mega-mondo-budget Hollywood spectacular.

Reading this book and others on writing, producing and selling movies can provide valuable background. Taking classes can be good preparation for specific parts of the process. Working on other people's movies (regardless of the budget) can be an education in itself on what to do and what not to do.

One of the best sources of information we've found is people who have made a feature before, whether on film or digitally. They're generally more than happy to talk to you, even if some of the film folks are still a bit skeptical about the digital revolution. They'll mention a few pitfalls to watch out for, recommend some cast and crew people, suggest who else to turn to for free advice, and maybe even volunteer to help. At least, that's been our experience.

If there's one thing we learned, it's that dreams are contagious, and you should try to infect as many people as possible with yours. You have a

3

long, challenging journey ahead, and you'll need their help if you're going to start — not to mention finish — a digital movie.

Regardless of the length of your journey, there is a destination — the moment when the finished movie is projected in front of an audience. And at this moment you can see the fruits of your labor — your dream — come to life. The audience laughs. They cry. They gasp. They applaud.

And your dream has become reality.

THE SCRIPT
(IF IT AIN'T ON THE PAGE...)

Analogy #1: Just as the basement is the foundation for your house, so too is the screenplay the foundation for your movie. A strong foundation makes for a stronger house and a stronger movie. However, unlike your basement, you can't fill up your screenplay with extra stuff you're not using. There's just no room in your digital movie, in your shooting schedule, or in your budget.

Analogy #2: Your screenplay is your roadmap. It tells you, your cast, and your crew where you're headed and how you're going to get there. Without a good roadmap, you might make it to your destination but not before wasting a lot of time and money — two commodities that are in short supply.

A dramatic feature-length movie is only as good as its screenplay and rarely any better. While this is certainly common knowledge, you'd be amazed at the number of filmmakers (and we're not just pointing fingers at Hollywood here; independents are just as guilty) who dive into production with a screenplay that simply isn't ready to be shot.

Therefore, be prepared to spend a lot of time on your script. It's a difficult process, but you'll be happier about it in the end, and the results will show in your finished production. Making a good movie out of a bad script is not unlike the proverbial sow's ear and silk purse — it's simply not going to happen.

The basics
While this chapter isn't intended to provide an exhaustive course in screenwriting, it will give you the basics you need to construct a script that can be shot on your ultra-low budget.

(For further reading on the finer points of screenwriting, along with sample formats, please refer to the appendix. There are a number of excellent books out there on screenwriting; however, notable screenwriter and author William Goldman offers this sage warning about everyone's advice on writing a successful movie: "Nobody knows anything." For every absolute rule someone states about screenwriting, you can always find several examples of successful features that have broken that rule. The appendix also lists where you can buy or download screenplays of existing movies, which can be an excellent educational resource.)

Story

As an independent moviemaker with no budget to speak of, story is your friend, your biggest asset, and your secret weapon. The reality of making movies on this scale is that you're not going to impress a distributor or festival planner with your big-name stars (unless you're married to one), your exotic locations (unless you live in one), or your stunning crowd scenes (unless you have a stunningly large family). You simply don't have the bucks for them.

That leaves you with story, the one place where you can compete head-to-head with the Hollywood big kids. You can have a better story in your $8,000 digital feature than there is in some $100-million box-office bomb starring the latest rock star/actor in a remake of some baby-boomer Saturday-morning cartoon.

Story is your best-selling point. If the story is great, shortcomings in lighting, videography, sound, set design, and so on will be forgotten as the viewer is drawn into the story. Consider the early films of D. W. Griffith or Charlie Chaplin: no sound, only natural light, black and white, static camera shots. Yet they are still powerful, entertaining, and remembered today because they presented engaging characters in interesting stories.

The three-act structure

We're big fans of the three-act structure:

Act 1 (otherwise known as The Beginning), in which you establish motivation and set the scene, which leads to a catharsis, crisis, or conflict that requires the main character to make a decision about what he or she wants to do.

Act 2 (also known as The Middle), in which the main character faces challenges and obstacles to carrying out that decision, leading to a "scene of recognition" in which the character reaffirms his or her commitment to the decision.

Act 3 (you guessed it, The End), in which the story reaches its climax, and the main character succeeds or fails to achieve what he or she wants.

Of course, this isn't the only way to structure a screenplay, but it's tried and true, and 90% of the most successful and well-loved movies follow this pattern.

There are, of course, exceptions to the rule. Quentin Tarantino took the classic three-act structure and turned it on its ear with *Pulp Fiction*, which contained a three-act structure, but ordered them as Act One, Act Three, and then Act Two. Even a classic dramatist like Harold Pinter has put a spin on the three acts, structuring his film *Betrayal* (and the play of the same name) so that we see the story's conclusion at the beginning of the film and then work our way backwards so that the beginning of the story occurs at the end. If you have a bold, innovative, stunning new screenplay structure in mind, go for it. It just might be your ticket. If you haven't been struck by a bolt of inspired genius, stick to the proven, audience-tested structure.

Writing for a tiny budget
While the traditional three-act screenplay structure can apply to any movie, there are special considerations that you must be aware of in crafting your ultra-low-budget feature script. And we do recommend writing the script specifically for a tiny budget. It's easier to make your limitations invisible if you aren't imposing them on a bigger-budget story.

With that in mind, here are some of the building blocks for your screenplay:

Creating unique characters
Any respectable movie needs interesting characters that the audience cares about. This is doubly important to your project. Unique, unusual, remarkably true-to-life, or endearing characters will help you attract an audience, which in turn will help attract attention to your movie. But of more immediate concern, juicy roles will draw the high-quality actors you need. This is a case of one strong asset attracting another. Actors live by their resumes, so the better the role, better the actors will be who want to audition for the role.

Along this same line of thought, give good lines to all the characters, even the waitress in the walk-on role. Speaking parts are the currency

7

of an actor's resume. Since you can't pay them much — or any — money, give them something good for their reel.

The late Jim Varney did a whole series of silly *Ernest* movies on the strength of a character he created in a popular car ad. Jeff Goldblum virtually launched his career with "I forgot my mantra" in Woody Allen's *Annie Hall*. Even Richard Dreyfuss had a memorable line in his early, minuscule appearance in *The Graduate*. ("You want me to call the cops? I'll call the cops.")

Bottom line: Give all your actors something interesting to play.

Mystery
A bit of uncertainty in the plot line can really help propel your story forward. Don't tell the audience everything at once. Let the story be revealed. Make the audience want to see the next scene to learn the truth about a character, to see how a scheme unfolds, to find out what that crazy person was building. A little mystery can go a long way towards preventing your story from slowing down. But — and this is a big but — make sure the answers are worth the wait.

Twists
Keep your audience engaged in the story by occasionally turning the plot direction on its ear. (The heroine in peril was actually married to the villain! The priest is the blackmailer! The dog can talk!) If they are concentrating on the story, they're less likely to notice that you couldn't afford a room at the Ritz for that romantic scene and are instead shooting in your parents' attractively paneled basement rec room.

Dramatic tension
Don't forget to create conflict between your characters. Who are you most likely to watch, the couple in the corner quietly holding hands or the ones flailing their arms and shouting at each other? Make use of that rarely-admitted-to human instinct, voyeurism. This is an easy point to forget, but the fact is that if your characters agree on everything, you don't have much dramatic tension. And without dramatic tension, you won't have much of a movie.

Building drama or comedy
Many of the strongest movies set the stage for their climax in the first

act, sometimes even in the first moment of the story. Usually this means that some essential characteristic or life experience of the protagonist is presented early in the story. This aspect of the person then becomes a pivotal challenge for the character as the story's climax unfolds, causing the story's ending to resonate back to the beginning. An example is *The Truman Show*. In the early scenes of the film, Jim Carrey's character can't leave his island home for a job assignment because he has a lifelong fear of water after the childhood experience of seeing his father fall from a boat in a storm and drown. At the story's climax, the character must face his deepest fear and sail a boat in a raging storm in order to achieve his goal. Way cool; do this if you can (and we don't mean sail a boat in a storm).

Testing your story

Test your stories on your friends — the ones who will tell you if it stinks. If you don't have any friends who are that honest, find people you don't know well. If your story wins them over, it's good. The point is, make sure you have a tale that people want to be told, because at its heart, moviemaking is storytelling.

You can also get actors to read your script in a public reading — basically readers' theater — or join a writing group, and read it to other writers. You'll get feedback, and even better, it will turn your wince detectors up to full sensitivity. It's like having a new friend over to your house for the first time. You find yourself cringing at every bit of peeling paint and every stain in the carpet as you look at your house through another person's eyes. Reading the script aloud will do the same for your story. You'll know where it drags or where it becomes implausible because you'll wince. Just keep track of where it happens, and go back and fix those spots.

🎦🎦🎦

These are the things you need for a successful screenplay. Next we've got the list of things you can't have if you want to finish your ultra-low-budget movie.

Cash constraints can be gratifying to overcome, and we think they bring out the true creativity of a production team. If you can just throw money at a problem, you tend to take the first solution that comes to mind, usually the one that's been done a dozen times before. If you have to come up with a novel solution to your problem, you've usually added a new creative element to your movie. A tight budget can squeeze those creative juices out of you. So, here's a list of constraints to inspire your best ideas.

Number of characters
Limit yourself to three main characters, or, barring that, don't include more than three main characters altogether in a scene or have them all interacting at the same time. For instance, if you have a party scene, break up the conversations into subgroups of three or less. Why? You don't have time or money to do more.

Equipment rentals mean every minute you spend in production is like having dollars slip through a hole in your pocket. Your cast and crew will be giving up real pay to essentially work free for you, and inevitably their neglected spouse, a bill-wielding landlord, an unexpected illness, their waning interest, or real work will cause them to leave your production. The longer you shoot, the more likely you'll lose key people. And the number of main characters in your movie directly affects your production time and production costs.

Here's how it works out. Your fiscal and temporal resources (money and time) will only allow for a three-to-one (3:1) or four-to-one (4:1) shooting ratio. A 3:1 ratio means you can shoot only three minutes of tape for each finished minute of your movie.

For example, let's say you're shooting the climactic scene where Rhett walks out on Scarlett (apparently you've ignored everything we've said about historical costume dramas and crowd scenes). With a 3:1 shooting ratio, this gives you just enough tape to shoot the scene in a master shot showing both of them, and then to shoot two other takes with different camera setups for a close-up of Rhett and a close-up of Scarlett. That's 3:1, with no margin for error.

If Rhett said "Give a hoot" instead of "Give a damn" in the master shot, you can do a second take — which would move you up to a 4:1 ratio for this scene and force you to shoot some later scene in a 2:1 ratio to compensate. Or you can make sure that you get him to say "Give a damn"

10

in the close-up. Most of the time you'll try to work in a 3:1 or 2:1 ratio to save time and tape for that tricky shot that's going to need a 5:1 ratio. So what's shooting ratio got to do with the number of main characters in your script? Let's add Ashley to the scene with Rhett and Scarlett, and you'll quickly realize that you're into a 4:1 shooting ratio — a master shot and three close-ups (Ashley, Rhett, Scarlett). And that assumes there are no mistakes that require a retake. The more group scenes like this in your script, the more your expenses for videotape and equipment will rise and the more your production schedule will stretch out. The sad fact is that you can't afford either one.

Here are the numbers. We find that each camera move for a new setup consumes about 15 minutes to adjust camera, lights, focus, and whatnot. With an extra setup for each of the 20 to 25 scenes you need to shoot a day, that adds up to about 5 hours of lost production per day. Over four weekends of shooting, that's almost two more weekends spent on extra setups (emphasis on the word "spent" because it comes out of your wallet).

"But what about retakes from the same camera setup?" you plead, "It doesn't take much time and the extra tape costs will be cheap."

Not necessarily so. While the tape costs won't be much, the time still adds up if this is your standard operating procedure. Back to the abacus. It would be hard to reset a scene and reshoot it in less than two minutes. Those 20 to 25 scenes you need to shoot each day translate into 60 to 75 setups a day in a 3:1 ratio. Already hard to do in a 12-hour day. Now use two minutes more on each of those setups, and you've just added 120 to 150 minutes — two hours or more — to each day's shooting. Keep this up and you'll have to sleep on the set to get any rest. While you can afford an occasional retake, don't get the cast, crew, or director used to it. Stick to a 3:1 ratio if you want to get your production done for $8,000.

So does this mean you can only afford to do a movie with two characters? By no means. But on the other hand, you probably aren't going to do a story about a baseball team whose players are inseparable.

In *Beyond Bob*, we had seven principal characters, because the script was not originally written to be done on an ultra-low budget. When possible, the script was rewritten to break up dialogue among smaller groups of

11

characters. We kept to a 4:1 shooting ratio only by making editing decisions in the camera and by breaking scenes into subgroups of characters. Rarely do all the characters appear in the same sequence, and if they do, they don't all talk.

While we limited ourselves to two or three main characters in the scenes of our digital movie, *Grown Men*, we completely abandoned the shooting-ratio rule and tried a different approach. Each of the four different story segments — which had different casts — and a framing segment were slated for two weekends of production with a 6:1 or 8:1 shooting ratio (thanks to equipment loans that kept us off the rental clock). This allowed us to spend more time creating nicely lit, well-composed shots. It also gave the actors more takes for each setup. However, time was still limited. Every scene was storyboarded so we knew exactly how many setups we had to get done in a day. This approach worked because we didn't need the same actors and crew throughout the shooting schedule, and because we didn't have to rent our major pieces of equipment.

The perfect number of characters in a scene from Grown Men. (Pictured, Peter Moore and Susan Vee. Photo courtesy of Granite Productions, Unlimited)

We still think a 3:1 shooting ratio is a good balance between cost and results if you're paying for rental equipment. By keeping the cast in each scene small, this is relatively easy to do.

Number of locations

To stay on an $8,000 budget, you'll have to do all principal videography in four weekends or less. Trust us on this one. In order to accomplish this, you have to control yourself on the number of shooting locations.

Now this doesn't mean you can't have a variety of locations, just that you need to have big chunks of dialogue occurring at a limited number of locations.

The main reason is time. If you move your entire crew from one location to another during one day of the shoot, you'll lose a minimum of an hour for each move, in addition to the travel time itself. This is more than merely an hour, because during that hour you're also paying equipment rental, you're losing daylight shooting time, and there's always the problem of having the crew and cast straggle off "to get a Coke." You also lose the momentum and pace your director has been trying to establish in order to shoot 12 pages of script a day. You don't want to do this. Enough said.

By keeping a couple of points in mind as you write your script, you can provide a nice variety of locations without wasting precious production time.

The first thing is not to introduce a new location without using it for a lot of pages of dialogue or action. However, this doesn't necessarily mean that you should only use one location in your story. Since you'll be shooting out of sequence, it doesn't matter when in the story you use a setting, just as long as it totals up to blocks of 12 pages — the amount you'll shoot in a day. This way, you can set up your crew and equipment at that location and shoot for the whole day. It's easy enough to switch locations overnight by just taking the equipment home and bringing it to the new location the next morning. No production time wasted.

If this seems like a stifling limitation, keep in mind that the same location can include many settings. For example, the house we used in *Grown Men* served up an easy half dozen settings. A location also can be altered to create a different mood for a different scene. You can change lighting, add props and furniture, change characters, or completely change the interactions between the characters. All of these will reinvigorate the scene, and the audience will scarcely give a thought to whether they've seen this location before.

You can also pick a bland setting and redress it to serve as more than one location. If you could afford a soundstage and set pieces (which you can't, so forget it!), this is how you'd shoot all of your interiors, for the same reason Hollywood productions do: to save the costs and time of moving cast, crew, and equipment. You can, however, find a location that can serve the same essential purpose for you.

For example, in *Resident Alien*, we shot in Dale's living room and workroom for one afternoon (we spent the morning shooting in his backyard, so the whole day really counted as one location). With the use of office partitions, a desk, a computer, a file cabinet, chairs, and careful camera angles, we transformed the neutral-colored walls of the living room into a welfare office. Not three feet away, again using a few selected decorations and pieces of furniture, we created the interior of a North Dakota farmhouse.

Another 12 feet away in a workroom with unfinished Sheetrock walls, we moved a few appliances, propped up a few more pieces of Sheetrock for additional walls, and — voila! — we had a motel laundry room in central Minnesota. Four hundred miles of travel in less than two dozen feet of distance. And no one has ever suspected when seeing the finished film. So if you're planning to repaint the living room, pick something nondescript.

You may have noticed that we've mainly referred to interior locations. That's because your script should primarily take place indoors, unless you live somewhere where the weather is reliable (we don't). On your fast-paced schedule, you need as much control as possible, so limit the outdoor dialogue scenes and try to locate them near an indoor location you can switch to in case of typhoon, blizzard, tornado, or other acts of God.

To compensate for shooting most scenes as interiors, you can add a large number of establishing shots to your script that won't need dialogue or extra lighting. (You won't have to rent a microphone or a lighting kit. If you own or borrow the camera, then these shots become virtually free.) You can even have your actors in the shots as long as there isn't dialogue. This second-unit shooting is cheap and can be done as time permits.

We shot the first ten minutes of *Beyond Bob* — which was all essentially silent exteriors — as second-unit work over the course of three months, after principal photography was completed. So if you want other interesting locations, just write them as simple establishing shots in your script. We've even used miniatures of locations and building signs to create establishing shots that helped give us the look of a bigger-budget movie.

Remember, every time you introduce a new location, think of where else in your story you can use it.

Write what you own
Another point you can never forget while writing the script is that you

have no money! Nada! Zippo! All of your money is going for equipment, tape stock, and food for the cast and crew. So don't write in any props or locations that you don't own, can't beg or borrow, or can't sneak into long enough to get your shot.

Forget about that old truism, "Write what you know." You need to write what you *own*. Daniel Myrick and Eduardo Sanchez took this concept to new minimalist extremes when they made *The Blair Witch Project* using little more than a tent, backpacks, and a state park. (They earned extra-credit points when they returned the video camera they purchased to shoot much of the production... and got a full refund.)

Clearly, expensive set dressings are not going to be your strong suit. They're simply too time-consuming and expensive. However, you can enliven your scenes by using unique props and costumes.

On *Grown Men*, one story segment is set in the apartment of a character who flits between artistic pursuits. Taking advantage of this character trait, we filled a warehouse work space with a variety of art to create an interesting setting. Several local artists were thrilled to loan their work in exchange for screen credit and a chance to reach a larger audience. Props worth thousands of dollars can be just a phone call away.

Also look around where you live. It may be old hat to you, but unless you live in Los Angeles or New York, it's a unique regional location for the rest of the world. What is mundane to you may never have been seen by most audiences. Trent Harris, in his offbeat film *Plan 10 from Outer Space*, used local Mormon statuary in his hometown of Salt Lake City as truly memorable settings for several of the movie's scenes.

This is one of the biggest reasons we're fans of regional moviemaking. Ninety percent of the films released look like the terrain within 100 miles of Los Angeles. There are thousands of unique settings, urban and rural, that are rarities on the screen. So when you think of locations for your scenes, pick settings that are unique to your neck of the woods. What is an expensive location shoot for Paramount is a cheap, backyard set for you. Your neighborhood can add hundreds of thousands of dollars of visual impact to your movie for next to nothing. This kind of thinking will have distributors guessing you spent a million bucks on your digital feature.

It's also possible to use what you don't have to your advantage. When Kevin Smith made *Clerks*, he had complete access to the convenience store that served as his primary location. The one drawback was that he only had use of the location at night, and his story took place during the day. Not having the budget for lights to create the illusion of sunlight, he took this disadvantage and made it his character's problem. Dante, the beleaguered store clerk, arrives at work to find that someone has jammed gum in the lock that secures the metal shutters over the front window of the store. As a result, he can't get the shutters opened. This is just one of the many problems that plague Dante throughout the day. Smith took a problem and turned it to his advantage as part of his story.

Night vs. day & big vs. small

Here's a simple mathematical equation: Lights = money. Because you have limited money for your production, it follows that you will have limited lighting. How does this affect the scripting process? Let us illuminate.

The first requirement is to not write scenes set in large locations that must be lit artificially. Now, if you're reading carefully, you see that this doesn't prevent you from using large locations. You can use the Grand Canyon during the day; thanks to the sun, you don't have to rent lights to do it.

Night shots seem like a cheap idea, but they actually may require a lot of money — that is, light — to make them visible on tape. Again, if you're reading carefully, you'll notice we said "may require." If you limit the size of the area you are trying to light, the simple lighting kit you can afford (four 1000-watt lamps) will be more than adequate. We even simulated a blinding UFO landing using this lighting kit by limiting the area we were lighting.

We were also able to shoot underexposed shots during the magic hour (just after sunset but before dark) to simulate night. We could see headlights on vehicles and details in the dark trees and cars without using any artificial lights.

So, the lesson here is to write scenes requiring artificial lighting only for small locations or small parts of large locations. Keep in mind that large locations must be shot in daylight, during the magic hour (this will have to be a short sequence that can be accomplished in less than an hour), or as miniatures that you can afford to light.

Surely you are thinking these are enough shackles to place on one project. Dream on.

Other constraints

These are only the budgetary constraints you must suffer through. They'll seem easy once your project is facing the list of "artistic" requirements most potential distributors look for. Most of these requirements are so lowbrow (more blood, more girls, more blood, more bikinis, more blood, more sex, more nudity, and did we mention more blood?) that we were glad we didn't pander to them.

Make a movie that's your vision, that you're proud of. When you face the inevitable rejections, you can sleep nights if you've followed your dream. It's hard to justify risking your hard-earned savings and thousands of hours of your personal time just to make a return on your investment. If you're only in this for the money, there are better investments that are a lot less work.

But just because most of this advice from distributors is fecal doesn't mean there aren't some valuable points.

The best piece of advice we've heard is to get your story moving in the first five minutes. *Resident Alien* doesn't kick into gear until about 15 minutes in. This is a long time without the aid of a well-known star or stunning visuals. We've been fortunate that most people are willing to wait for the good stuff that follows. However, attention spans are short in the world of distribution and increasingly so among audiences as well, so it's important that your story hits the ground running.

This is why we rewrote the opening of *Beyond Bob* to show Bob's comic (yet tragic) death in a hang gliding accident. It's a fast, fun opening that grabs the audience's attention and keeps it while we set up the story and the other characters over the next 20 minutes.

You need to make sure something intriguing, startling, or dramatic happens in the first five minutes to draw the audience into the story. And then you darn well better use the next 85 minutes to build on that opening. Ideally, the viewers will be so captivated by your story that they'll never get to think about it being an ultra-low-budget movie again until it's all over. By that point, they won't care if you had a big-name star or a Riviera locale.

17

Finding the write stuff

So what do you do if you're not a screenwriter, but you have everything else it takes to make a movie? Obviously you need to find a screenwriter, which really won't be that difficult. The tough part will be finding the right screenwriter.

As with every other crew and cast position you'll need to fill, we recommend that you opt for a person's excitement about the project and a positive attitude over experience. Not that we're knocking experience. Experience is great — when you can afford it. The main problem with experience is that by the time someone becomes really experienced in something — like writing, editing, photography, whatever — they often expect to receive a paycheck that is commensurate with their skills. And who can blame them? You can't, but you can't afford them, either.

The people you're looking for are the ones who are really excited about the project and who appear to have the basic skills necessary to get them through their tasks. In our case, it was often people who had experience in movie production, but were usually one or two steps down from the position they were taking on our project. For example, a production assistant becomes a production manager, a boom operator becomes a lead sound person, or an assistant editor becomes an editor. These are people who want to move up but haven't really had the opportunity. That is, until your digital movie came along.

The same will probably be true of your screenwriter. Odds are you aren't going to get a working, professional, card-carrying Writers Guild member to write your script for you. First, because you can't afford them, and second, because as union members, they can't work on your decidedly non-union project.

So how do you find this budding William Goldman? Well, if you followed our earlier advice (tell people that you're making a feature), you may have already heard from a couple of writers. Word travels fast, and the word about feature-length movies seems to travel at supersonic speed. (We even had someone call us from New York to inquire about the possibility of being an extra in one of our productions. In Minnesota. Trust us, word travels fast.)

However, if writers haven't started seeking you out, there are a number of ways to beat them out of the bushes. Here are a few:

- Many colleges and universities offer scriptwriting and playwriting courses. Call the professors at a school near you, and see if they can recommend any of their students. You may even get the professor interested.

- If there is a chapter of the Independent Feature Project where you live (see the appendix), check with them about putting an announcement in their newsletter or on their bulletin board (cork, voicemail, or computer). In the announcement, specify what you're looking for ("an ultra-low-budget script") as well as what you're not looking for (for example, "no slasher, horror, or exploitation," if that's your plan). This will save you and the respondents a lot of time.

- If your city or state has a film commission or office, talk to the people there. (We've provided contact information in the appendix.) Generally, film boards are in the business of bringing big-buck movies into your area, but most of them also do their best to help out local folks interested in movie work. At the very least, they'll have a directory of local production talent, which will come in very handy later on. Odds are they'll even know who the up-and-coming screenwriters are in your area and will help put you in touch with them.

- If all else fails, you can place an ad in one of the Hollywood trade papers — *Variety* or *The Hollywood Reporter*. However, we'd recommend that this be your avenue of last resort, for a few key reasons. First, it costs money to place an ad, and you don't have any money to spare — certainly not to be placing ads. Second, you will be inundated with scripts. Your mailbox will be stuffed. Boxes of scripts will land on your doorstep. Your answering machine will explode from overuse. Your home will be swallowed by paper. Your body will never be found. Perhaps we exaggerate, but not by much. And finally, 99.99% of these scripts will not be written for your budget level. And cramming a million-dollar (or 20-million-dollar) script into an $8,000 budget is not a pretty sight. Imagine Orson Welles in a Speedo.

If you feel you must take this approach, be sure to specify "ultra-low-budget" in your ad. This will tell the reader two things: Don't bother sending big-budget scripts (they will anyway), and don't plan on getting paid. Also specify what you do or don't want. We've put the addresses for these trade papers in the appendix. Contact them for information on ad rates (and don't get mad when we say we told you so).

Once you've found your screenwriter, you need to settle on your story. He or she may have a story or script that can be adapted to your budget. If so, great. Or you may need to outline the parameters and let the writer go off and stew on it for a while. Most writers like a challenge, and writing for an $8,000 movie certainly qualifies.

Of course, you may already have a story that you'd like the writer to adapt. This is a fine approach, with a couple of caveats:

If it's a story you made up, you're in great shape, because that means you own the rights to it. You can do whatever you want with it.

If it's a story that's in the public domain, you're also in good shape. "Public domain" means that the author is dead and has been for a good long time. As such, no one person owns the rights to the material; it is now owned by the public. Shakespeare is a good example of a writer whose work is in the public domain. Danielle Steel is not.

However, with writers who are dead but not nearly as dead as Shakespeare, it's often tricky to figure out what's in the public domain and what isn't. If it's older than a hundred years, you might be okay, but you'll want to check with the Library of Congress on the copyright to make sure.

If the story you're interested in adapting isn't in the public domain, you're going to have to get the rights from the author, and that's going to cost you money. Probably.

For example, if you've got your eye on a Michael Crichton or John Grisham story, forget it. These guys are out of your league. But if the story is by a less well-known author, you may be able to work something out. Regional writers are — not so surprisingly — great resources for regional stories and may be interested in seeing their work transferred to the big (or semi-big) screen.

As with everyone you bring on board, you'll need to establish a contract with your writer so it's clear who owns what rights and what is expected of you and what is expected of the writer.

One final housekeeping note: Whether you write the script yourself or contract with someone else, be sure that you copyright the material and that the writer registers it with the Writers Guild of America.

Technically, anything original that you write is copyrighted the moment you write it. However, it is a good idea to go through the simple copyright procedures when your script is finished. To copyright your script, write to the Library of Congress and ask for their Form PA. You can find their address in the appendix. As of this writing, it costs $30 to register a copyright.

You should also register your script with the Writers Guild of America. This registration doesn't take the place of copyrighting, but it does provide you with an additional level of security should there be any question about the ownership of your script. Send them an unbound copy of your script, along with $20.00 (for nonmembers). Their address is in the appendix.

An alternative is to mail a copy of the script to yourself by certified mail so it has a delivery date. Don't open this package, just put it away as proof of a date by which the script was completed.

🎥🎥🎥

Part of the creative challenge for the screenwriter of an ultra-low-budget movie is how to turn every penny into a screen image. The right script for your digital movie is literally worth hundreds of thousands of dollars in apparent value for the finished production, so it's not a creative challenge to take lightly or do quickly.

As you — or your new best friend, your screenwriter — shape the script, think of what it costs to do everything, and then think about how you can reuse that expense several more times to get maximum screen value for it.

Remember, your screenplay is the support structure for the rest of this project. Build this foundation with the strongest material you can find; it's got to carry a heavy load.

21

THE BUDGET
(AND HOW TO BUDGE IT)

Figuring out how to shoot a 90-minute digital movie for $8,000 is a lot like losing your job and finding out you can live on $100 a month.

All those things that were essentials suddenly become luxuries you have to do without. You sleep on your best friend's couch. You dine at the grocery store on the days they have free food samples. You accept and even ask for handouts and favors. You distill your existence down to bare necessities. To succeed within this budget, you will have to discover how to make a movie using only the barest of necessities.

Making an ultra-low-budget digital movie may give you freedom and let you keep your integrity, but you've got to swallow a lot of pride and inhibitions along the way. And you have to discard many of your preconceived notions about moviemaking.

More than once as we planned and shot our movies, we found ourselves following the model of the silent films of the 1910s and 1920s. There were few rules about how to make a film back then, and most movies were done on shoe-string budgets. They didn't have years of "standard practices" to constrain them.

To create your budget and your production, you have to throw off nearly 100 years of accumulated ideas about moviemaking. You don't need dressing rooms for the stars. You don't need most "standard" crew positions. You don't need a day to shoot one scene. You don't need that lighting truck or camera dolly. You don't need to follow the "rules." Once you've broken free of these mental shackles, you'll find developing your budget is a lot easier.

It's best to start your budget by including only items that would prevent you from starting and completing your movie:

Essentials
- Script
- DV camcorder, batteries, zoom lens, tripod,
- Tape stock
- Cast (unless your movie is about inanimate objects)
- Very abbreviated crew
- Good food and drinks for cast and crew (to prevent mutiny)
- Editing equipment (a computer-based, nonlinear system)
- Music score
- Recording studio time for music recording
- Recording of sound effects, foley, and dialogue looping
- Final master tape output

Once you start adding up the numbers, you'll be appalled to see that these items will chew up most of your budget, and any moviemaking experience you have will be screaming that you've left out a bunch of important stuff. We know. This is where you apply your creativity. You start looking at the list and figuring out what you can get for free, borrow, get for a discount rate, or can defer payment for until your movie grows up and starts earning its own money. Once you've done this (don't panic — we'll give you some more help on this), you will have an even more paltry sum of money available to spend on the almost-essentials.

While the list of essentials included the items you need in order to make a salable feature-length movie, the list of almost-essentials will be governed more by the unique aspects of your project. You may be able to do without some of the items on this list or make limited use of them.

Almost-essentials
- Lighting equipment (If you can shoot in natural light, you can get away with just light control devices such as bounce cards, scrims, and reflectors.)
- Shotgun mike, wind screen, and boom pole
- Token payments to cast and crew
- Video dubs (for the composer and for use in dialogue looping, foley, sound effects, and special-effects production)
- Titles (do-it-yourself ones)
- Publicity photos, publicity packets

- Photocopying for scripts, maps to locations, cast and crew phone lists, etc.
- Preview videotapes for distributors and film festivals
- Postage for publicity and preview tape mailings

If you still have a few pennies left after including all the essentials and almost essentials, then you can move onto the luxuries:

Luxuries
- Wardrobe rentals or purchases
- Makeup
- Models and miniatures
- Vehicle rental
- Location rental
- Camera dolly
- A small-name actor or personality for a cameo role
- Festival entry fees
- Film market entry fees

You'll notice that a lot of Hollywood essentials don't appear in this budget list. No big-name stars, no exotic international locations, no sound stage, no insurance, no gala premiere, no music-and-effects sound mix for foreign release, no stock footage, no cute little chair with the director's name on it, no toadies to fawn over the producer. There simply isn't enough cash or minutes in your production days for these non-essentials. So readjust your perspective, and move on.

The budget for our first digital feature was a hybrid consisting of a standard budget and a lengthy list of freebies from friends and relatives and from people and businesses we know through our day jobs in audiovisual production. This was great because the cost savings allowed for the rental of specialty equipment (dolly, special lighting, etc.) and the extension of the shooting schedule to ten weekends. This longer schedule was possible because the movie is essentially five different stories.

Also, because we had set up a nonprofit organization to do movie productions (finally acknowledging the truth in ten years of financial ledgers), we were also able to have our director, producer, actors, crew, and writers work as volunteers.

25

This was all well and fine for us, but it won't work for you unless you decide to do your production through a nonprofit organization and unless you have the same kinds of business connections to help trim the budget to the bone. So, we've created a realistic, no-frills, no-freebies budget for producing your digital movie, based on current costs for rentals and purchases. The good news is that digital video equipment keeps getting better and cheaper (causing more perfectly usable "obsolete" equipment to go on the bargain table every day), so you'll have even more options for cutting budget costs in the future.

This budget presumes you're a for-profit enterprise, so it includes three possible types of payments to your cast and crew: deferred payments with signing fees, wages, and stipends.

Deferred payments — in the event that you make a profit — are for staff positions that can be filled with independent contractors. With them there is a signing fee of a small amount of cash.

Minimum wages are included for cast and crew positions that must be employees according to federal Internal Revenue Service rulings. Minimum wage currently amounts to about $6.00 per hour including social security, unemployment compensation and workers' compensation insurance.

Cash stipends are an alternative to wages if you choose to have the cast and crew be interns instead of employees. Then they just receive a token cash payment. These categories will be explained more in the section on employees in the business chapter.

Though we've included the wage figures, you'll see that you can't stay within an $8,000 budget if you pay your cast and crew. The business chapter will give you ideas on how to avoid these wage costs, but they are included here to give the full budget picture. This budget will give you a reasonable cost for producing your movie without any donated help, equipment or supplies. You can easily chop out items that you can get for free or already own. Try to get as much as you can for free, and try to already own as much as possible. Here's how you'll spend that extra $8,000 you have rolled up in the corner of your sock drawer.

The budget

ITEM	CAST AND CREW *DEFERRED [D]* *SIGNING FEE [F]* *WAGES [W]* *STIPEND [S]*	CASH
Screenplay and rights	$4,000[D], 0[F]	
Producer	4,000[D], 0[F]	
Director	4,000[D], 0[F]	
Lead Actors		
3 Actors	2,592[W], 60[S]	
($864 x 3[W], $20 x 3[S])		
Supporting Actors		
4 Actors	1,728[W], 80[S]	
($432 x 4[W], $20 x 4[S])		
Day Players		
5 Bit Parts	360[W], 25[S]	
($72 x 5[W], $5 x 5[S])		
5 Walk-ons	120[W], 25[S]	
($24 x 5[W], $5 x 5[S])		
Extras	0	
Crew, Equipment and Supplies		
Unit Production Manager/ Script Supervisor	1,248[W], 20[S]	
Production Assistant	768[W], 20[S]	
Art Director	500[D], 5[F,S]	
Set-Construction Coordinator	120[W], 10[S]	
Set-construction materials		100
Model Builder	500[D], 5[F,S]	
Model-building materials		50
Wardrobe Supervisor	120[W], 10[S]	

Wardrobe rentals/cleaning		0
Makeup-and-Hair Supervisor	204[W], 10[S]	
Lighting Gaffer/	768[W], 20[S]	
Boom-Mike Operator		
Light rental		545
Lighting supplies		215
(purchase)		
Director of Photography/	1,032[W], 30[S]	
Videographer		
3-CCD digital video camcorder		1800
(purchase)		
2 camera batteries and charger		275
(purchase)		
Fluid-head tripod rental		210
Scene slate		0
Second-unit tripod		75
(purchase)		
Sound Recordist	768[W], 20[S]	
Sound mixer rental		105
Microphone, boom pole, windscreen,		390
batteries, cable rental		
Vehicles (on-camera and production)		0
Meals on location		500
Locations		0
10 DV 60-min. tapes		110
Production stills		55
(film, processing, prints)		
Storage vault rental		0
Video, Sound, and Music Editor	3,000[D], 20[F,S]	
Nonlinear edit system		1,500
(purchase)		
Editing software		600
(purchase)		

Software to create film look		0
Video dubs for composer, dialogue looping, sound effects, special effects		10
Composer/Music Supervisor/ Songwriter (synchronization rights)	3,000[D], 5[F,S]	
Singer (synchronization rights)	30[W], 5[S]	
4 Session musicians ($30 x 4[W], 5 x 4[S])	120[W], 20[S]	
2 Back-up vocalists ($30 x 2[W], 5 x 2[S])	60[W], 10[S]	
Music recording		250
1 CD music master		10
Sound effects, foley, dialogue looping		15
Titles		0
Sneak Preview		0
DV deck rental for final output		265
S-VHS deck rental for submaster		65
1 full-size DV tape (124 min.)		25
3 S-VHS tapes		25
1 5-minute BetacamSP or 3/4" U-Matic tape		10
20 Preview cassettes		40
Publicity photos (5x7)		95
Publicity packet costs (15)		50
Publicity packet writing		0
Photocopying 18 scripts		100
Miscellaneous photocopying		100
Postage for publicity packets and preview tapes		110

Cast and Crew Costs

Total deferred salaries	19,000[D]
Total signing fees with deferred salaries	35[F]
Total wages	10,038[W]
Total stipends	400[S]

Equipment and supplies costs

Total equipment and supplies $7,700

☙☙☙

Based on the budget amounts above, here are three possible budgets for your feature-length movie, depending on whether your production is for profit or nonprofit, and depending on the employment status you choose for your cast and crew.

Three budget options

1) Production with employees and independent contractors

Total cash costs	17,773

      (equipment, supplies, employee wages, independent contractor signing fees)

Total deferred costs   19,000

2) Production with interns and independent contractors

Total cash costs	8,100

      (equipment, supplies, intern stipends)

Total deferred costs   12,000
      (screenplay, producer, director only)

3) Nonprofit production with volunteers

Total cash costs	7,700

      (equipment, supplies, all cast and crew are free volunteers)

If you have priced out any of the services or products listed in this budget, you're probably saying, "Impossible! There's got to be a trick." Yes, lots of them.

Pinching the pennies (until Abraham yells)

There are a several basic principles to use when whittling down your budget so it fits your bank account: You have more time than money. Use what you already own. Make it or borrow it if you don't have it. Use other people's waste or surplus. Dicker for everything you have to buy. Rent equipment when business is slow. Use crew members who own their own equipment. Also, don't make it a secret that you're throwing your personal resources into the project. This will encourage everyone in the crew and cast to add what they can for the benefit of everyone.

Because you're going to spend a lot of money renting and purchasing budget items, we'll start with some general thoughts about these activities.

This budget assumes that you are shooting your production over four weekends, the times when no one else is renting the equipment. Most rental houses will give you an entire weekend for the cost of one or one-and-a-half days' rental; you can get the most out of that rate by picking up the equipment late on Friday afternoon so you can shoot some night shots that evening.

You may be able to get better rental deals if you ask for a bid on the whole package you want to rent for four weekends. You might get an even better deal if you use their favorite four-letter word, CASH. Some rental houses have cash flow problems while they wait 90 days for their invoices to be paid. They may trim your bill to put some cash in the till. Sending out a formal bid form will make them think you're getting bids from their competitors even if you're not. However, it's a good idea to get multiple bids. No matter what the rental or purchase price, plead poverty and ask for a deal. A painful wince at the price and saying "We're on a really tight budget. Can you do any better?" will get you an almost-automatic 5 to 10% discount at all but the most hard-hearted businesses. And from there you can bargain for better. You've got to have the chutzpah to keep pushing for more and more — or in this case, less and less. ("Chutzpah" is best defined by the old joke about the kid who killed his parents and then pleaded for mercy in court because he was an orphan.)

31

If you can be very flexible and if you're feeling really lucky, make a deal to rent the equipment dirt cheap if no one else rents it for the weekend. When you offer this, be sure you're talking to the owner, who is going to recognize extra income. The salespeople don't necessarily care if they rent anything or not. They're not paying the overhead. Odds are that most of the equipment sits idle on the weekend, so this is a pretty safe rental deal, and one the owner is likely to consider.

Remember, only suckers pay list price.

Because of the low cost of much of the equipment in the digital video format, you don't necessarily have to deal with rental houses. Many professionals own their own equipment and may be willing to rent it to you for prices well below the going rates. They have a lot of money tied up in their lights or sound gear, and often it's gathering dust, not income. Before they rent to you, you'll have to demonstrate to them that you are conscientious and won't trash their $2,000 lighting kit. If they agree to rent it to you, be sure to get instructions from them on how to take care of and use their equipment. And then follow their instructions. You will soon be colleagues with these people, and you want only good things said about you. So don't burn any bridges.

You also might find while you're arranging a rental that this professional becomes intrigued and excited by your project. Since you're working weekends when these professionals usually aren't working, they may be willing to join your crew for the experience and the fun of working on a movie. A videographer friend of ours offered his services and his digital camcorder to shoot *Grown Men*. In the course of the production, he brought in other people who provided a top-of-the-line camcorder, audio gear, trucks full of lights, and even a Steadicam system with operator. Feature movies are infectious.

You also can get some equipment and supplies for lower prices from retailers outside the movie industry. For example, we bought photoflood bulbs for $1.70 from a wholesaler that sells all types of bulbs; photo supply stores wanted $3.00 for the same bulb. Instead of renting a boom pole for $10 a weekend, consider buying an adjustable painter's pole for $15 at the hardware store. You'll have to modify the screw fitting (a $3 roll of duct tape will do this if you're not handy), and you'll save $25 for more essential supplies. Moviemaking gives you all kinds of opportunities to use your imagination.

Squeezing the budget
Let's get down to specifics on the budget. We'll go point-by-point through this budget for a 90-minute digital movie.

Screenplay and rights
This area is important in budget trimming for two reasons. The first we've already discussed in the chapter on designing the script. What you write in the script is going to affect what you have to include in the budget. Hopefully, you'll write or have someone write a script that limits your expenses and showcases what you have at hand. But when you get to really creating your budget, keep in mind that changing the script will change the budget. If you find yourself trapped in a financial corner in the budget, you may need to look at revising the screenplay. This may be an affront artistically, but it's the kind of ruthless act that is needed to get a small story to the big screen. It's painful, but look on the bright side — at least you get to do it and keep control. If someone else were producing the story that means so much to you, they'd make changes, too — ones you probably wouldn't like. It takes courage to keep your freedom, so if there's no way out of a financial corner, write an escape route.

The other budget-slimming aspect of story and rights is limiting your cash payment for the script or have it donated free for a nonprofit production. As screenwriters, we can tell you this will be easy to do, especially with writers who haven't been produced. We've said this before, and we'll say it again. It would be great to pay all the people on your project what they are worth, and you will — just not in cash. Your currency is experience and credentials, and for people new to the movie business, these rewards are worth almost as much as cash. Your screenwriter (who may be yourself) will be thrilled to see her or his words brought to life. Other than a deferred payment if there are profits, that will have to be enough. In the case of a nonprofit production with the screenplay donated, the experience and credentials alone will be reward enough.

Cast and crew
In this budget, we included a bare-bones crew and a generic cast of three

lead roles, four supporting roles, and ten bit parts and walk-on roles. Of course, you'll want to adjust this to match your cast, but keep in mind that it will be hard shoot 12 pages of script a day if you have more than three main characters. If your list of cast and crew is much larger than the one in this budget, think about revising your script. There's only so much that you can do with an $8,000 budget.

When we did deferred payments for staff who qualified as independent contractors, we made sure there was a signing fee that gave those crew members just enough cash so that they didn't feel like it cost them money to work on our productions (basically, gas money). For ourselves, as director and producer, we took no money. Since we were financing the production, it would have meant paying ourselves.

For the staff who were independent contractors, the contract arrangements gave them a portion of any profits, but we made it clear that profits were a long shot at best. We also arranged it so we, as producer and director, would share in profits only after everyone else did. This made it very clear to everyone that we weren't out to make a profit off their almost-volunteer labor. This helped create an atmosphere of camaraderie that was needed to get us through the tough spots.

Most of the cast and crew can't be independent contractors under federal rules, and minimum wage will not be a minimal amount. Paying these wages will more than double your production budget and your paperwork. If you decide to go this route, you may need to hire a payroll person or a payroll service because doing the required withholdings, payments, and form filing is a real job — one that you won't have much time for during your hectic four weekends of production. For these wage calculations, we assumed that four weekends of production add up to 128 hours (four hours on Friday evenings and 14 hours each for Saturdays and Sundays). Some jobs require many more hours and some require much less. Wage costs were assumed to be $6.00 per hour. Following is a quick list of the hours for the wage employees based on our production experience:

- *Lead actor* — 128 hours (4 weekends shooting) + 16 hours (rehearsal) = 144 hours each ($864)
- *Supporting actor* — 64 hours (2 weekends shooting) + 8 hours (rehearsal) = 72 hours each ($432)

- *Day Player* — 8 hours (1 day shooting) + 4 hours (rehearsal) = 12 hours each ($72)
- *Walk-on* — 4 hours (1/2 shooting day) ($24)
- *Unit Production Manager* — 128 hours (4 weekends shooting) + 80 hours (preproduction) = 208 hours ($1,248)
- *Production Assistant* — 128 hours (4 weekends shooting) ($768)
- *Set Construction Coordinator* — 20 hours (as needed) ($120)
- *Wardrobe Supervisor* — 20 hours (preproduction) ($120)
- *Makeup-and-Hair Supervisor* — 24 hour (2 hours each shooting day) + 10 hours (preproduction) = 34 hours ($204)
- *Lighting Gaffer/Boom Mike Operator* — 128 hours (4 weekends shooting) ($768)
- *Director of Photography/Videography* — 128 hours (4 weekends shooting) + 20 hours (preproduction) + 24 hours (3 days of second-unit shooting) = 172 hours ($1,032)
- *Sound Recordist* — 128 hours (4 weekends shooting) ($768)
- *Singer* — 5 hours (studio recording session) ($30)
- *Session Musicians* — 5 hours (studio recording session) ($30)
- *Back-up Vocalists* — 5 hours (studio recording session) ($30)

If you decide to have your cast and crew be interns, the stipend you pay should be enough to give them bus fare or gas money to get to the set each day. Beyond that they are getting a learning experience for which they didn't have to pay a tuition fee.

We did *Grown Men* as a not-for-profit endeavor, so everyone volunteered their time. Total cast and crew costs, zero. We were careful to have cast and crew sign releases that gave all rights to their work to the nonprofit organization. That way there would be no barriers to distributing the finished production.

Just as we did, you will probably feel embarrassed that you can't offer real payment to these talented performers and technicians. You're probably thinking that you'd be too ashamed to ask anyone to work so hard for little or nothing in return. Don't underestimate the value of the experience and credentials you are offering.

One of the most gratifying parts of producing your dream movie is that you can also help other people realize their dreams in the process. So don't worry if the money is small; the opportunities are large.

For example, one of our lead actors talked to her actor friends in Los Angeles. They couldn't believe they'd made the trek to Hollywood and were still struggling to break into movies while she had stayed in the Midwest and had gotten the lead in a feature film. She's gone on to work on a larger feature film and a popular British TV series.

One of our unit production managers, who had been the assistant to John's agent prior to working with us on two films, now makes her living in Hollywood. She has worked on the Academy Awards and Emmy Awards programs for many years, the *America's Funniest Home Videos* television series, the World Cup final-game ceremony, the Super Bowl half-time show, and low-budget feature films, to name a few. She's a very talented person, and having two feature films on her resume didn't hurt when she was knocking on doors.

Several of our lead actors have gone on to perform lead and supporting roles in Hollywood low-budget films (meaning million-dollar budgets), larger films, and a prime-time television series.

Our composer, who had never done a movie music score before doing two of our films, used a CD of those sound tracks as his ticket into UCLA's Film Music program. Before he even graduated, he was writing scores for other movie productions, and he has gone on to score numerous low-budget Hollywood films and has assisted some of the industry's top composers.

We're not saying that their work with us paved the way. But it didn't hurt.

Of course, even the small fees you'll be paying your crew will add up. It will add up to big money if you decide to have wage-earning employees. So keep your cast as small as the story allows and work with the absolute minimum crew size in order to reduce the cost of personnel. Also, a smaller crew can keep up with your fast production schedule. (Ironically, the more helpers you add to your crew, the slower it moves.)

You may have a story that calls for extras. A contraction and two words of advice: Don't pay them. Amazingly enough, even after a hundred years of moviemaking in this country, people are still thrilled to be in a movie, even if it's just a scene. Just put their name in the credits. We had dozens of people who volunteered to skate for hours in the middle of the night on a July Fourth weekend for *Beyond Bob*. It was far from glamorous, but only a handful went home before we finished our shots. For budget purposes, the one thing you have to remember about extras is that you can't afford to feed them, at least not much. You can provide lemonade and cookies, but that's it. So when you are preparing your shooting schedule, plan to have extras start right after a meal and to be finished with them before the next meal. It's crass, but necessary.

Finally, don't be discouraged that you can't afford a big-name star. You can afford lots of actors who may become stars. The pre-stardom films of Julia Roberts and Tom Hanks are making money for somebody. You might be able to get the services of a celebrity from outside the entertainment field who will do your movie as a lark. Bill Gates in a cameo as a computer repairman would be a hoot. A little creative thinking and connections through friends of friends might find you a recognizable name without paying for a star.

Set construction
Looking over our budget, you may be asking, "How the heck did they do set construction for just $100?" Our secret is "We didn't build any." In truth, we did do some limited set construction on our movies, but we usually used an existing location and just created a false wall to change the look of the interior. In the case of *Beyond Bob*, we wanted to divide a combined kitchen and sitting room into two separate rooms. We built a quick and crude wood framework to support a couple of sheets of wood paneling that had come loose from our director of photography's basement wall. If you've ever seen a Hollywood set, the pressure is off. You can get away with murder. Even the crudest sets look 100 times better on tape.

If you have to do some set work, look for borrowed or discarded materials. Haunt the dumpsters at construction and demolition sites. (Yes, you will sink this low to get your movie done.) Commercial construction sites are the best because they often discard items that still look new, such as lumber, sheetrock, paneling, carpet, cabinets, bathroom fixtures, and electrical wiring. Much of this material still looks good enough to serve on a movie set. Routinely check dumpsters at businesses for your furniture needs. Tons of repairable furniture are thrown out every time the office staff decides it looks too old-fashioned. You can even find computers and other high-tech-looking trash for those science-fiction projects. Dumpsters are a do-it-yourself set-building kit for low-buck moviemakers. Just add nails or sheetrock screws. (Our preference is sheetrock screws. Using screws and an electric drill, you can assemble and disassemble sets in minutes.)

A word of caution: When dumpster diving, be sure to wear good solid boots, heavy gloves, and even a dust mask. Watch out for hazardous items; this is garbage after all. A small stepladder can help avoid the embarrassment and danger of leaning too far into a dumpster.

Model building

We only included a small amount for materials for model building. You can either do it yourself or find model makers through your local hobby store. Offer to pay for materials, and they'll go to town. This is their passion and getting money to do it will make their day. In our case, Dale did most of our model work, and we didn't spend much on materials because he's a pack rat. The man just can't throw away anything that looks potentially useful. (Guess who had all the information on dumpster diving?) This is a trait that has kept his marriage lively. We'll talk more about models in the chapter on special effects, but for budgeting you should know that live-action shots that are difficult to set up can sometimes be accomplished as miniatures, saving lots of time and money. This is how we once created and lit a night scene showing a line of jets on the tarmac at an Air Force base, something we couldn't have afforded to do for real even if we had permission.

Wardrobe

You only need a fistful of dollars to get the wardrobe you'll require, especially if you've written a script that doesn't call for Halston designer gowns. There are several methods to pay little or nothing for your costumes. Use what you have, borrow, buy cheaply, make it, rent it, or, as a last resort, be slightly unscrupulous.

If you've written the script yourself, it will be easy to use what you have. You should have written in your old prom dress or that beekeeping hat Uncle Jim bequeathed to you. Also ask actors if they can provide their own costumes. If they are working actors or just the wild-and-wonderful people that actors usually are, they probably have a closet full of interesting clothing that fits them. The exotic dancer who performed the lead in one segment of *Grown Men* brought a selection of her professional wardrobe to a rehearsal at John's house, but not before mistakenly knocking at his neighbor's door and asking for John. We didn't need to arrange for any other costumes for this performer, and the resulting neighborhood gossip could be considered the first step in a word-of-mouth publicity campaign.

Borrowing opens up a world of attire to you. Friends and relatives of anyone connected to your project become sources of clothing, uniforms, and professional gear. For *Beyond Bob*, we literally got the shirt off the back of Dale's minister, and most of the costumes in *Grown Men* came from the actors and their friends. Think of it as thousands of dollars of wardrobe just out there for the begging.

You can even ask local stores and local designers to loan clothing in exchange for screen credit and any publicity that it will garner. We've found that independently owned stores get in the spirit of the project more than chain stores, which discourage most initiative and independent thought in their employees. You also can find fledgling designers at technical colleges, who are happy for the exposure, or by asking around at fabric stores and funky clothing shops. We got some unique costumes from an up-and-coming designer recommended by a sales person at a clothing boutique. Screen credit and any publicity that mentions the clothing designs can return the favor for the designer's career.

You can ask people working in a profession to borrow their special clothing and accessories, or you can approach suppliers of professional gear. It's called product placement, and Hollywood overdoes it daily. We got some name-brand roller skates (Oberhamers — we're still repaying the favor) this way for no cost, and they even let us keep them after the shoot. You can thank businesses by sending them a photo of their clothing or equipment being used in the movie for their company bulletin board or newsletter.

Professional wardrobe used in Grown Men. *(Pictured, David Fields and Melissa Kashmark. Photo courtesy of Granite Productions, Unlimited.)*

If you are forced to spend actual money on some of your costumes or accessories, head to thrift shops, garage sales, and used clothing stores. In most cases costumes don't have to look brand new, and an imperfect fit can be made presentable with safety pins, needle and thread, or even gaffer's tape. By doing a little hunting, you'll find that you can buy more than a pocket for pocket change. Before you go bargain hunting, strip off those preconceived costume ideas and be open to finding some surprising and stunning new concepts in the rag bin.

For technical and scientific costumes, consider disposable coveralls, gloves, footwear, and head gear from safety equipment suppliers. This disposable clothing is the real stuff, but it's meant to be cheap. We needed the science-nerd look for two characters in *Resident Alien*, and we got the desired look by buying orange disposable coveralls for $3 each. To this costume we added a 50-cent used belt, borrowed safety glasses, and inspired casting of nearly-identical bald guys (taunting our hair-challenged producer), and, voila! — we had convincing techno-weenies for only $3.50 each.

Specialty costumes, like the alien space suits we used in *Resident Alien*, can be hard to find in friends' closets or at the neighborhood tuxedo shop. However, if there's a modicum of sewing talent handy, you can make specialty costumes. You can even do it without sewing talent. Our alien space suits were made from thrift-shop long underwear, foam rubber, contact adhesive, cardboard, and spray paint. Sure, the spray paint tends to rub off. Sure, the costumes deteriorate pretty quickly. Sure, the actors don't have a full range of movement. But the space suits lasted long enough to get the shots we needed, they cost less than $10, and they looked like hundreds of dollars on the screen.

You can rent costumes, but this is an avenue of last resort and only permissible when a particular costume is so critical to your project that you are willing to sacrifice other resources for it. Since an $50 costume rental costs as much as renting the shotgun microphone for a day, ask yourself *Am I willing to shoot 12 minutes of my movie without recording usable sound?* This should tell you how important the costume is. If you do need a costume badly enough to rent it, you'll need to get the best deal possible. Actual costume shops are probably too expensive unless you can get the owners to give you a deal in exchange for publicity and screen credit. Theater groups will sometimes loan their costumes for a reasonable fee. You can also try making arrangements with a local high school or university drama program. We found that uniform and specialty clothing shops sometimes are willing to rent items they stock, but their prices were often high, and their willingness to strike deals was low.

The last method for getting free costumes is not without its own type of payment. Being unscrupulous can allow you to buy clothes on your credit card, use them, dry-clean them, and return them. We did this. We still feel guilty.

Initially, we approached a large department-store chain's headquarters to trade screen credit for costumes. They were not interested because they felt it was too much work to review the screenplay for appropriateness. However, we needed an extravagant (and expensive) peignoir for a 30-second scene, and we were out of time to make arrangements to borrow the costume. So we took advantage of the store's generous return policy and put it on the plastic. We shot the scene, knowing full well that if we damaged the lacy item, we'd own it. We dry-cleaned it and returned it. Picture a balding, 30-year-old producer returning this racy getup to the saleswoman with the sad phrase "It didn't work out." That's a movie scene in itself.

The problem with this method is that you continue to feel guilty, especially if you were raised Catholic — as we were. (We probably mention it here out of need for confession.) If we ever get a big-budget project, we'll buy our costumes at this store to make amends, and we try to do our personal shopping there to assuage our guilt. It's about the only thing we've done on our productions of which we are not proud.

Selecting your wardrobe may or may not require a wardrobe supervisor. If you have very limited costumes — such as two characters lost in the desert wearing just shorts and T-shirts — the director, producer, and production manager can select costumes. A more extensive and fashionable wardrobe benefits from the attention of someone with a flair for clothing. Even if you have a wardrobe supervisor, you don't need this person on the set except to deliver the proper wardrobe to the location and maybe to stay around for repairs if there are delicate items being used. Otherwise the production manager can supervise wardrobe changes, which helps you avoid having one more crewperson to feed, move, and keep out of the way.

The time you spend getting good costumes will pay off in the finished movie. Costumes play an important part in creating the screen image of every single scene and the overall look of your movie. You can easily add $100,000 to your apparent budget on the screen by using these low-cost methods to get a top-notch wardrobe.

Makeup and hair
We've done one production with a makeup-and-hair supervisor and two without. Whether or not you need one on your set depends on the unique needs of your production. If you have a very small cast and simple hair and makeup that doesn't change, and experienced actors, the cast can do their own makeup and hair styling.

If you have a larger cast or makeup and hair that need changing during the shooting day, you'll probably need this crew position. It is a comfort to the actors to have someone else watching these details, but you have to weigh it against adding another crewperson who will slow down the march of your little rebel band of digital moviemakers.

The first thing you must do is discourage your makeup-and-hair supervisor from tweaking and primping the actors before every shot. When you're trying to shoot up to 100 shots each day, a minute to do makeup on each shot wastes 100 minutes of production time. And the difference is rarely discernible in the end. Except for makeup effects (bruises, bags under the eyes, and fragile hair styles), makeup and hair can be spiffed up after lunch break, and that's good enough. On the finished movie frame, hairstyles gone wild are more noticeable than lip blush wearing off, so concentrate on hair the most. This advice will insult makeup professionals, who do an important job well. But remember you're operating in subsistence moviemaking. Only the vital elements. You can get only 90% of what you want, and you have to be willing to sacrifice the other 10%. Touching up hair and makeup definitely falls into the 10% category.

If you have professional actors or a professional makeup-and-hair person (or beautician or hairstylist), they likely can supply the makeup you need out of their basic makeup kit. Everyone on the production should be in the "My uncle's got a barn, and I've got footlights" mode, so ask if they can scrounge or donate the needed supplies. Only pay for what you have to, and definitely don't pay for a shopping spree at the cosmetic counter. It's okay to say you can't afford something. This will cause the makeup person or any crew member to use their creativity to find a solution. Our makeup supervisor scrounged a lot of the makeup for *Beyond Bob* from the set of a made-for-TV movie that shot in town. Their crew was routinely throwing out barely-used makeup supplies — another example of Hollywood waste and how to profit from it.

Lighting and lighting supplies
You can't have enough lighting. That is to say, you can't have as much lighting as you want or need, because you lack the necessary money and electrical power. You won't be working on a soundstage equipped with its own electrical substation, and you probably can't afford a portable generator, much less the truck and the time to pull it around. So accept the situation. Your power shortage actually works well with your money shortage. You couldn't afford to rent more lights even if you had more electricity.

Fortunately, you can get by with a small, lightweight, not-too-expensive lighting kit because of the low-light capabilities of digital video cameras.

We've worked with a kit that includes four 1000-watt lights (called "1Ks") that can be flooded or spotted, such as Arriflex or Lowel DP lights. These same lights can be outfitted with 650-watt or 500-watt lamps if you find you're singeing the actors' eyebrows in tight locations. The kit contains barndoors for blocking the lights' spill, stands, and extra lamps. With tax and insurance this kit cost us about $115 a weekend.

In the budget, we've also added one weekend's use of a 2000-watt Lowel Softlight for lighting larger locations. We were able to light an entire roller rink using only existing light and two softlights. These lights are an extra expense — about $50 a weekend with tax and insurance — so try to group all of the large locations together so you don't have to rent this light continually.

For outdoor daytime shooting, the only lighting equipment we used was a 38-inch silver-white Flexfill, which is a collapsible reflector. It's great for filling in harsh shadows when shooting outdoors. We also used it as a reflector on indoor settings. It cost about $35 dollars for four weekends with tax and insurance.

Now you may be tempted to skimp on other equipment and add more lights, because your director of photography really wants some 5Ks. Forget it. Here's the mathematical reason: Most residential and commercial circuits are 15 amps or 20 amps. At 120 volts that means you have 1800 watts (15 amps x 120 volts = 1800 watts) or 2400 watts (20 amps x 120 volts = 2400 watts) of power available. Using more watts or continuously using up to the maximum wattage will cause fuses to blow or circuit breakers to trip. It's easy to see that a 15-amp circuit can only support one 1000-watt light reliably. A 20-amp circuit can handle two, or it can handle one 2000-watt softlight, but not both. Switching to 500-watt lamps in the lights will give you less light, but you can run three of them on a 15-amp circuit or four on a 20-amp circuit. In most locations, you'll be running a lot of extension cords just to make two or three circuits available. You see that four lights will max out your power.

Our budget also included some expendable lighting supplies:

- a $13 roll each of black, white and gray gaffer's tape (useful for taping everything from cables to the floor, correction gels to windows, and troublesome clothes to the actors)

- a dozen "practical" bulbs (These are 150 to 200-watt tungsten bulbs that fit standard light fixtures for brighter light sources within a scene; beware of overheating the light and shade.)

- a 2' x 3' piece of daylight-correction gel to color the tungsten (incandescent) light to match sunlight (3202 Full Blue CTB from the Rosco company)

- a 4' x 3' piece of 105 Roscolux tough spun (a fabric-like material similar to tissue paper but without the same flammability) to soften and reduce the intensity of the lights, and a 10' x 58" length of 3401 RoscoSun 85 for correcting daylight coming through windows to match the tungsten lights.

This last item is only needed if you are dead set on the camera being able to see out windows when you are shooting interiors. This is a $115 choice because gels are not cheap. The gels and spun are cut into smaller sizes to be used on several lights or windows at the same time.

From our personal supplies, we scrounged other important lighting gear: wooden spring-type clothes pins to clamp gels and spun to the barndoors, black construction paper to make flags for blocking light, leather gloves to avoid cooking hands when moving hot lights, extra 15-amp and 20-amp screw-in fuses, and three-prong to two-prong electric-plug adapters.

We also built some lighting gear. For locations that were hundreds of feet from the nearest power outlet, we built some 100-foot extension cords from 10-gauge copper cable used in home construction. They were wired to fiberglass electrical outlet boxes, which were nailed to squares of wood for stability. Use the cable that's intended for wet locations (type UF). You'll need heavier-gauge cables for longer runs (otherwise you'll overheat the cable, blow fuses, and not get enough power to the lights). As with all extension cords, protect them from damage and keep them off wet ground. These cables were not designed for use in the rain — but that's the least of your troubles, because neither are your lights or camera equipment.

To weight down lights and other equipment, we made sandbags rather than rent them. We put a plastic bag three-quarters full of sand inside the cut-off legs of worn-out jeans and sewed the ends shut. This was better than spending $20 a weekend to rent them, and it made decisions on what to wear easier.

As with all the equipment rentals, you can get a substantial budget savings on lighting if your crewperson owns the equipment you need. This allows you to limit your costs to replacing burned-out lamps and buying the gels and spun. This approach also gives you an efficient lighting person who knows and cares about the equipment.

Camera equipment

After all our harping on how you can't afford this and that, you were probably surprised that our budget recommends buying a digital video camcorder rather than renting it for your shoots. Frankly, we were a little surprised when we figured out the costs ourselves. Here's how it worked out: To rent a DV camcorder, such as the widely available Sony DCR-VX1000, it would cost about $880 for four weekends. You'd need to rent the camera (cheaper than a playback deck) several more times to make VHS copies for selecting your takes and to digitize the footage into your nonlinear edit system. This will take a minimum of four separate days of rentals costing almost $600. That's $1,480, and you won't have a second-unit camera available to do establishing and insert shots, to shoot miniatures or special effects or title elements, to record intermediate outputs from your nonlinear editing system, to use for recording CD-quality sound effects and dialogue replacement, or to redigitize footage when the gremlins of the edit system attack.

If you spring for another $600, you can purchase a good-quality $1,800 DV camcorder with two extra five-hour lithium-ion batteries and a charger to keep unused batteries charging while you're shooting. The benefits of a second-unit camera, a playback and record deck for your edit system, and an audio recorder will be worth $600 — and money you might end up spending anyway having to rent the camcorder for extra days. You may also be able to rent out your camcorder to other moviemakers to recoup some of your own costs.

The camcorder needs to have three CCDs to capture a high-quality image. The sizes of these imaging chips range from 1/4" to 1/2", but the size doesn't matter much. Having three of them to separately capture red, green, and blue components of your images is the most important factor in creating a top-notch picture. Your camcorder also needs to have a zoom lens, zebra striping to show proper exposure, audio metering, time code, and manual controls for the focus, white balance, exposure, shutter speed and audio level. It must have an IEEE1394 (also called FireWire and i.Link) DV in-and-out connection. Connectors for composite video and audio input and output are also important for

46

bringing in audio elements and for outputting working copies to VHS tape. Though not essential, some of these cameras will also shoot digital stills that can be used for publicity photos, especially on a Web site.

Prices on these DV camcorders keep dropping, so you'll be able to get better and better camcorders for this $1,800 in the future. Right now, the Sony DCR-TRV900 is available for this price and has all the essential features, but check around for what's new on the market (and what it has done to lower the price of camcorders already on the market) before you buy. Also, look beyond your local video store. There are many companies selling nationally on the Internet who offer some great deals. It's fine to support the local businesses as long as they support your local moviemaking with a similar price break. Keep in mind that you may be required to pay local sales tax if you purchase equipment and supplies out of state. In some states, this requirement doesn't apply to Internet sales. Be sure to factor in any tax and shipping costs before you decide where to buy this big-ticket item.

If your camcorder can take a screw-in filter, you may want buy an ultraviolet haze filter. This filter is virtually clear glass and doesn't noticeably affect the image. However, it's a cheap filter, and if something accidentally hits the camera lens, the filter will take the blow, not the lens itself. It's easier to live without this filter than without a lens during the shoot. Get one, and leave it on the lens all the time. Most camcorders include a neutral-density filter to cut down light levels in bright daylight. If your camcorder doesn't have one, you'll probably need to buy one for shooting scenes outdoors on sunny days.

There are lots of tempting features for digital video camcorders, such as DVCAM and DVCPRO formats, interchangeable lenses, professional configuration of controls, XLR (three-pin) sound connectors, etc. These are all very nice, but none of them are essential to getting your movie done, and they will blow your budget if you try to buy or rent them. Now if someone wants to give these things to you, that's great. However, consider what it will do to other parts of your budget. We had a Digital Betacam camcorder loaned free to us for shooting *Grown Men*. This gave us stunning visual quality in a wide-screen format, but it wasn't really free. The tape costs were three times higher. Be sure you really know what freebies will cost you in the end.

47

One advantage of the compact DV cameras is that they look much like the camcorders used by the parental paparazzi at kids' soccer games. Consequently, you can avoid dealing with curious passers-by and hassles about permits on public streets and other such nonsense. You can set up your shots, shoot, and disappear before anyone really notices you. One team of gutsy moviemakers shot the movie *Windhorse* about the modern-day struggles of Tibetans under Chinese military occupation. Using their small camcorder and silent hand signals, they shot street scenes in Tibet virtually under the noses of Chinese officials. (You may not want to risk permanent residence in a foreign prison on your first digital movie.)

To support your camera, rent a tripod with a fluid head. Fluid heads don't give you the jerky camera moves that friction heads do. Now, we really debated on this rental because we also put the purchase of a $75 tripod in the budget to use for second-unit shooting. There are some not-bad consumer tripods with fluid heads in this price range. They will be good enough for those second-unit shots that are just a simple pan or a static shot. Our debate was that you'll spend $285 for renting and buying tripods, but for about $400, you can own a wonderful Manfrotto tripod with the 501 fluid head and ball-claw leveling. For this budget, we opted to save $115, but if you're thinking of renting out your camera, having a professional tripod with it might pay for itself pretty fast. You decide.

We didn't recommend a camcorder with a changeable lens because you'll be using a zoom lens for your videography. While prime lenses that are a single focal length do give better image clarity, a zoom lens speeds up your production. You can reframe a shot in seconds without having to change lenses. Even Ingmar Bergman used this technique to work faster. Good enough for us.

Don't bother renting a camera slate to mark the beginning of shots. Use a child's chalkboard or cut up a discarded white board. Anything legible that you can write scene and take numbers on will do the job. A real slate looks cool, but on your production, "cheap" is the ultimate cool.

Sound equipment
There aren't many corners to cut on the sound-recording equipment you'll need. Even big-dollar features don't get a lot more elaborate than

what you will be using. We're always amused to see behind-the-scene shots of the latest high-tech production using the same sound-recording techniques we used on our movies.

Thanks to the CD-quality sound recorded by digital video camcorders, you won't need to rent a tape recorder. But because of the compact sound controls on small DV camcorders and because you don't want the sound recordist breathing down the videographer's neck on every shot, you'll want to rent a small portable mixer to control the sound levels away from the camera.

To get sound to the mixer, you'll need a good shotgun microphone, such as a Sennheiser MKH-416 (or an ME-66, ME-67, ME-80 or equivalent microphone). You'll want to put that microphone in a shock mount to prevent picking up noise from the boom pole. As we mentioned earlier, you can find substitutes for the boom pole, but make sure any alternative poles are light enough for your boom operator to hold overhead all day. Whenever you are shooting at outdoor locations, rent a "zeppelin" windscreen to cut wind noise. It works much better than a foam windscreen, so pay the extra dollars. It's worth it. You can save money by not renting the windscreen if you know the entire weekend will be shot indoors.

The last things you'll need are headphones for the mixer, 200 feet of mike cable, and at least three sets of batteries for the mixer and the microphone. Sometimes you can have another set of headphones for the boom pole operator, but don't spend any extra money for it. We never used them, and our boom operator still knew where to point the mike with a little advice from the sound recordist. On *Grown Men*, the sound recordist with headphones also operated the boom mike. Only rarely was it necessary to adjust sound levels during a take, and if the levels were set high enough to get the quiet sounds, louder sounds could be cut down by aiming the shotgun microphone slightly to the side of the sound sources.

A word about using wireless microphones: Don't. It may seem like a great idea: You don't have to follow the actors with a microphone, and you can cut out the boom operator, saving a crew position. Unfortunately, these systems use tiny lavalier microphones that are more apt to sound tinny than other microphones. They are super-susceptible to sibilance, so they sometimes hiss on "s" sounds. (This last sentence would be a good test.) Clothing and chest hair rustle against the mikes. They are hard to hide and still get good sound. The radio-receiver units for these microphones sometimes pick up truckers' CBs and radio signals from the French underground. In short, they are not worth the trouble.

You'll get better sound more quickly and with less trouble using a boom mike. We tried them again for some segments of *Grown Men*, and, while the sound quality was on a par with the shotgun mike, they were still a royal pain. Basically, if your actors are going to move, lavaliers are going to pick up clothing noise, unintended body sounds, heartbeats, and the scratching of skin or hair rubbing against them. There's a good reason most big productions depend on shotgun mikes.

As with other equipment, you may find a person who personally owns a mixer and mikes. Try to rent cheaply from them or get them to join your crew and bring along their equipment.

Vehicles
We didn't budget anything for vehicles. We used what we had. John needed to buy a new used car shortly before we began shooting *Beyond Bob*, so he bought the kind of car we wanted the main character to drive. In *Grown Men*, John's latest car also did duty on camera. If you've done your scriptwriting well, you'll be using vehicles that are available to you free. If you need something exotic, try to find someone with a car compulsion who owns one. They are as excited by cars as you are about movies, so they are usually glad to drive theirs in the movie for you as long as it's not a crash scene. You may be able to talk a local car dealership into providing a vehicle, but beware if they start talking about insurance. You'll be buying a camcorder instead of insurance.

As for larger vehicles to haul equipment, you'll soon discover you don't need any. The equipment you can afford will fit in the trunks of cars.

Meals
Don't skimp on the quality of the food, just the price. We've included some sample menus in the appendix that don't require expensive ingredients, but

are good, hot, substantial meals. You can buy the food in bulk to save costs and prepare it yourself to avoid the extra cost of prepared food. Fortunately, Dale's wife Kathy is a very good cook and a tolerant woman. She, along with her sisters and in-laws, prepared and served meals for the cast and crew on our first two productions. These days, few people actually make meals from scratch, so even the simplest homemade meals taste like Mom's finest to them.

For the cast and crew, these meals almost made up for the meager pay and long hours. In fact, some cast members from our first film agreed to work on the second film only if Kathy was making the meals. Others said it was the best they'd eaten in years. Now don't be thinking we made gourmet meals. This was just standard fare prepared by human hands rather than extruded from vats in a factory. On *Grown Men*, our nonprofit status was parlayed into free food from many local restaurants and grocery stores, so that snacks and drinks were the primary food costs for several weekends.

Basically the budget includes a snack for a Friday-evening shoot and three meals a day for the Saturday and Sunday shooting days. Six meals and a snack for about 20 people for $125, or about 89 cents per person per meal. This may seem like a miracle, but it's not that hard to do if someone makes it.

The snack and breakfasts can be simpler, so you can save some money there to add a little to the lunch and dinner meals. If you plan menus for your entire production ahead of time, you can buy larger quantities of food at lower prices. For drinks, fruit-juice concentrates and generic-brand pop are cheapest (though we ultimately bought some name-brand pop because of crew complaints). For the nonperishable items (canned goods, chips, pop, coffee, tea, baking supplies), buy them as they go on sale during the months ahead of the production. Meats, cheeses, and fruit-juice concentrates can be bought on sale and frozen until needed. Frugal shopping, filling but inexpensive menus, and home cooking can make these meals a high point of your production and a low expenditure in your budget.

Locations
We found it pretty easy to get use of private locations for nothing. Most

people are thrilled to see a movie in production, though they quickly learn that it is tedious, hard work, even on fast-paced productions like ours. It's fun for them to tell the neighbors about hosting the movie crew. If you live in a town where movie productions are common, you may run into more people asking for money to use their property. You can't afford it, and tell them so. They may relent. If they still want money, move on. Sometimes losing your first choice leads to a better, more interesting choice. At least, try to look at it that way because you lose a lot of first choices making a feature-length movie with no visible budget.

We found small towns to be very accommodating. They don't usually ask for permits to shoot in public areas, and we even were allowed to work on some residential streets after a casual conversation with the police chief and notifying the neighbors who might be inconvenienced. Friends, neighbors, and relatives are also good sources of locations, as are state and federal parks.

Be mindful of distances when you plan your production. You can't afford to put up your cast and crew overnight, and if you drive a long distance to a location, the rental dollars you spent on your equipment will be ticking away every minute you're on the road. It's best to select sites that are near to your cast and crew and clustered together for easy grouping on the production schedule. We're fortunate that where we live there are landscapes ranging from rocky cliffs to secluded woods to city skyscrapers to urban decay to suburbia to cows in the fields, all within one hour's drive. If you look at your own hometown area with the eye of an outsider, you'll probably discover a great variety of unique settings for your movie as well.

We believe a cardinal rule of using locations is to be courteous and careful. Don't use things without asking. Take great pains not to damage anything. Clean up when you are finished. And be friendly to the owners and neighbors. When actors are waiting for their next scene, encourage them to chat with the natives. This is part of the thrill of having a movie crew shoot at your home, and it builds goodwill that allows you to come back for retakes if necessary. We think it is irresponsible of moviemakers to leave property owners unhappy. This poisons the waters for future productions and gives a bad name to all independent productions. To our knowledge, there aren't any locations that wouldn't welcome us back.

Tape stock

Tape stock prices are often in a state of change. In the course of one year, mini-DV tapes dropped by $2 a tape. Look at a variety of sources to find the best price on the market, and don't forget to check the Internet. In the appendix, we've listed some suppliers who generally have good prices.

In order to figure out how much tape stock you actually need, count script pages. Each full page works out to one minute of screen time. You'll be amazed how accurate this is if you use standard script format (see the example in the appendix), but be cautious of lines like "We see the Crimean War begin." This may require more than a few seconds of screen time.

Let's assume you have a perfect script... meaning 90 pages long, 90 minutes in length. Since your camera will most likely use mini DV cassettes and the 60-minute version is the best price, that's one and a half tapes. You'll be shooting in a three-to-one ratio (3:1), meaning you'll shoot three minutes of tape for every minute of the finished movie. So at a 3:1 ratio, you'll use 270 minutes of tape (90 x 3 = 270), or four and a half hours of tapes, or five tapes for production. By the same calculations, a 4:1 shooting ratio will require six tapes. You'll obviously need more tape if your script is longer. (If your script is longer than 100 minutes, it requires cutting to fit a $8,000 budget. Trust us; this surgery is much easier and cheaper to do now.)

We've thrown in another four tapes in the budget to cover intermediate outputs from your edit system. There are also VHS tapes for dubs to be used for music and sound work, a full-size DV 120-minute tape and two S-VHS tapes for the final output, and 15 VHS tapes for preview copies. The 120-minute DV tape will be extra expensive, because it has a memory chip in the cassette. For your 60-minute camera tapes, there are versions available without the memory chip that cost about a third less. Buy those. You don't need the features offered by the memory chip.

Production stills

You'll be sorry later when you do publicity, but you're going to be giving short shrift to still photos of your production. As the director and producer, we've taken photos during the shoots, but the results have been lackluster because we were busy helping with the movie magic when the interesting photo opportunities happened. We thought of getting someone who wanted to take photos for the experience and having them click away, but we were concerned about having another person to feed on the set and one more body to slow down a crew that needs to be lightning fast. We opted for one less person on two of our movies, knowing we'd regret it when it came time to assemble a publicity package, and we did.

On *Grown Men*, we did have a friend shoot some publicity photos on a couple selected days and got some nice shots. We recommend picking one day in your production schedule that promises to be photogenic and having a volunteer paparazzo tag along for the day. Another approach is to shoot your publicity stills later as staged shots. We did this to get poster shots for our movies. Any way you do this, only budget enough for 5 rolls of 35mm film and processing. There's not money for an extravagant publicity kit, so there's no sense in having hundreds of photos to choose from — all you need is a handful of good ones.

Storage vault rental
When we shot on film, we felt the need to safely store our negatives and master soundtracks in a film vault. It costs about $100 a year. Since it doesn't cost us extra, we've stored our digital movie's master tapes there too. However, we think you can skip this expense. Just take care to store your tapes safely. It's wise to store them in double plastic bags (in case of roof leaks or exploding water heaters) inside sturdy containers. Make sure the tapes are well away from magnetic fields, such as refrigerator magnets, electric motors, and coils of electrical cord. Steel drums buried in the backyard are pretty secure if the Environmental Protection Agency doesn't dig them up for analysis.

For added protection you can rent another DV camera or deck (which ever is cheapest, of course) and shell out for enough extra tapes to make a copy of each original master tape. (Aren't lossless tape formats grand!) Then have this set of tapes stored at a different geographic location that is far enough away not to be struck by the same hurricane, lava flow, locust, or tornado that is going to nuke you and your master tapes. Don't forget to flip the record lock-out tab on the camera tapes the moment they come out of the camera to avoid artistic devastation resulting from clumsy fingers on the VCR controls.

Nonlinear edit system

Along with digital video camcorders, computer-based nonlinear edit systems are responsible for rewriting the manual on how to do independent movies. They produce professional results, have all kinds of high-end features, and are no more expensive than buying a personal computer. You can own your editing system for less than it cost us to rent a 16mm flatbed editing table for our film, *Beyond Bob*. And we got a good deal.

Right now, we've budgeted the iMac DV Special Edition with 400mhz speed, 13GB hard drive, 128MB RAM (random access memory), DVD drive (which also reads CD-ROMs and audio CDs), and USB and FireWire ports. It's equipped with enough hard-drive space, speed, and memory to cut your digital movie and mix its soundtrack. There are more powerful Macintoshes and PCs that can do the same job, but not for so little money. Of course, by the time you read this, there will be faster computers available, which means you can get a better system for the same money, or you can buy this system cheaper and cut your budget even more. Either way, you win.

If you're looking at other systems, be sure they can successfully run video-editing software in the real world, not just in their carefully worded promotional brochures. It's best to see the system work or at least talk to someone using the same gear you're going to buy.

Assembling your own system is an option, but one that can be fraught with hazards because video demands a lot from a computer system. For example, hard drives must have a 3.6MB-per-second *sustained* data rate for audiovisual editing. Lots of drives can meet this requirement for average rates (meaning they go faster and slower than this speed but average out to it) but they may not be able to sustain this rate (meaning they never run slower). Another difficult selection is a capture card to get your digital video into the edit system. They come in an ice-cream-shop variety of flavors, and not all will do the job for you. Before putting together your own editing system, get a complete list of specification from a working system to use as your blueprint. We'd hate for you to spend a big chunk of your budget and end up with a high-tech space heater. For those of you that want to limit your risks (as if producing an independent movie weren't risky!) buy an integrated system like the iMac DV SE that is ready to rock and roll. Also, get as much hard drive size and RAM as you can for the money available.

While this iMac system comes with iMovie editing software, don't plan on editing with it. Unless your digital film is an ersatz home movie, iMovie won't have the controls and features you need to do a professional-looking and professional-sounding project. However, it can capture stills and create QuickTime movies for a Web site.

You'll need to add professional video-editing software like Adobe Premiere or Apple Final Cut Pro to play with the big kids. John edited *Grown Men* with Final Cut Pro, and Dale produces digital videos with Premiere day-to-day in his paying job. Final Cut Pro seems to be more crash-resistant, but Premiere works well too, and costs about half the price. Of course, prices are likely to drop, so shop around. Try to get useful free software in the deal. Sometimes high-quality image-editing software, such as Adobe Photoshop Limited Edition (Can you say "special effects"?), is thrown in as a promotion.

We didn't budget for software to create a "film" look for your digital movie, even though there are some products available in the $250 range. There's a cheaper trick that gives your footage a pretty decent shot-on-film quality. In Adobe Premiere, just reduce the speed of your shots to 99% of normal speed. It barely affects running time (one minute over a 90 minute movie); it causes no noticeable speed lag or shift in voice quality; and the result is a respectable film look.

Expect your editor to want the latest editing software and a real-time system that doesn't have to render transitions and effects (always more expensive — usually lots). Be ready to negotiate with and explain budget realities to whomever will be doing the editing. If that's you, don't let anyone hear you talking to yourself. They already think you're loony for making a feature-length movie, and you don't want to give them more evidence for the commitment hearing.

Video dubs
You'll need video dubs of your movie for your composer to write the music score, for actors to loop lines that were badly recorded, for timing

sound effects not recorded on location, and for doing postproduction special-effects shots. All this for $20 or less? Sure. Just buy VHS tapes, record edited segments of your movie out to your DV camcorder, and then duplicate them on the VCR sitting under your TV.

Music recording
Dramatic changes in audio-recording technology have led to the growth of home studios and ultra-low-budget music production. This means there are lots of composers who have their own recording capabilities, and you may be able to eliminate much of this budget item except for tape and CD supplies. If you get the final music soundtrack on a CD, then you won't have to acquire any additional equipment to digitize it into your editing system. If your composer can't do the recording, then you have to start looking for the blue-light specials.

Start by thinking small and looking for special arrangements. We've recorded music tracks in the basement studio of a freelance audio engineer. The sound booth was tiny and the cheapest in town, and the results were as good as with a larger studio. It's the quality of the microphones and the recording and mixing equipment that are most important.

There's only enough money in this budget item for about five hours of studio time, though you may be able to arrange a lower rate by agreeing to work only when the studio has no other bookings. Either way, your composer isn't going to have weeks of time in the studio to complete your music tracks. She or he is going to have to record on the musical equivalent of your 3:1 shooting ratio, with very few takes of live performances. Any editing will need to be done on the video-editing system. Plenty of rehearsals before entering the studio will make this feasible.

When we needed to record an orchestra and a big band, our composer arranged for free use of the studio and recording equipment at a technical school for audio engineers and musicians. Good connections and lots of friends can help with these kinds of expensive items.

Sound effects, foley, and dialogue looping
Thanks to the CD-quality sound that digital video offers, you can do the

recording of any sound effects and foley (sounds for the actors' motions) and the "looping" of replacement dialogue using your camcorder. The on-camera microphone may be adequate for sound effects and foley work; however, to make sure the sound quality of the dialogue matches the location recordings, rent a low-cost tabletop microphone so you can get farther away from any camera noise. While a sound booth at a recording studio will give you the best quality audio, you can get very usable results in a quiet room with blankets or drapes hung on the walls to quiet echoes. This makeshift sound booth will also work well for dialogue looping, helping you limit your costs to rental of a microphone for one weekend. If you can borrow one from a school, church, library, friend, or business, you can zero out this budget item.

Sure this means you'll make some compromises, but that's life in the ultra-low-budget lane. Remember that your audiences most likely will be seeing your movie on video, which means sound from a 3-inch TV speaker. Great sound is wasted there. Good sound is the order of the day.

Titles
Thanks to the power of your video-editing software you can make titles that rival those of any feature film you've ever seen — at no added cost. Even elaborate animated ones are within your grasp if you have animation skills. Simple animated ones can be produced even if you're new to animation.

Sneak preview
A sneak preview is a good way to test how your movie will play to an audience, to see if its comedy, drama, suspense or romance works the way you intended. Of course, there's no money to do this. Of course, we have a free alternative. There are three ways we know to do this for nothing. Start by outputting the edited version of your movie to DV tapes and combining them onto a VHS cassette. It doesn't have to be a perfect version to get some helpful audience feedback.

The first option is to loan the tape to people who are your intended audience, whose opinion you value, and whose candor you can count on. This probably won't be the most helpful feedback, because most responses will be about how surprised these people are that you've been making a "real movie." Also, you won't be involved in the process, which is one of the most helpful aspects of a sneak preview.

The second option is to invite a group of people (same credentials as above: intended audience, valued opinion, candor) to your home or any nicer place you can get for free, make some popcorn, give them soft drinks, and show your movie. Many audience reactions will be "Wow, I didn't realize you were making a *movie* movie," but you may get a group dynamic going in the response. More important, you will be there to observe their real reactions and your own. Their reactions will reveal when you really drew the audience into the story. If you don't see it, you probably didn't do it. Your reaction will be the "wince factor." When you find yourself cringing at an upcoming scene or special effect or line of dialogue or performance, it's probably one you should fix. Just like in script writing, you can convince yourself that the problem areas are not really problems, but the blinders fall from your eyes when you sit down with a real audience. Use this unvarnished look at your movie to make it better.

The third option is to use your salesmanship or the kindness of friends to arrange for your movie to be projected free in a theater for an audience. This can be done from your VHS tape or from your mini-DV tapes with a quick tape change after the first 60 minutes. We were able to arrange for a sneak preview of *Beyond Bob* as a fundraiser for the local Independent Feature Project chapter. They arranged for the theater, the video projector, and publicity. They collected a small admission fee to add to their funds, and we got a preview audience. You can use some of your photocopying funds to make up short response sheets for the audience to fill out after the movie, but these comments were of less use than what we learned observing the audience and our own winces.

Final output and preview cassettes

When it comes time to get your movie out of your nonlinear editor, you'll find it can get complicated. We'll run you through the procedure later, but for budget purposes, you need to know that at the end of the process you'll need to rent a DV recording deck that can take a full-size DV tape that is 124 minutes long. (Your camcorder uses mini-DV tapes that are a maximum of 60 minutes long — a little short for your 90-minute movie.) During the same weekend, you'll be renting an S-VHS deck (at a lower rate than the DV deck) to create two duplication submasters, so you can make future preview copies by renting the less-expensive S-VHS deck again. Depending on how many copies you'll be making in the future, you may want to spring for a $200 S-VHS deck instead of renting one at about $65 per weekend. As long as you have the DV rented, use it with your home VHS record deck to make 20 preview copies for festivals, distributors, and publicity kits.

You're also going to need video copies for other purposes. For any TV previews, such as talk shows or news interviews, you'll need a 3/4" U-matic, S-VHS, or BetacamSP video version. You don't need the whole movie in this format, just two or three good selected scenes that you've edited out of your movie for this purpose. You can make an S-VHS preview tape when you have the S-VHS record deck for transferring your full movie to this format. Make a copy of the preview scenes on mini-DV format too.

To save on transfer costs to make a 3/4" U-matic or BetacamSP version, ask the TV station if they will transfer it to one of these formats if you bring them a mini-DV or an S-VHS copy. It only takes them a few minutes, and they will consider it as preparation for the interview or news story. If you provide the blank tape stock, then you can walk away with a preview that you can use at the next TV station. You can buy this tape stock half-price from a company that sells recycled, evaluated tapes. They take used tapes from TV stations and production companies who don't use a tape for more than one pass. They erase and evaluate the tapes so they are as good as new. Look to the ever-informative appendix for a listing of such companies and some other low-cost tape suppliers.

Publicity photos and packets

Patience is a virtue. It also saves money in a world of "we can get it there overnight if you pay $20 more." For our publicity packets, we selected photos from the ones we'd shot on location. While not a sterling collection, they were interesting enough to get them published in more than a dozen newspapers and magazines. We recommend "modest but pithy" as the theme for publicity packets. Don't waste money on 8 x 10s. Most publications can do everything necessary with a 5 x 7 color glossy photo. It will also cost extra to do them in black-and-white, so don't. We had several magazines and newspapers use them in color, and it presents no problem for publications using black-and-white images. The patience comes in when you get them printed. Forget the expensive labs who serve studio photographers. Go for the mail-order labs or the drug store labs. Check the appendix to find our favorite ones. We got our 5 x 7s for $1.25 each. A couple had poor color balance, so we sent them back for a free reprinting, which turned out fine. Sure, we had to wait two weeks to get them all, but time was something we had in large supply.

The publicity packets themselves consisted of pocket portfolios (bought at a discount office supply store) with the movie's title on the front. This title art was photocopied onto full-sheet adhesive labels (same store) and then cut to size and pasted on the folders. We handcolored some of the title text with highlighter markers. Inside we included the publicity photos and photocopied sheets with synopsis, cast list, and a feature article on the production for reporters to plagiarize. We wrote these ourselves and copied them at the cheapest duplicator we could find. Each of our packets cost less than $9.00: five photos ($6.25), folder (.25), about 20 pages of text ($1.20), mailing envelope (.50). Add to that the $18 we spent on the box of 50 label sheets. These kits looked professional and got us as much publicity as we could get from a packet.

The Internet is your friend when it comes to publicity packets. You can avoid almost all of these costs if you have access to a scanner to scan your photographs. As you move into the publicity mode, your nonlinear editing system will become your Internet publicity machine. All of your written materials, your scanned photos, and any logo can be e-mailed directly to entertainment reporters anywhere in the world or put on a free Web site where they can find them... at no cost. If your kit is a quality job, they won't mind getting it. You can even create some short QuickTime or AVI files on your Web site showing brief segments of the movie. Indicate in the publicity kits that preview copies of the movie are available, but save money, and only send them out if a reporter is interested enough to request one.

Photocopying scripts and miscellaneous photocopying
You'll need one full copy of the script for each main performer and supporting role, so you may be able to trim script copying costs if your cast is small. The bit players only need the pages they are in. You also need copies for director, producer, unit production manager, director of photography, sound recordist, art director, wardrobe supervisor, makeup-and-hair supervisor, editor, and composer.

Miscellaneous copying will include maps to locations, call sheets for the shooting days, release forms, shot-log sheets, and dozens of items that will crop up before, during, and after production. Try to get a photocopying shop to do all of your copying free or for a reduced rate in exchange for being listed in the screen credits. Your local Independent Feature Project office may have a deal with a local photocopy shop; check with them for details.

Postage for publicity and preview tapes
You'll want to send the publicity packets by first-class mail. Don't get sucked into the "send it express" or "fax it to me" syndrome. Planning ahead or waiting until the next printing deadline for a publication will eliminate these unnecessary costs. The people you're mailing the material to want it today so it can sit on their desks for two weeks until they get to it. First-class postage and a mailing envelope will cost about $2 per publicity packet if you keep the size small, totaling $30 for 15 packets.

You're going to need to mail your preview cassettes around to distributors and festivals. We recommend the U.S. Postal Service's Priority Mail. A VHS cassette in the free box or envelope provided by the Postal Service will cost about $3.50 to ship, and it will arrive in 2 to 3 days. You can save about 50 cents by going Parcel Post, but you give the postal workers a week or so to use your video as a stress-relief device. For 20 preview cassettes, mailing will cost about $70. What's left in your postage budget will be chewed up easily by remailing the few preview cassettes that are returned and by sending out those letters requesting bids for equipment prices. Eventually you'll find yourself dipping into the grocery money for postage.

Video-to-film transfer
You may notice that there's no line for a video-to-film transfer in the budget. Darn tootin' there isn't. Creating a motion-picture version of your project will more than double your production costs. Transferring your digital video image to 16mm with mono soundtrack or 35mm film with stereo soundtrack will cost from $100 to $900 per minute. A 35mm transfer costs about 50 percent more than a 16mm transfer. For this $9,000 to $81,000, you'll end up an image negative, an optical-sound negative, and one answer print of your movie.

Obviously, this is not a cheap path to take, and you'll want to be quite sure it's necessary before you run down it. For any feature-length movie, there are two major routes of distribution: release on film or release on video (tape or DVD). Film releases are designed for big festivals that don't accept video (a dinosaur attitude that is rapidly teetering toward extinction) and for showings in theaters. We chose to stay on video because movies as small as ours have a hard time even making it onto the screens at art-house theaters these days. Even movies from some major studios go directly to home video without ever flickering onto a theater screen. We knew that any potential distributor would preview our movie on video and that it most likely would be distributed in the home-video market. If a distributor is really excited to do a theatrical release of your movie, the cost of the transfer to film can be built into the distribution deal. Whether you pay for it yourself or the distributor pays for it (which really means it will be taken out of your potential profits), get bids from several vendors before selecting someone to do a tape-to-film transfer. A little Internet research will give you loads of information about the best way to prepare your digital movie for transfer at different postproduction houses and about the merits and weaknesses of different transfer procedures.

As more theaters and major producers investigate projecting digital movies on movie-theater screens, this topic will probably evaporate from your list of things to decide. So unless you're seriously committed to having your production end up on film stock, we recommend staying in the digital video format and seeking your fortune there.

🎥🎥🎥

If you've done all the begging, finagling, dickering, and shortcutting we recommend, you now have a budget of $8,000 or less. Congratulations. You've just taken one of the biggest steps towards making your feature-length movie a reality. You've set realistic expectations for the kind of digital movie it can be and created a plan for making it happen. You're on your way to a successful production. Savor the moment after you've completed your budget. Sit back and just visualize what it will be like shooting your movie, what it will be like to see the story you love on the screen in front of an audience. Spend at least five minutes with this vision so you can remember it well, because you're going to need it. This vision of your goal has got to last when the realities of funding, organizing, and launching your production come stomping into the room.

We hit those realities right away on our digital movie. We didn't have $8,000 lying around ready to use on the date we set for starting production. Our solution? Figure out how to shoot it for a lot less. Here's what you can do if you find yourself in this situation.

How to shoot it for less

If you throw out all the postproduction — that's everything after "Storage vault rental" in the budget except for photocopying — you'll get rid of close to half of your budget expenses, leaving your cash need at $4,990. You won't be able to do any editing, music-track or sound-effects work, titles, sneak preview, final output, or publicity. But you won't be ready to do any of that work until after you finish shooting anyway. And once you've got your principal shooting done, you can set the postproduction schedule to match your ability to raise cash.

If this dollar amount is still an insurmountable mountain to climb, then shorten the mountain. Fire up your networking skills and start talking to people about the movie you want to shoot, especially people who own DV cameras. If you can get use of a camera and tripod for free (and possibly the videographer with it), you can shoot your movie for $2,980. If you also can get your lighting and sound equipment donated, your shooting budget will be under $2,000. That's between $40 and $60 a week for a year. That's a part-time weekend job for a year or less. This is a hill you can climb if you really want to shoot your movie.

Of course, the hydra of the remaining budget costs will rear its ugly heads at a later point, but you can lop them off one at a time if you're persistent... and you keep working weekends at the video store.

THE BUSINESS
(Ultra-low Budget, Inc.)

When we first dreamed of making our movies, we never dreamed of becoming accountants. We never dreamed of becoming corporate officers or contract lawyers or corporate tax preparers.

To us, these weren't dreams. They were nightmares. That's not to impugn any of these professions; they're just not ones to which we aspired.

But just as your dreams at night sometimes cast you in unusual roles, the dream of making your own feature-length movie may put you into some unexpected professions. We found ourselves pushed, pulled, and thrown into all of these jobs as we got into the business end of making movies.

Now if you're as passionate about making movies as we are, you're probably thinking about skipping this chapter and saying to yourself, "I don't want to be in business. I just want to make my movie." We said that too, but it didn't help. We still ended up in business, and you will too if you plan to have your feature shown somewhere other than your basement. This is one of the dark chapters of making a movie, so you might as well come to terms with it now because it's not going away.

Here's the bad news of this book for anyone in love with making movies: it's a business.

During the ten years that we've spent producing our feature-length projects, at least seven years of that time has been drained away running a business. Sometimes it seems like producing and shooting movies is just a sideline. But no matter how grisly it is, this work has to be done. Even gourmet cooks have pots to wash. And since you're going to be a gourmet cook working at a diner, you probably can't afford to have someone else do your dirty work.

Now, we're not saying we've got the inside track on the business of business. It remains the one area we are least certain about. However, we avoided having any really scary discussions with tax collectors or other people's attorneys, so we make the bold presumption that we did okay.

Nevertheless, before we started our production of *Grown Men*, we switched tracks in the business area. We incorporated as an educational nonprofit organization to produce the movie. There were several considerations that led us to that decision. We were tired of doing corporate tax filings; we were not making profits as a business; we couldn't accept volunteers or donated services and materials as a for-profit business; and we acknowledged the fact that we aren't very entrepreneurial by nature. So we've seen both sides of this fence, and there's some green grass in each place.

What follows is how we took care of business — both for-profit and not-for-profit — but it comes with a warning: results may vary. The bad news is that almost every state has different rules related to business and nonprofit issues. The Internal Revenue Service (IRS) has consistent rules, which may be interpreted differently by individual IRS personnel. The good news for you is that we work in Minnesota, which has some of the more stringent rules and most aggressive tax structures. (We're not complaining, mind you — both lead to an above-average quality of life.) This means that some issues we faced may be nonexistent where you work.

The details of our experience aside, you can't ignore business issues without suffering repercussions later. You will have to investigate to find the best solution for your personal situation under the current laws and tax structure. Our two approaches are just a few of many strategies. They might not be the best ones for you.

Trust us on this point. You'll be glad you took care of business issues when the distributor who wants your movie asks, "Are all the rights clear on this film?" It may be the difference between getting your movie distributed and not.

Business decisions
There were four main factors that motivated the business choices we made:

1) **Money.** As always, we couldn't afford to spend any money that wouldn't show up on the screen somehow.

2) **Rights.** We wanted to produce movies that were ready to be sold as professional productions, meaning we clearly owned all rights to our productions and could sell them.

66

3) **Legal Liability.** We owned houses and cars that we didn't want to lose in a lawsuit.

4) **Tax Obligations.** We didn't want to spend the rest of our days in tax jail (where you can either make license plates or produce movies that explain tax laws).

Because these four factors are often joined at the hip, please excuse some repetition in our ramblings. It's important to know how each of these factors will affect other decisions you must make.

Money
If the point hasn't been made already, let us reiterate: Money and the lack of it are going to be the undercurrent that affects every decision you make. To complete a feature-length digital movie for a paltry $8,000, you can't spend a penny that isn't going to somehow improve the look or the sound of your movie. This means a big list of people you can't hire (but need) and things you can't buy or rent (but need).

Professional help
At the business end of film production, lack of money primarily translates into not being able to afford lawyers, accountants, and tax preparers. This means you'll need free help to set up your business or nonprofit, develop contracts and releases, keep your books, and prepare tax statements. Since we didn't have friends who could do this work for us, we had no options. We learned to do it ourselves.

There are a number of how-to books and Web sites that are immensely helpful with everything from basic accounting to incorporating a business, to starting a nonprofit, to boilerplate examples of essential documents. We've listed ones we've used in the appendix, but don't let this list limit you. There are many fine works out there in your local library and on the Internet. Keep in mind that most libraries can borrow from bigger or more specialized libraries if they don't have what you need. Library books and Web sites are resources that fit your budget.

We also asked other people who had done this before for their ideas, warnings, sample contracts, release forms, articles of incorporation, and such. We took a local class on incorporating a nonprofit organization.

We learned that we could take the work of other people's expensive lawyers and tailor it to our needs. We also learned that being a lawyer doesn't mean you can write good contracts or release forms or articles of organization. We've seen contracts and release forms with serious holes that could really hurt both parties. Personally, we believe that complex legal language creates more misunderstandings than it prevents. We feel that plain language will make it less likely that you'll have problems with contracts, release forms, and other written agreements. That's been our experience for ten years.

Lack of money will probably force you to do your own accounting, bookkeeping, and tax preparation too. But they're not so bad when compared to being trampled by stampeding wildebeests. Truly, these tasks are the most boring, confusing, and terrifying work on a film production. And you'll need to do them even if you are operating as a nonprofit organization, though there are some shortcuts available. Do whatever you can to find someone who loves doing these jobs and get them to take on the task. Dale, as producer, reluctantly took on these duties and learned basic corporate accounting and tax preparation in the trenches. (We think this is what caused his hairline to retreat and go AWOL.) Even if you hand over these duties, be sure to learn enough about the books to know where the money is going. (There are too many stories of accountants flying off to Rio... not that they don't deserve the break.)

If you're forced to do your own taxes, take heart. Surveys of professional tax preparers have shown extreme differences in the final tax returns they prepared. Just do your honest best and hope the IRS treats you kindly.

As for the accounting, it's one of those mystic arts, but it is learnable. If you start with a basic accounting text the way we did and spend a few evenings studying it, you'll soon understand the basic principles of accounting... or you'll renew your efforts to find someone to do it for you. Many textbooks also include helpful examples of lists of accounts, general ledgers, ledger entries, and year-end reports, which are the basic tools of accounting. If you are computer literate, there are accounting programs that will do most of this work for you once you set up the accounts.

Insurance
Working on an $8,000 budget means your production will do without

liability insurance, completion bonds, or errors-and-omissions insurance, unless you scrape up more money. There's only one of these that we would suggest you even consider, but you should know what they all are.

Liability Insurance Liability insurance is the basic coverage that pays for damage or injury you cause, such as dropping an electrified Klieg light into a hot tub full of bathers. Not having liability insurance has prevented us from using some locations, has caused us to pay out of pocket for some minor damage to buildings, and has caused us to lose more than a few hours of sleep. The cost of this insurance will add a significant percentage to your tiny budget, but if you're planning to do especially risky work or are accident-prone, it may be worth rounding up the extra greenbacks to pay for it. If you happen to work in the audio-visual field, you may already carry annual production insurance that you can apply to your movie, or you may be able to add a cheap rider to your existing policy. Unless you have one of these policies in your pocket ("Is that an insurance rider, or are you just glad to see me?"), you'll be on the high wire without "the good hands" to catch you. That's what we did. You just have to be very cautious, safety conscious, and careful with borrowed props, costumes, and locations. The one liability insurance we got was a low-cost damage option on our rental equipment. Given the cost to replace this equipment, it was worth doing.

Completion Bonds Completion bonds are essentially insurance policies that will pay over-budget costs in order to guarantee investors that you will complete the production. Forget it. Anyone putting money into an $8,000 movie had better recognize that this is a long-shot proposition. There are a hundred minor things that can cripple a fringe production like yours, and only three things that will get it finished — the tenacity of your production troupe, good luck, and the kindness of strangers. And you're depending on all of these. You and everyone on your production are rolling the dice that your skills and creativity are going to win big. There are simply no guarantees, and any investors should recognize that they are betting on you, plain and simple.

Of course, you couldn't afford to get a completion bond anyway. Even if you tried, the completion bond company would probably shriek with laughter. It's the equivalent of smoking unfiltered cigarettes, flying home-built jets, bungee jumping, ... and then applying for life insurance.

69

Completion bond companies don't want to pay to finish your movie, so the only way they will give you a completion bond is if your production uses the safest, time-tested production procedures. Wrong universe! You're going to do something that is completely alien to completion bond companies. You're going to break most of the rules to make something out of nothing. And that's only going to happen if you and your investors close your eyes really tightly and repeat "I believe. I believe. I BELIEVE!"

<u>Errors-and-Omissions Insurance</u> This is liability insurance that protects you in case you failed to get all the necessary rights and releases from performers, used copyrighted material without permission, included libelous material, didn't get location releases, infringed upon a famous title, or based your screenplay on someone else's published work. Simply put, it's insurance to protect against you — the producer — having not done your job.

There are three reasons we didn't bother with this insurance. First, we did our job right and got all the necessary rights and clearances. Second, no one will issue this insurance to you unless you have done your job right. ("Sure, we'll insure you against dying while deep-sea diving now that you've given up diving.") Third, this primarily protects the distributors, so our feeling was, let them pay for it if they're so nervous. If someone is insisting on errors-and-omission insurance, give them copies of your paperwork, and make it part of the contract that they will pay for the insurance.

Employees

As a business, lack of bucks will prevent you from having employees, especially union ones. You can't afford employees because you have to pay them at least minimum wage — except for corporate officers, sole proprietors, and partners, who can forego salary. If you were a union production, even at the union's low-budget rates, you'd have to pay union scale to cast and crew. That alone would use up all of your production money and more. So if you come from a long line of union activists, either give up this ultra-low-budget movie idea now or steel yourself for some tense family reunions.

The employee issue is a real problem for low-budget independent productions these days. When we started making movies, we were able

70

to have all crew members be independent contractors and defer their salaries to be paid out of any profits — if there were any. Everyone on our productions was okay with this arrangement, because we were all doing it for the experience, not the money. Well, it can't be done that way today. This was one big reason for us to start up a nonprofit organization to do productions as educational experiences. Here's what happened to independent contractors — the condensed version, as we understand it.

The federal Internal Revenue Service (IRS) audited the film-and-video industry's practices and found that most people — actors, crew, directors, producers, etc. — were hired as independent contractors who were responsible for paying their own income tax, social security withholdings, and such. The IRS also found that many of these taxes and withholdings weren't being paid. Then the IRS looked closely at the nature of these jobs and found that most of them met the statutory description of employees, not independent contractors. So today, only a few positions, such as director and producer, can qualify as independent contractors on a production. This may sound like arcane tax talk, but it significantly affects your production. If you have employees (actors and crew), you have to pay them minimum wage and maybe overtime if you manage to shoot more than 40 hours on a given weekend. (We did 32 hours.) You'll also have to withhold income tax and social security and pay for workers' compensation insurance. As you saw in the sample budget, this very quickly adds up to all of your production money being spent on salaries.

We've come up with five ways to deal with this issue on an ultra-low-budget movie. We've only tried the last one, and the other three legal ones fall in the ideas-that-might-work category. You might come up with others of your own, but in any case, check out your plan with state and federal employment regulators before you go forward. Federal rules continue to change and so do state requirements, so you'll need to scan the sea before you set sail. Here's the skinny on the five approaches:

- Ignore the rules and just work with little or no salary for all cast and crew. Bad idea. This could earn you big fines and payment of back salaries, and maybe even some jail time as a corporate officer who willfully violated the labor laws.

- Pay wages and find a way to come up with double the budget for

71

your digital movie. Also, you would have to do a lot of paperwork for taxes and withholdings. This might spur you to hire a payroll service or payroll staff person.

• Hire all cast and crew as student interns who are paid only a small stipend as they work on your production to learn and earn resume credentials. This might work, especially if you have an inexperienced crew. However, this method should be checked out thoroughly with state and federal employment officials before attempting it.

• Make the entire production a partnership venture, so everyone on the cast and crew would be partners in the production. As owners, they and you could forego salaries. This would be like everyone on the production owning a corner grocery store together, making business decisions together, contributing to the costs equally, and sharing in the profits equally. It could work with the right people, sort of a digital-movie commune. The downside is that this business structure would put your personal assets on the table if there were a lawsuit or some financial liability. ("Daddy, why is that man repossessing my trike?")

• Finally, create a nonprofit organization whose mission would be to offer educational experiences for cast and crew on independent movie productions. All cast and crew could be volunteers on the production. Equipment, supplies, and food could be donated, something that a for-profit business can't accept. This was the approach we chose, because it fit with our personal goals of making movies... not making money. And everyone gains experience and resume credentials whether the project is for-profit or not-for-profit. Obviously, this isn't right for everyone, but current employment rules make it very hard to do an ultra-low-budget movie as a business.

One downside of this approach is that your workers might work harder and better if they see this as an entry-level professional production. If you're asking them to volunteer their time and effort, it could affect how they view the project, and working professionals might be less likely to sign on. This means your crew and cast might be less experienced. But that can be an asset. They won't know that you can't make a feature-length movie for no money.

On *Grown Men*, we found that experienced people and novices alike were happy to work on this nonprofit production, and many brought equipment with them for free. For the most part, everyone treated it as a serious production, and only a few people failed to show up. However, we did not shoot our digital movie on a grueling four-weekend production schedule, so we don't know for sure if this volunteerism and goodwill would hold up for a month of movie boot camp.

Obviously, the employee issue is going to play a major role in your decision about the business or nonprofit organization you'll use for your movie production. You'll need to select an approach that you can afford and an approach that will let you meet your moviemaking goals. And then you'll want to check it out thoroughly with state and federal employment officials so your movie dream doesn't become a business nightmare.

Rights

The next major factor affecting your business or nonprofit activities is the securing of rights.

Not securing all necessary rights for your digital movie is going to put you at a severe disadvantage when you try to distribute it. It might even tie up your production in legal actions. And it's a problem you can avoid.

Rights are a matter that you'll want to pay attention to from day one. A lot of decisions you make will relate to getting rights to present your finished movie, and you'll need to diligently gather them as you wend your way through preproduction, production, and postproduction. So fire up the photocopier. There are forms to copy.

Contracts, release forms, and letters of approval are the three ropes you're going to use to hog-tie those pesky rights. The performance rights you're looking for include the screenplay, the performances of your cast, the work products of your crew, the music and sound effects (if they come from a recorded library) in your soundtrack, any copyrighted material used in the movie (images — such as photos or prints that are more than just background, readings or dialogue from other sources, snatches of music or images on the radio or TV), and the locations you use (excluding public property, but be aware that seemingly public areas such as shopping malls are privately owned). Get the approvals before you commit these items and performances to tape. If you don't and can't get the rights later, you've wasted precious production time.

We started securing rights as soon as the first crewperson joined us on our production. Everyone, including the director and producer, signed a release form that gave full ownership of their work to the organization producing the movie. We used this ownership clause to secure rights to the cast's performances, the crew's work, the screenplay, and the music tracks. On our first two movies, our composer, who wanted to potentially use the music again, only granted us synchronization rights. Synchronization rights mean you can do anything you want with the music as long as it stays connected to the movie images. If you want to release a hit single, you have to get more rights. Given that we were getting thousands of dollars of original music for next to nothing, it seemed like a fair compromise. We also bought some previously recorded music for a few scenes, and for this we also used a contract for synchronization rights only.

Release forms also will take care of the rights to use the images of extras, unpaid performers, and locations. If you're shooting in a public place, you technically don't need to get permission to use the images of people who could have been seen by anyone in that public place, as long as you don't highlight them (close-ups of people adjusting their undergarments will just buy you trouble). Some productions post signs that warn people entering the area that they may be included in a movie, but that presumes the moviemakers have gotten permission to shoot in that area in the first place. Guerrilla productions like ours only get permission if there's no permit fee from the city or whomever, so this may draw too much attention to your work. If you decide to feature someone in particular, you better get them to sign a release form or make sure they're not identifiable. Also, get signed location releases for every privately owned site you shoot on or shoot at. Do this in advance of your shoot dates to avoid those ugly high-stress negotiations while your cast and crew are waiting. Samples of individual, group, and location release forms are included in the appendix.

Approval letters are all you need to get use of various copyrighted items. For example, we featured an existing hang-gliding book in one of our productions. To obtain approval, we just wrote to the publisher, explained the movie and the context to them, and they sent a permission letter.

Sound effects from recorded libraries don't require any forms. When we've used them we just bought the sound with synchronization rights from a production house and got a receipt. Be sure to tell them you want it for a feature-length movie, because some libraries aren't licensed to be used for feature productions. Of course, being in the proper low-budget mindset, you're planning to record all of your sound effects with your DV camcorder anyway.

If in any situation you can't get the rights you need (worldwide, exclusive, without restrictions, in perpetuity), stop. Do not pass go. If you can't persuade that performer, crewperson, landowner, or copyright owner, don't even think about using their stuff. Find another solution. Otherwise, you'll regret it when you have to go back and beg that person for the rights so you can sell your movie.

The last point you need to consider about rights is holding on to them once you've gotten them. You or your organization automatically own copyright to your production. Under U.S. law, you don't have to register it or even put a copyright notice on it in order to own your movie's copyright. However, it is advisable to register it with the Library of Congress' Copyright Office to make it clear to everyone who owns the movie and to establish the time when it was created, in case any legal disputes arise later. It's also a good idea to put the copyright notice at the beginning or end of your movie. It should read "Copyright (year) (the copyright holder)."

Legal liability
Nobody wants to be sued. As a result, many of your business decisions will be aimed at reducing your potential value as a lawsuit target. For a business on the razor's edge of viability — which we guarantee you'll be if you're trying to make a feature-length movie for eight grand — a lawsuit could mean the untimely demise of your dream. For a nonprofit, it could mean that you have to close up shop as well. And don't be foolhardy enough to think that it couldn't happen to you. Law schools are graduating more lawyers than ever before, so many so that their employment possibilities are getting almost as poor as those for moviemakers. But lawyers do have one advantage: A town that can't support one lawyer can support two. They know how to make their own work.

Because of the diminishing job possibilities in established companies and law firms, lawyers are now forced to do what screenwriters and other underemployed professionals have always had to do, which is work on speculation. Just as we have written entire screenplays with only the hope of selling them, lawyers without work will undertake lawsuits just for the possibility of getting a percentage of any settlement. The upshot: Anyone can get a lawyer to sue you today. And lots of people do.

You do have some automatic advantages in this area. For the most part, you'll be in the turnip category, as in "you can't get blood out of a turnip." However, people who automatically smell money around moviemaking may mistake you for a worthwhile candidate, and frivolous lawsuits are as costly to defend against as valid ones. The other advantage is that you're small, fast-moving, and out of sight quickly — at least something good about not being able to maintain a high profile. Because none of these factors will guarantee your safety, it's wise to build in whatever protection you can. Here are three steps we took.

Incorporation
If you're going to make this movie for professional sale, you'll end up with some business structure eventually, and by default if you don't actually decide. Basically, you have six choices: individual proprietorship, partnership, limited partnership, S-corporation, C-corporation, and nonprofit corporation. Don't go to sleep on us now. There's going to be a test at the end of the chapter.

If you embrace inertia and ignore business concerns, you'll probably end up being legally classified as an individual proprietorship, which means that you'll personally own the business and all its assets. A partnership is very similar, except that two or more people personally own the business and divide the assets. Even these simple business structures have legal and tax requirements, so ignoring business will put you into some trouble with local, state, and federal authorities. Though these business structures have simplified accounting and tax requirements, they didn't meet our main criteria: protecting homes, cars, and personal assets from being taken to pay business liabilities. So we reluctantly rejected these simpler forms of business.

Limited partnerships are used to finance many independent film productions. These businesses are made up of two groups of partners.

The first are general partners, usually the filmmakers, who run the business and have all the duties and liabilities of a regular partnership. The other group is the limited partners, who are just putting money into the project for a share of the profits. Because their participation in business decisions is limited, so are their financial and liability risks. Different states put different restrictions on how these limited partnerships can be set up. There are also federal limits on the number of limited partners you may have and how you invite people to become limited partners. Too many partners or a general public invitation to become partners will land you in regulations governing securities (stock), and your business won't meet the requirements of a limited partnership. Limited partnerships are complicated beasties that should probably be set up with a lawyer's help. Unless that help is available free to you, forget it. Also, as a general partner who runs the business, you'll find that this structure won't protect your personal assets.

The S-corporation is a corporate structure under which the business' assets are included in the shareholders' personal coffers for tax purposes. This simplifies the business income and tax reporting, but complicates your personal taxes. This was a tempting choice for us, but because it intermingles the business assets with your personal assets, a lawsuit or bankruptcy might also be applied to your personal assets. ("Sorry about losing the house, honey.") Too risky for us.

So, on our first two films, we bit the bullet and became a real C-corporation, just like GM, 3M, and MGM, but without the medical plans and the golden parachutes. This means that all government agencies viewed our movie-production business as a "person" or entity that was wholly separate from us. As a result, if we wanted to put personal money into the film production, we had to loan it to the corporation or purchase stock shares, in spite of the fact that we were the sole shareholders and the corporate officers. It's a little hard to get into this mindset, but you catch on eventually.

As a C-corporation, there is a significant amount of recordkeeping and tax reporting required (and federal corporate tax instructions are not a pretty sight), but you are afforded almost complete personal protection from lawsuits, bankruptcy, creditors, and the like. However, this doesn't mean you can act irresponsibly. In extreme cases of corporations flagrantly violating the law or endangering employees or communities, the corporate officers have been held liable, even sent to prison. But if

77

you act in good faith and take steps to protect people's safety, the beat-up Toyota in your garage should be safe from seizure.

Now, becoming a corporation may seem like a daunting task, but it's actually pretty easy. We had to file some boilerplate articles of incorporation with the state's Secretary of State Office, apply for state and federal tax numbers, and set up stock ownership....

Brief tangential discussion: Stock is tricky and heavily regulated. If you don't sell stock outside of the state in which you're incorporated, if you don't publicly offer to sell the stock, and if offers and sales are only to residents of your state, you are exempt from registering with the federal Securities and Exchange Commission under the "Intrastate Offering Exemption" of Section 3(a)(11) of the Securities Act. On the state level, you'll likely have to file a registration form U-7 that was adopted by the North American Securities Administration Association as a uniform state securities registration form for small corporate stock offerings. But not all states have the same requirements, so check your local laws and rules. Also, the sale of stock on the Internet and other stock-sale innovations are causing the securities laws to change with some regularity in order to keep up, so don't assume this information is still accurate. Use this as a starting point to see for yourself what the latest requirements are. The U.S. Securities and Exchange Commission Web site is a good starting point. It's listed in the appendix. End of digression and back to our story.

...We found a great little guidebook prepared by a state university that gave us all the steps in layperson's terms. It's called *Simplified Business Incorporation: A self-help manual,* and it's listed in the bibliography. It's specifically designed for Minnesota businesses, so you'll want to look for a similar publication for your state.

There are small business assistance offices in most states and the federal Small Business Administration to help you get started. Some of them even publish free guides to setting up a business and may even have financial assistance, though filmmakers are not usually considered a good investment risk. The Feds and some states offer free training programs on taxes and other business issues. So do universities, business schools, and vocational technical colleges, but not for free. And don't forget the public library; that's where we found the incorporation guidebook. Ask the reference librarians for help. These people love ferreting out information the way you love moviemaking, and they're usually delighted to be asked to use their skills.

If we haven't been too specific about the actual details of incorporating here, it's because it constitutes its own book, and you'll undoubtedly have more, less, or different steps to take where you live.

Even early Homo sapiens grew weary of stalking giant cave bears for food, and tried a quieter life of growing corn and potatoes. After nine years of hunting for corporate profits and wrestling with the hairy behemoths of corporate taxes and corporate recordkeeping, we opted to cultivate a nonprofit organization instead — since profits had been elusive and small anyway. Of course, the nonprofit organization would own any movie productions done under its auspices, but a corporation owned the productions we did under its name, so the situation didn't really change much.

There are a some definite advantages to being a nonprofit corporation. You have the same protection of personal assets that a C-corporation offers, but unlike a C-corporation (or any other for-profit business structure), you can accept donations of money, services, equipment, and food, and people can work for you as volunteers — all the stuff you need to make an ultra-low-budget movie. They are no harder to create than a business corporation — as long as you have a nonprofit purpose in mind — and the paperwork can be a lot easier. If you want to try moviemaking as your full-time gig, you'll be happy to know that nonprofit organizations can have staff that are paid for their services. (You can opt out of the corporate rat race and still seek your fortune. Many people have done it for years.)

To set up a nonprofit organization, start by reading up on your state's rules for creating a nonprofit organization. Also read the federal rules, because you have to meet both sets of requirements in order to qualify for federal nonprofit status and exemption from federal income tax. Following are the general steps for setting up a nonprofit corporation (But remember, like the tourist attractions, the state song, and the official rock, the rules are different in most states):

1) Your corporation must be organized to carry out a nonprofit purpose. The acceptable purposes under section 501(3)(c) of the federal tax code are: charitable, religious, educational, scientific, literary, testing for public safety, fostering national or international amateur sports competitions (but not providing equipment or facilities), or prevention of cruelty to children or animals. (Note that prevention of cruelty to screenwriters isn't a tax-exempt activity.)

2) You must file in your state for a unique corporate name, articles of incorporation (also called "articles of organization"), and corporate bylaws. Some states will provide sample articles and bylaws (check their Web sites or Secretary of State offices), but you must pass muster with the IRS, so check out the boilerplate examples in Publication 557 (Tax-Exempt Status for Your Organization) on the IRS Web site (see appendix). It's best to stick pretty close to the examples so that your requests for state corporate status and federal tax exemption aren't denied. It costs money to incorporate — in most cases a couple hundred dollars — and you usually have to pay to revise your articles of incorporation or bylaws. So do them right the first time and save some bucks. To assist you, there are some nonprofit organizations that help other nonprofits get set up. (No kidding!) Ask around in the local nonprofit community. There is also advice on the Internet, but make sure it's for the state in which you are incorporating. A good shortcut is to ask for a copy of the articles of incorporation and bylaws for an existing nonprofit that is similar to the one you plan. You can modify those articles to create yours.

3) File Form SS-4 with the IRS to get an employer identification number (EIN). You'll need this number to set up a bank account for your organization and to do the required filings if you hire any employees. You may need a state identification number as well, such as a sales tax number, so be sure to check with your state.

4) File Form 1023 (Application for Recognition of Exemption under 501(c)(3) of the IRS code) and Form 8718 (User fee for Exempt Organization Determination Letter Request) with the IRS. The filing fee is based on your likely budget average — a $500 fee if you have a budget average over $10,000 per year for four years, or a $150 fee if less. See, you can save $350 by having an ultra-low budget.

5) Annually file a Form 990 (Return of Organization Exempt from Income Tax). If you have less than $25,000 of receipts in a year, you don't have to file this form. If your income is more, you have to complete the form, but it's a lot simpler than a for-profit-corporation tax form.

6) Annually file state income tax, sales tax, and nonprofit registration forms. In most cases you don't have to file state income-tax forms if you're exempt from the federal forms, and you only have to file sales tax forms if you have taxable sales. Be sure to ask your state to make sure you know all the forms you are required to file.

After you have obtained your nonprofit status, make sure you operate within the purpose you set out for the organization. If you don't, Special Agent "Red" Tape may show up at your door in his sunglasses and black suit to discuss how you've erred and what penalty you have to pay. (And don't mention our names. We warned you, after all.)

Now, one last thought on incorporating: Delaware. You may have noticed that lots of companies that send you direct mail or run late-night TV ads for greatest hits albums are listed as Delaware corporations. That's because Delaware has proclaimed itself the "corporation capital of the world."

You can become a Delaware corporation for about $100 within 24 hours, or you can pay extra for two-hour service. (Would you like fries with that Certificate of Incorporation?) Check the Web site of the State of Delaware Division of Corporations (see appendix) for complete incorporation details, including boilerplate articles of incorporation for several types of corporations (stock, close, non-stock, foreign, nonprofit, unleaded, low-fat, etc.) forms for creating a limited partnership, fee schedules, and a description of the corporate franchise tax (which is tons simpler than most states' corporate taxes). The only thing missing is a screensaver with a tasteful photo of Delaware's governor, though he did smile at us very pleasantly from the Web site.

If you're considering going the Delaware route, there are a couple of points to consider. First, you must have a registered agent in Delaware. You can get one from the list on the State of Delaware Web site. For as low as $500 some agents will do all the incorporation filings and send you a kit that includes corporate books, a corporate seal, and necessary forms. For an annual fee as low as $50, they will be your registered agent in the state, and some will even send you reminders when annual fees and forms are due. Check the going rate before you get in too deep. Second, there's a minimum annual franchise tax whether you make any profits or not. It starts at about $50, depending on the corporation type and size. (In our state, we don't have to pay income tax if we haven't had any income.) Third, you'll be subject to Delaware business laws, so you'd better become familiar with their requirements. Fourth, to operate in your home state, you'll probably need to file some legal notices as a foreign (out-of-state) corporation. You may even be required to do some type of tax filing as a foreign corporation. Fifth, if you have legal troubles, you may have to handle them in Delaware. And sixth, we've never done this. It only cost us $150 to incorporate in Minnesota ($70 as a nonprofit). We did it ourselves without legal help, and when we didn't make profits, we only had to pay sales tax. And there's no minimum annual fee. Delaware is home to many corporations, but make sure you know the obligations you will have in that state and in your home state before you make it your business home.

If your mind works like ours, the urge to run and hide under the desk is becoming overwhelming about now. Regulations, taxes, legal notices, thumbscrews, and charging mastodons are all listed deep in our primitive brains as things to avoid as fast as our legs can carry us. It's your basic fight-or-flight decision. We could have chucked the entire project when faced with this business stuff, but the rewards from making a movie were great enough that we turned and fought our way through the paperwork and legal language, and we're glad we did. So take heart; success comes to the brave. On the bright side, the remaining steps to protect yourself from legal liability are all easier.

Liability waivers

The second step we took to protect ourselves from lawsuits was to include liability waivers in all our contracts and release forms with the cast and crew. This was to avoid lawsuits from inside our production group. Of course, we still took steps to minimize risks of injury, but there's always a chance of an accident. These waivers are not ironclad by any legal definition, but it puts the people you're working with on notice that they are responsible for their own medical and accident insurance and that they have acknowledged that they are accepting any risks of injury. If nothing else, they will all think twice before they ask a lawyer about suing you, and therefore won't be advised that they could sue you anyway. If they do sue, that's when your turnip status comes into play.

There are a couple of secondary benefits to this waiver. When you get location releases signed by property owners, some ask about insurance (which you don't have). It helped us to be able to say that we had this waiver for every person on the production crew to avoid lawsuits for injury. Of course, the waiver won't absolutely prevent legal actions, but lawsuits would probably involve the production company first and the property owner second.

By this point, you're probably beginning to realize that the only real protection from lawsuits that you can have is to make sure nothing happens that anyone can sue you over. To ensure this, take precautions on the set to make sure risks are limited. If you have dangerous-looking scenes, do everything you can with special effects, visual tricks, and safety equipment to prevent real injury. In our film *Resident Alien*, an important scene takes place on a roof at night, which worried us a lot. The first thing we did was find a one-story building with a roof that had a low pitch, almost flat. We assigned one person to hold the ladder whenever someone went up or down, and Dale, as the producer on the set, spent all night reminding people they were on a roof and warning them when

Shooting for safety on the roof for Resident Alien. (Pictured, l to r, actor Patrick Coyle and director of photography Scott Lee Dose.)

they got too close to the edge. Because of technical problems, we had to reshoot this sequence, so we actually did it twice without mishap. We were very, very careful and very lucky.

Copyright

Our third step to avoid legal entanglements was scrupulous attention to copyright laws. We're always amazed how many professionals in the media business ignore the laws which protect their own work. In case you have any doubts, *you can't use anything you didn't create without getting permission*! No, you can't borrow that music; no, you can't use video footage running on TV; and no, you can't just lift a few lines from a novel or another screenplay. Granted, there are some gray areas in satire and parody, in public domain material, and in documentary or scholarly usage of material, but you aren't likely to have the lawyerly resources to make sure you have clear rights to use these items. So don't.

For low-buck producers such as ourselves, there are only two feasible options (unless you have free use of a copyright attorney): Create something original or get written permission to use it, which often comes at a cost. Creating something original is easiest. There are lots of creative people looking for outlets for their work. They will love you for asking them to create music, artwork, or poetry for your movie. For example, we had at least six composers ask if they could do our music tracks for free. You can also ask these people to give you permission to use music, art, or writing they've already done.

For minor items, like a newspaper masthead with a column by one of our characters, we just made up a bogus newspaper on the computer. For a club scene that had TVs visible in the background, we ran a video of one of our previous movies on the monitors. When we wanted our characters pictured on *Entertainment Weekly* magazine, we asked permission, and the publisher granted it after reviewing the final layout. (Of course, this was when the magazine was just starting out and looking for publicity. *Rolling Stone* turned us down flat.) Often pleading poverty and being friendly will get you permission for free if it's not something that's normally sold for performance.

There's one detail that you must not forget: For all the wonderful original writing, music, and pictures, be sure you have a contract or release form signed by every artist stating that you own all rights to that material or at least all rights to use it in your movie. Get these from the composers, painters, musicians, photographers, graphic artists, and everyone else. And then file them away safely. We've never had to pull these out, but we can if there is any question about rights. Don't overlook this essential task.

If something is copyrighted and is identifiable on your set, get permission or replace it with something you have created (and photocopying it is not creating it). It will save you lots of worries in the future.

Even though we were very careful, we got a scary letter on our first film, *Resident Alien*. It was from an attorney for a larger docudrama by the same title. In stern legal language, it warned us that our title infringed on their production. It urged us to select another title.

This was not a pleasant letter. Our production money was gone, titles were done, and our title fit our story perfectly. We also knew that you can't copyright a title unless that title is so famous that you would instantly be stealing sales that rightly belonged to the original production (so you can forget about calling your film *Casablanca*). We definitely couldn't afford an attorney to respond, but we wanted to resolve the issue.

This is where being writers and people who know the value of humor came in handy. We mustered our best legal language and wrote back a letter thanking them for asking whether *they* would be infringing on *our* film's title. We went on to say that since our films had different audiences and since we couldn't copyright titles, we felt we could coexist in the marketplace. We closed by wishing them good luck with their *Resident Alien*.

Fortunately, the attorney and his client appreciated the ironic humor and the validity of our arguments. We got back a cordial letter that parroted our language about co-existing and wished us luck with our *Resident Alien* which proves that the pen is mightier than the lawsuit. Our point is, don't mess with copyright. Every distribution contract that's come across our desk has a clause in which you cross your heart and hope to die if you don't own all rights to the material in your movie. This is when you'll be glad you didn't borrow that shot from *Star Wars* and that you remembered to get all those release forms signed.

Tax obligations
Swallow hard kiddies, and hold onto those armrests. Ready to hear some really terrifying tales? We're going to talk about federal, state, and local taxes and how they affect the business choices you need to make. This is scarier than anything you'll see on the late-night horror show.

Actually, the scary part about taxes is the not knowing. Not knowing if there's a tax out there that you've forgotten to pay. Not knowing if you've filled out the forms properly. Not knowing if the IRS SWAT team is going to kick in the door and seize the paltry gains that you've managed to wring out of your creative efforts. Our advice is to relax and ask questions.

85

Like most things governmental, there's a lot of fear about taxes that is unnecessary and unwarranted. Dale has worked in government for more than 20 years, and he's not very threatening (unless you ask him to spend money wastefully). And he promises that zombies don't suck the souls of civil servants every morning as they come to work. Government work is just like any other work. Some people are good at their jobs; some are poor. Some are friendly and helpful; some are cranky and officious. The point you need to remember is that the tax man (Notice that there's not much clamor for equal gender access to this term?) and tax woman are people you can ask for help.

There are three main types of taxes that may affect you, presuming you don't buy real estate as part of your production: sales/use tax (and this may not apply to out-of-state sales, sales for resale, or when you buy something for your movie that will be taxable when it's sold later); employee taxes (social security, workers' compensation insurance, state and federal income tax withholdings); and state and federal corporate income tax.

Taxes have mainly affected our business and our nonprofit corporation in three ways: where we do business, whether we have employees, and what type of accounting we do.

We live in and on the fringe of the Minneapolis and St. Paul metropolitan area in Minnesota. We incorporated our moviemaking business in the fringe community because there were no extra sales taxes to pay for a domed baseball stadium (also it was where there was a corner in the basement for an in-home office).

For our business, we operated with no employees except corporate officers — the two of us. And the corporate officers declined any salary until the company was profitable (which it never was). With no employee salaries, we avoided having to track and pay employee taxes, such as workers' compensation insurance, social security tax, and withholdings for state and federal income tax. For the nonprofit corporation, we've operated solely with volunteers. Especially keep this part in mind. Taking on that first employee will probably generate enough paperwork to require at least another part-time employee. We've decided that if we ever reach the point of taking on employees, one of the first to be hired will have to be an accountant/bookkeeper/tax preparer, and if they can sew costumes, that's all the better.

The third taxing effect on our business and nonprofit has been accounting. You will be dealing with large enough sums of money that the state and federal revenue departments will want to know what you're doing with them as a business and as a nonprofit. Even if you've decided to go the individual proprietorship route, you'll still have to keep records for tax purposes. There's no escape. They've got you surrounded. So surrender, and learn how to speak the victor's language. We set up an accounting system that was designed to keep track of our loans and to tabulate the end-of-the-year information we needed to report on our corporate income tax. This system will become your best friend or your worst enemy, or both.

Beyond this basic tax advice, you just need to get the forms and read the instructions. It's all right there in gobbledygook. If you thought personal income tax forms were incomprehensible, wait until you get a look at business tax forms. They don't even try to make them friendly. (Nonprofit tax forms are much friendlier probably because even IRS employees might need a meal from a nonprofit soup kitchen some day.) But take heart, at least you won't be paying a professional tax preparer to make your mistakes for you. So relax, be honest, and do your best on the forms. That's what everyone else is doing.

It also can be helpful to call the IRS or your state department of revenue for advice when you get stuck. They don't want you to do it incorrectly, so they'll usually help if they can. And be sure to keep a record of the helpful person's name, because surveys have shown that the advice from the IRS tax person is wrong a lot of times.

The problem is that special interests and political deals have made our tax system into a combination labyrinth and morass that no one fully understands. So where the rubber meets the road in the IRS office, there's some poor soul like us just trying to figure out this mess. When you call her or him up, express your fear and your desire to do the right thing, and treat him or her as a person. You'll likely be pleasantly surprised by the results. We were. Time for an example.

We had dutifully applied for a state sales tax number when we incorporated, but were told to wait until we had a product for sale. So we went into production for three years and reapplied when we had a finished movie to sell. We got the forms, and as we read through them, we realized that the film stock and processing we had been buying out of state was taxable. This was a hefty chunk of sales tax (about $800) because film was one of our major expenses. Worse yet, some of this tax was three years overdue with a 20% per year penalty. Dollars were mounting.

With faint hope that we could avoid some or all of this tax, we called the state sales tax office and found compassion. The tax guy was actually impressed that we had discovered our oversight (their oversight, too, since they wouldn't send us the information we needed at the beginning) and that we wanted to do it right. He advised us to just pay the tax as if it wasn't overdue. We took his name and thanked him, and avoided more than $500 in tax penalties. This just goes to show you that tax people are human too, and they respect people who try to do the right thing. They also like it if you don't scream and spit at them.

Now, just a word about grants, for those of you who are able to pry loose some free money. Remember that even though someone gave you this money to do all or part of your movie, you'll still need to operate as a business or nonprofit organization if you want a salable product in the end. If you're a nonprofit, the grant may be large enough to push you into the bracket for filing an income form, and you'll certainly need to show it in your accounting books. If you're for-profit, you'll probably have to report the grant on your personal income taxes and give some of the money away in taxes right off the bat. Because grants are usually given to one or two individuals, not to companies, you are probably going to be an individual proprietorship or a partnership.

Even though the grant money was free, as soon as your business or nonprofit hires people, you get into the employee issue. You'll still need talent and location releases; you'll still need clear rights to music, performances, and images; and you'll still be a target for lawsuits. And if you have the good fortune to make sales of your movie, you'll likely have to pay sales tax and income tax. Sorry. No escape from the business demon or the tax incubus.

We know this business stuff is a big turnoff. But no art comes without suffering, and this is just part of your penance. Hopefully, our experiences can help alleviate some of your pain in going through the process. Also, keep your eye on the goal — a finished and distributed feature-length movie. Knowing your destination makes a bumpy trip more tolerable.

Just to summarize, here's a quick checklist of the business or nonprofit decisions you need to make and tasks you need to do to set up and run your filmmaking business.

Decide:
- Business structure: individual proprietorship, partnership, limited partnership, S-corporation, C-corporation, nonprofit organization
- Worker status: independent contractors, employees, student interns, volunteers
- Location of business
- Cute, serious, funny, or suggestive name for your company

Tasks:
- Read up on starting a business or nonprofit and on basic accounting.
- File necessary business or nonprofit start-up papers with a state.
- Set up a partnership agreement, a limited partnership agreement, or articles of incorporation if these apply.
- Sell and issue stock to your shareholders if incorporating as a business.
- Get tax and employer identification numbers from the state and federal governments.
- Set up accounting books, and begin keeping accounting records.
- Prepare contracts, liability waivers, and talent-and-location release forms, and get them signed.
- Get rights to all music, sound effects, images, performances, and work for your movie.
- Request the appropriate sales tax and income tax returns from state and federal governments.
- Pay sales, income, and (if necessary) employment taxes on both state and federal levels.
- File for copyright protection on your script and finished movie.
- Lie down in a dark room with a cool washcloth on your forehead.

THE MONEY

("Hello, Uncle Burt? You Don't Remember Me, But...")

When we made *Resident Alien* and *Beyond Bob* ($28,000 and $26,000, respectively), we thought we'd gone about as low as you could go, budget-wise. So, can you imagine our elation when we realized that we could complete *Grown Men* for in the neighborhood of $10,000? Well, obviously we decided to move right into that neighborhood.

But that $10,000 had to come from somewhere, and so will the cash you need to get your movie off the ground and into post. You've got to buy or rent a camcorder, sound equipment, lights, tape stock, and get your hands on an editing system. And pay for lots of costs in between.

Yes, you've reached that point. You have the idea, the script is written (or percolating), you've worked out your budget, set up your business or nonprofit structure, and now the next big step looms before you. And you're asking yourself, "How the heck do I come up with the money to do this?"

A darn good question. A tough question. A question with many possible answers. Most moviemakers follow one or more of the following well-worn paths: investors, credit cards, scrimping, grants, favors, and found money.

Investors
The biggest problem with investors is that they generally want their money back. It's annoying. Some of them even want their money back plus a profit.

Apparently they don't understand movie investments.

While as a moviemaker, you're in a position to offer your investors many things — the thrill of being an integral part of an artistic experiment, the joy of watching talent bloom, the sheer excitement of being involved in the moviemaking process, and seeing their names in lights — a guaranteed payback is, sadly, not on your list of deliverables.

So when you begin scouring your hometown for investors, you'll want to seek out people who are clearly much more excited about the process of making a digital feature than its profit potential. If an investor is simply looking for a fast or hefty return, it's best to suggest that they look elsewhere.

However, if they're committed — to you, to your idea, or to a local asylum and have granted you power of attorney — they can become some of your strongest allies.

The other problem with raising money via investors is that in many cases it actually costs money to raise money. And on a no-buck digital feature, there is no loose change jingling in your pockets for such shenanigans.

Limited partnerships have historically been the financial vehicle of choice for independent moviemakers, and with good reason: They're sleek, they're relatively fast to put together, and they keep the moviemaker firmly in the driver's seat. In a limited partnership, the moviemaker is the general partner (the one who makes the decisions) and the investors are the limited partners (the ones who put their money in and sit quietly). However, limited partnerships require voluminous paperwork, and with voluminous paperwork comes lawyers, and with lawyers come fees.

You see the problem.

So while a limited partnership may be an efficient way to raise your money, it's usually not a cost-effective method, because it can also siphon off your resources at the same time.

The fact is, you could easily spend $5,000 on the legal work necessary to put together a limited partnership. Or, you could spend that same amount and shoot your feature. Take your pick.

If you're determined to take the limited partnership path, the best advice we can offer is to find a lawyer who will take care of all the aforementioned voluminous paperwork for free or on a deferred basis. The same is true of other similar methods for raising money, such as taking on stockholders in your corporation (make this a small number or you'll end up in very deep paperwork and legal requirements), loans, nonprofit donations, or even a full partnership. Be sure you understand the legal ramifications of each structure because they will have consequences further down the line.

Once you've figured out how you're going to set up your money-raising apparatus, the next step is to go out and actually start knocking on doors to find your investors. (Beware. In some states, there are rules governing how many doors you can knock on, especially for limited partnerships and stock offerings.) Doctors, dentists, businesspeople with a love of movies, women who've outlived their rich husbands, old rich guys with young second wives who are dying to get into movies... these are the traditional supporters of independent moviemakers.

And the beauty of funding an ultra-low-budget movie is that it doesn't take a large number of investors to pull together the cash you need. If your budget is $8,000, all you need are ten friends with $800 each. Or five friends with $1,600 each. Or four friends with $2,000. Or one really good friend with $8,000. The money is out there; you just have to go ask for it.

⚟⚟⚟

Once you've found your investors, don't abandon them while you dive into production. Keep them apprised of your progress and give them an opportunity to share in the few moments of glamour and excitement that are part and parcel of the process.

They should be invited to the set to watch production, and if extras are needed, they should be asked if they'd like to take part. If you're sending out updates in the form of a newsletter to the cast and crew during postproduction, the investors should be added to the snailmail and e-mail lists. All the investors should certainly be invited to preview screenings, and they should be given a place of honor at the premiere. In short, you should involve them in the process so that they can get something out of it other than a profit (if even that).

Credit cards
Yes, we've all been tempted.

You get one or two or five envelopes a week that exclaim "You've already been approved!" And who doesn't crave approval?

So you tear it open, and there's a simple form to fill out that will make any number of delightful and convenient credit cards wing their way to your abode. And you look at the generous credit limits — $1,500 here, $2,000 there, trusting souls offering you $5,000 — and you do the math. Before you know it, you've got a plan.

Here's one word of advice: Don't.

Here are four words of advice: It's a bad idea.

Here are eleven words of advice: You're going to lose your shorts and maybe even your house.

Sure, you've heard the stories about moviemakers who put their movies — and their credit ratings — on the line. They rolled the dice, and they won!

Yeah, sure. And we've got some prime real estate in Florida that can make you a fortune.

It's not just the risk factor that concerns us. We all know that moviemaking is a crap shoot. We actually like risks. It's that it just isn't a smart plan.

Let's say that you decide to finance a portion of your movie with credit cards, about $5,000 worth. If it's the $5,000 you need to finish the movie, you're in trouble. Why? Because even if you can finish the movie in a month — edit it, do the soundtrack, complete your publicity materials, cutting great deals at every point — it's going to be at least another month before you sign with a distributor (and that's being very optimistic). And then there's a minimum of three months before they work it into their distribution schedule (again, wild-eyed optimism). And then there's another four to six months before exhibitors send in the money they owe you (optimistic doesn't begin to describe what *that* is).

That's ten months. You're paying 18% interest (if you're lucky) on $5,000 for ten months — minimum. And what if you can't get the movie finished that quickly? And what if you can't find a distributor? And what if, what if, what if, what if?

Of course, if you want to put yourself in some deeply serious trouble, use the $5,000 to *shoot* the movie. That will tack on another six months to a year to that ever-mounting interest monster you've created.

The stories that have circulated about moviemakers charging entire features on their credit cards are good copy, but they're also simply bad business, grossly exaggerated, flat-out not true, or about moviemakers who like to play "chicken" with freight trains.

If you want to boast that you charged your entire feature on your Bloomingdale's card in your press releases, go right ahead. We won't let on. But the next time you get one of those "You are already pre-approved" mailings, do the smart thing. Just say no.

Scrimping

Scrimping is an unpleasant word. Say it out loud once, and you'll see what we mean. "Scrimping." It has an unpleasant ring, doesn't it? It sounds like a particularly demeaning part of a fraternity hazing: "Yeah, first they shaved our heads, and then we had to climb down into the sewers and spend the night scrimping."

Scrimping is not fun. It requires sacrifice. It requires discipline. It requires saying no to common urges, such as the urge to eat out, the urge to buy extravagant non-necessities, the urge to get a new pair of sneakers when your current sneakers are only five years old and the holes in the bottom aren't really all that big as long as you stay out of puddles and wear two pairs of socks, which also have holes in them.

Can a person really scrimp together a budget for a digital feature? That depends on the person, their income, and the willingness of their significant other to join in the festive mood of scrimping and living like a pauper. As Ben Franklin said, "Two can live as cheaply as one, but they have no idea how cheaply they can live until they try to scrimp together the money for a digital feature." We're paraphrasing, of course, but you get the idea.

Diligent, concerted, and ongoing scrimping can put an extra wad of cash in your pocket every month, and that wad could add up to a big part of your budget.

Scrimping can take many forms. You can bring your lunch to work instead of eating out. At two to four dollars a day, that gives you an extra $500 to $1,000 a year. You can buy food in bulk at co-ops. Or you can stop buying those expensive breakfast cereals and treat yourself to oatmeal, the breakfast of scrimpers!

Even when you're scrimping dutifully, money can still slip away incrementally — a few dollars here, a few dollars there, add up to a big part of your income. You can use this incrementalism to your advantage, however, by having an extra $50 or $100 deducted from your paycheck every two weeks as part of your tax withholding or simply increasing your W-4 tax deduction (creating a sort of forced savings plan). At the end of the year, your refund will include an extra $1,200 or $2,400, which can buy you all sorts of digital luxuries, like tape stock, a camera, or an editing system.

Of course, many would argue that letting Uncle Sam hold your money for a year doesn't earn you an iota of interest, while even the worst bank savings account will pay you something for the honor of holding your money. True enough. The value of the Uncle Sam savings plan, though, is that once you fill out the form, it's out of your hands. The money is taken out every two weeks, whether you think about it or not. And it's not available for you to use on something else. Most people don't have the discipline to set aside money every month; if you do, then skip the tax deduction step and do it yourself. Some companies have employee savings programs that will take a set amount out of your paycheck and put it in a savings account. The result is the same — a bit more money toward making or finishing your movie.

Another scrimping method is to join a carpool to cut down on parking costs. Changing your own oil in the car will also save you some cash. If your climate (and commute) permits, you can simply get rid of the car and ride a bike to work. You'll save on gas, auto repairs, and insurance, and as an added bonus, you'll start to get yourself in shape for the grueling rigors of movie production.

They say art is sacrifice. And they also say that scrimping sucks. They're right on both counts.

Grants
Grant money can be a great financial resource for an ultra-low-budget moviemaker, particularly if your project is out of the mainstream or focused on a particularly unique niche of our society. Granters are always looking for noncommercial, personal movies that examine or celebrate cultures, population segments, or lifestyles the commercial media generally ignores.

While you may not be able to raise your entire budget this way, a grant can help you get started or help you finish, depending on the grant program. Some programs are devoted to supplying seed money, giving you the dollars you need to get your project off the ground but not necessarily enough to complete it. However, one person's seed money can be another person's entire budget. Twenty thousand dollars may be only enough to help a $500,000 feature film set up shop; it's more than enough to get you all the way through production and postproduction, plus enough left over to take a nice cruise.

Regardless of what kind of funding you're asking for, we should point out that there's a trick to getting grant money. This is a secret, so please don't spread it around because then everyone will know about it, and it won't work anymore. In fact, after you read this section, you may want to tear these pages out and eat them, just to be on the safe side.

Ready for the secret? The trick to getting grant money is this: Follow the grant instructions.

Seems obvious, doesn't it? Yet every day moviemakers submit grant proposals that blithely, even blatantly, ignore the grant instructions. And not just the fine print. Often the big print as well.

In most cases, these grant requests are turned down. Ignored. Or even mocked. Yes, it's true. Grant panels will openly mock incorrectly filled-out grant proposals (behind closed doors) and then unceremoniously discard them. It happens every day in foundation board rooms across the country.

It's a shame, isn't it?

Well, no. Actually, it's great. Because if you fill out the forms correctly and others don't, it will be their applications piling up by the dumpster and yours that gets moved ahead for further review.

That's the second secret of getting grant money: Grant committees are just itching for a reason not to give you money. It's not because they don't like you. Or your project. It's because there are so many requests for grant money — and so little money to go around — that they need an easy way to wade through the piles of plastic binders and find the proposals that are completely and totally deserving of their largesse. And the easiest criteria for eliminating contestants from this pool is to toss them out for rule violations.

Let's say they ask for a one-page project summary, and you, in your foolish arrogance, submit a three-page project summary—well, you're outta there! Kiss your grant hopes good-bye! They can now move on to more deserving candidates. Or perhaps their pedantic instructions insist upon three letters of recommendation, and you submit only one. Heads up! Another grant proposal headed for the wastebasket. They shoot... and you don't score!

Submitting your proposal late. Failure to include an innocuous piece of paperwork. Your name at the bottom of the page instead of the top. Who knows what will set off the finicky grant people?

You do, that's who.

You now know how to get the edge over most of the people applying for grants. Read the instructions and follow them to the letter! Not everyone will. Filling out the paperwork correctly doesn't guarantee you success, of course, but it does put you head and shoulders above the rest of the crowd.

At that point, your project and its merits will have to speak for themselves. But at least they'll have an audience.

Favors
Favors are the currency of independent moviemaking. They're the oil that keeps the gears running smoothly. They're the sip of cool water in the middle of a desert.

Favors can come from anyone and anywhere. A video producer with a camera package lets you use it on weekends. A relative gives you the key to their empty cabin, a perfect location for your movie. An old friend from junior high who now works at a rental house cuts you a great deal on lighting equipment. Your ex-brother-in-law has access to some editing equipment and comes to your rescue.

While you probably can't produce an entire digital feature on favors alone, regular trips to the favor bank can save you oodles of cash along the way.

Calling in some favors resulted in getting a nightclub, dancers, extras, and even a Steadicam during the production of Grown Men. *(Photo courtesy of Granite Productions, Unlimited.)*

Of course, building up an account at the favor bank doesn't happen overnight. You must invest in the favor bank, just like a savings account at a regular bank. Do favors for other people in your moviemaking community by helping out on a shoot, lending some equipment or advice, or offer your talent and your services. All of these favors are an important investment for you and for the rest of the moviemaking community.

By the time you're done with your feature, you'll undoubtedly be overdrawn at the favor bank in a big, big way. So be sure to get back out there and start investing again, offering your help to those who helped you. Your moviemaking community needs you. And with any luck, you're going to need them again as well.

Found money
Found money is great. It's that sudden influx of cash that you didn't expect which suddenly makes it possible for you to get your movie off the ground.

Found money was a great asset on all of our feature projects. The trick with found money, however, is to quickly invest it in your movie before you realize that you have some actual need for it — like home repairs, car repairs, or a new pair of sneakers and socks.

Found money comes in many shapes and sizes. Here are some situations that could best be described as found money.

- An ailing, distant aunt dies, leaving you $8,000 (after probate and taxes, bless her heart).

- You win the lottery with a ticket you found on the sidewalk while picking up a nickel because you've been scrimping lately to get a movie project off the ground.

- The hours you spent diligently preparing and mailing in all those Publishers Clearinghouse Sweepstakes entries finally pay off when your mail carrier proposes to you, and you discover that your new fiancé is really an eccentric millionaire with a penchant for independent moviemakers.

Of course, there are moments during the money-raising process that may cause you to feel panic or even desperation. During these moments, you may feel as though you would do anything for money. *Anything.* There are a few situations that do not qualify in the strictest sense as found money, and we recommend that you don't succumb to these temptations when money gets tight:

- Your distant, ailing aunt asks for a second opinion, and you arrange an appointment for her with Dr. Kevorkian.

- You accidentally place your younger brother's kidney up for auction on E-Bay.

- You enter a convenience store wearing a ski mask and carrying a prop pistol, and the goofy night clerk inadvertently gives you all the money in the safe.

🎥🎥🎥

No matter how you slice it, getting the money is one of the hardest parts of the moviemaking process — whether your budget is $8,000 or $80 million.

The mere size of your tiny budget provides you with a slight advantage, but on those dark days when no one is returning your calls and your friends and relatives turn icy when you enter the room, it is little solace. And no longer mere.

Along with distribution hell, the money-raising phase of the moviemaking process is one where you feel the least in control. It follows, then, that this is a time when you are the most vulnerable — to compromise, to inertia and entropy, to complete and total surrender. Resist these feelings with the full force of your psyche because giving in to any of them spells death for your project — and for a bit of your soul.

As Winston Churchill so stoically put it, "Never give up. Never give up. Never give up." If his Prime Minister gig hadn't panned out for him, he had what it takes to be digital moviemaker.

So hang in there. You never know when you're going to find that lottery ticket, persuade that investor, or receive a knowing wink and a smile from your mail carrier.

PREPRODUCTION
("*BEING COMPULSIVE IS NOT A BAD THING.*
I KNOW. I DOUBLE-CHECKED.")

He's making a list and checking it twice. Yes, Virginia, Santa Claus would be a welcome addition to any ultra-low-budget movie's preproduction team. He's cheerful, leaves nothing to chance, gets things done on schedule, and is able to perform miracles.

On our movies, we found that the producer, director, and unit production manager formed a triumvirate that was the guiding force of the production. These are the only three people who see all aspects of production, so it's natural that they do the preproduction planning and follow-through. These three members of your production team should be as compulsive as possible.

It's a pity that therapists around the world are trying to control compulsive behavior when independent moviemakers are looking for that very quality in their crews. (Hint: Look for people with clean desks and neatly stacked paper clips, organized by size, color, and age.)

You may want to add the director of photography to this team because so much of the planning is around creating images for your movie. You may want to include the screenwriter, who can offer insights into the vision and the intent of the story. We included our director of photography in some of our preproduction meetings, but not all, because there were hundreds of logistical details that we didn't want the director of photography to think about. She or he will have more than enough to worry about on your production just trying to make sure you've gotten usable and, hopefully, artistic images on tape.

These compulsive three, four, or five people have some basic production decisions to make before the meat of preproduction begins.

Digital or film
You wouldn't have picked up this book if you weren't giving serious thought to producing a digital movie, but you or your team may still be struggling with the question of whether to shoot digital video or film.

Even after we decided to shoot *Grown Men* on digital video, we found ourselves revisiting that decision as new considerations occurred to us. Preproduction is the time when you want to be sure you're committed to your path, so take time to sort out any nagging uncertainties. We'll share the points we discussed.

Video has long had a stigma in the feature-film world that's been a barrier to distribution. If an independent feature was shot on video, it was considered an amateur production that was relegated to cable access or maybe late-night broadcast TV. If an independent feature was shot on film, it was admitted to the next level and considered for distribution. About five years ago, we were approached by a local novelist who wanted our advice on doing an independent feature-length movie. He had a script, a cast, a crew, most of his props, locations, and a relative who would front him $40,000 to do the project. We were overjoyed for him and told him everything we knew about how to get it shot on film for less than the 40 grand he had available. But he had video equipment available to him, and the video sirens were calling. Although we advised him that he would never find a serious distribution offer if his movie were done on video, he ultimately chose video. We heard he completed the project, and that's the last we ever heard of it. No local premiere, no local news coverage, no nothing. Even short films got more attention than this. Our guess is that his efforts fell into the video abyss.

If he approached us today, we'd give him very different advice, because the world of movies has changed. You can hardly watch a movie these days that doesn't have some digital segment in it and that wasn't cut on a nonlinear edit system. Audiences have paid big money to see all-digital movies such as *Toy Story*, half-digital movies such as *The Matrix*, and mostly-video movies such as that juggernaut of profit, *The Blair Witch Project*. And for every one of these movies, there's some happy little distributor sitting on his office floor counting the piles of income. Is it any wonder that the distributors are no longer so picky about what medium you use to shoot your movie? Even if you shoot on digital video, you can easily (though not cheaply) transfer it to film, DVD, or streaming Web video. The independent movie has become format-independent as well, so choose the format that makes technical and economic sense for you. If you're checking your car seats for change in order pull together a production budget, we recommend digital video.

Because you'll be working with a compact digital video camcorder to shoot your feature — one that looks suspiciously like the camcorder Aunt Mary uses to tape the kids' birthday parties — you might face an attitude from your cast and crew that your production is not completely serious. Of course, you know that the size of the camera is no measure of the production... but some people on your team may not get it. You'll need to decide how to deal with this attitude so it doesn't affect the quality of the cast and crew's work. Here are a couple approaches that have worked for us:

- Explain to cast and crew that you will be shooting in a state-of-the-art digital format and that you'll be editing on a nonlinear edit system. If they aren't impressed, just continue to spout impressive-sounding technical specifications (just like the camcorder salesperson did) until their eyes glaze over (just like yours did).

- Be as organized and professional as possible, and hit the ground running the first day of shooting. When cast and crew see that you mean business about shooting 12 pages a day, they'll realize that they're in for a workout on a real production and that they'd better get cracking before they're left in the dust.

- Say things like "Film's dead, and Hollywood's not far behind" to build their confidence in digital video.

- Show them the dailies so they can see the professional-quality work. The skeptics in our cast and crew became believers after they saw a few scenes. They also worked hard to make sure they were as professional as everyone else.

The archival longevity of your movie may be an issue, especially if you're planning to become famous by being the last person standing from your era. (This is our plan, and we heartily endorse it.) The reality is that digital video, DVD, and most other digital formats probably won't stand the test of time. Even if you chiseled all those digital ones and zeros into a granite monument so they would never be accidentally erased by a refrigerator magnet, your digital movie would probably be lost. Digital formats depend on two fleeting elements: complex mathematical algorithms to compress and decode the image, and equipment that is rapidly changing.

Just try to get a 2-inch Quad video tape from the 1960s played back. You'll find only a handful of Quad machines still operating in this country, and this format was relatively simple by today's technical standards. At the rate of current technological change, most video and digital formats in use today could be difficult to play back 20 years from now. (Anyone remember 5 1/4-inch floppy disks?) In contrast, one film archivist commented "Give me a light and a lens, and I can look at any motion-picture film ever shot." So you have three choices: Embed in plastic a copy of your digital movie, a playback deck, and an early 21st-century power generator... oh, and be sure to include a note in several languages telling how to use them. Or you can pay to have a film transfer done of your digital feature. Or diligently copy it to the newest format every ten years or so. It also doesn't hurt to have it recorded in several formats in the first place as a hedge against obsolescence.

Video format
After you've decided to shoot a digital movie, you still have to decide what format. ("Will the decisions never end?" you wail. Frankly, no.) For us this particular issue was raised by the offer of free equipment in DVCPRO and later in Digital Betacam. This discussion might also be sparked by technical considerations such as longer tape length, fewer dropouts in the image, and 16:9 wide-screen format. We spent many hours and e-mails talking about the relative merits of tape formats and the production pathways that each would dictate. Which digital format to pick — Digital-8, DV, DVCPRO, DVCAM, Digital Betacam, DVCPRO50, HD or some other type?

In the end, all digital formats are good enough to make a movie (though not all camcorders may be up to the task). Heck, with the right story line, Hi8 footage was good enough to be the backbone of *The Blair Witch Project*. If Hi8 can do the job, then S-VHS, 3/4" U-matic, 8mm, and even VHS could do the job for some stories. Ultimately, it will come down to what you can afford, what's being offered for free, and what your vision is of the finished project. Just be aware that different formats will have different costs and production procedures.

For example, any of the analog formats (VHS, 8mm, U-matic, S-VHS, Hi8, Betacam) will require a media converter or codec (coder-decoder) to translate it to DV format when you digitize it into your nonlinear edit system. So you either have to use the codec on a DV camera or deck or buy a $400 media-converter box (such as Sony's DVMC-DA2) as part of your production budget. Once you pick a format, don't second-guess yourself. Just use it the best you can and make the best movie you can.

Shooting ratio
As we discussed in the budget chapter, your decision on shooting ratio has a direct impact on your budget and shooting schedule. To stay within an $8,000 budget, rental costs force you to shoot in four weekends. To shoot in four weekends, you have to shoot 12 pages of script a day. If you start doing two takes on every setup — keeping in mind that you'll be shooting 60 to 80 setups a day — you're not going to get your 12 pages done before the next day starts. So it's pretty much a no-brainer that to make your movie for $8,000, you have to decide on a 3:1 shooting ratio. Of course, you'll be able to get some shots in a 2:1 or 1:1 ratio, which would allow 4:1 or 5:1 coverage for a few other scenes.

Publicity
Another decision is to publicize or not to publicize. Whether 'tis nobler to suffer the questions of reporters and spectators or to work in relative obscurity and peace. We have chosen not to publicize our projects locally while we were in production for a couple of reasons.

Our budget level demands a non-union production, and we were up-front with our cast and crew about this. Several good people who were with the union chose to join us, and we did not want to get them in dutch with the union reps by getting a lot of attention while shooting. (Once you're done, nobody really knows if it was a union shoot or not unless they watch for the union "bug" at the end of the credits.) Most union reps realize that non-union work is where many union actors get their beginning credentials, allowing them to get bigger union jobs later. So they usually won't interfere if you don't call and ask them if it's okay to use union people on a non-union shoot (they have to say no) and if you don't rub their noses in it with a lot of publicity. (They'll feel obliged to interfere; it's their job.)

We also decided not to seek publicity during the shoot because it invariably attracts reporters asking questions and taking photos, both of which take time away from a cast or crew person who needs to be working. Reporters and other spectators also can create sound problems and get into shots. Suddenly, you need to have someone controlling the public too. You may even get the attention of official types who will feel the need to ask you for permits to use a public location you're shooting in. Now, whenever you're shooting out of doors, you can expect visits from the curious. Usually it's just the neighbors or a few passersby who'll get bored soon enough and move on. If you publicize it in the local paper, you could see dozens or hundreds of visitors. That's not a good thing for a production that doesn't have time for interruptions. And since we are generally in editing for more than a year after shooting, we don't benefit much from early publicity anyway.

However, you can benefit from a little national publicity. The two major industry trade papers, *Variety* and *The Hollywood Reporter*, both feature weekly Production Listings, which highlight all the movies currently in production, including their title, start date, primary cast, and major crew positions. Listing your production in the trade papers provides a number of benefits:

- It establishes a start date for your digital movie, which can come in handy if someone challenges the legality of your title. This happened on *Resident Alien*, and it was nice to be able to point to a published start date when someone questioned who had the title first — even though you can't copyright titles.

- It alerts distributors and sales representatives to your existence, and the more aggressive of them will begin contacting you to ask when they can see your movie.

- It introduces you to other movie professionals, such as composers, editors, and actors — many of whom are looking for work. While the vast majority will be turned off once they learn what your budget is, you may still find one or two who are looking for the experience or are simply turned on by your enthusiasm.

- Finally, it's a kick to see your little digital movie listed alongside the latest productions starring Hollywood's biggest guns.

To get your movie listed, simply call the papers and ask for a production-guide listing form. We've put the information in the appendix.

Time for a breakdown

After struggling with budget, business, and preproduction decisions, you may feel ready for a breakdown. That's okay. Preproduction is the only place it's allowed. In fact, it's required.

We're talking about the next preproduction step, the script breakdown. This is where your carefully crafted script — with its interwoven story lines, fully integrated characters, and gradually building emotional content — is brutally dissected. When the script breakdown process is done, the script will be lying there in front of you sliced and diced into its most elemental parts, all carefully labeled so you can plan your shooting schedule.

Actually, this process is a peaceful task that's perfect for the detail-oriented personalities on your crew, in our case the director, producer, and unit production manager. This is sitting-at-the-kitchen-table work that requires five distinct steps — four if you cut corners. As usual, we made a few changes to the standard Hollywood technique for breaking down scripts; some steps were simply unnecessary for such a small production. We've listed a very good reference source in the bibliography if you want to learn the Cadillac of script breakdown. We're giving you the Geo Metro version.

Step 1: Marking script segments

To start this process, you'll need a shooting script with scene headings that list scene number, interior or exterior, location, and day or night. You may have read or been told not to put scene numbers on a script you're trying to sell. True, but now that script is sold to you, and you need those numbers. Scene headings should look like this:

23. EXT. ROCKY CLIFF — DAY

or

125. INT. SHERIFF'S CAR ON ROAD — NIGHT.

If you've never understood why this was the required format for scene headings, you will after you've finished breaking down a script.

"Okay class, pencils up, ruler in hand. You may work in groups." Draw pencil lines across the page at the end of each scene. (Use pencil unless you never make mistakes. Wait, you're the one planning to make a movie for pocket change, aren't you? Definitely use pencil.) Remember that a scene occurs at one location at one point in time. Now look at the length of this scene, and mark in the margin next to the scene number how many eighths of a page this scene takes.

We know there's a lot of math anxiety in the world, especially when it comes to fractions. Far be it from us to make this a more anxiety-ridden world. Brief math refresher: A whole page would be eight eighths (8/8). Two pages would be 16/8. A half page is 4/8. A quarter page would be 2/8. And an eighth of a page would be 1/8. Anything less than an eighth of a page is still considered 1/8. Example: A scene running two-and-a-quarter pages is 8/8 + 8/8 + 2/8 = 18/8. Write "18/8" in the margin. (Math wizards, thanks for your patience. Just in case you're feeling smug, remember how many dates this skill got you in high school.)

As you break your script into scenes, watch for hidden scenes lurking within scene descriptions. Read the following scene description, and look for the hidden scenes.

24. EXT. BOX CANYON — DAY
Joe leaps from his horse and leads it to a sheltered spot among the rocks. He then scrambles up the loose rocks to the rim of the canyon. Removing his hat to avoid detection, he peers over the rocks. In the distance, there is a column of dust rising from the surrounding desert. Joe pulls a telescope from his saddlebags and looks again. Magnified, the dust column reveals itself to be Texas Rangers riding single file to hide their numbers. Joe quickly closes the telescope and runs for his horse.

Did you spot them? The first hidden scene is the distant shot of a dust column rising from the desert floor. The second is the closer shot of the Texas Rangers. Because these shots are actually at a different location than the main scene, they need their own scene heading. This is a common oversight in scriptwriting, and you should be watching for it. For the purpose of planning your shooting schedule, hidden scenes may happen on completely different days and locations than the main scene, so you need to break them out separately.

We've found hidden scenes in a variety of places: Shots of a television showing an image (the image needs to be shot separately); point-of-view shots of distant scenes; voice overs on radios, phones, and intercoms (no image to shoot, but you'll need to record the sound of the performers somewhere during your production schedule); and scenes that occur in doorways or looking out windows. This last item may not seem to fit, but consider the situation of using different locations for the interior and exterior of a building in your script. If a scene is viewed from inside the doorway, it is an interior at one location. If it's viewed from outside the doorway, it is an exterior at a different location. Unless you know that you'll be using just one location, list two scenes, an interior and an exterior.

When we found these hidden scenes without scene numbers, we just added a letter to the main scene number to designate them. In the scene above, the dust column shot would be 24a and the Texas Ranger shot would be 24b.

After you get into it, this is pretty easy, restful work. Enjoy it while you can. It helps to have more than one person working on it so you can discuss and decide how to shoot any ambiguous hidden scenes. Just plug ahead at this task until all script pages are broken down into scenes and lengths. Here's an example:

Script with scenes broken down

111

Step 2: Script breakdown pages

Almost all Hollywood films do this next step though it's one that we skipped. We were so compulsive and detail-conscious as a team, and our scenes were simple enough that we felt this step was unnecessary. Turns out we were right. But that was us. If you don't have the kind of production overseers (producer, director, unit production manager) who ask each other three times if they remembered the yellow sweatshirt for scene 16a, then you might want to consider doing this step. It will help you keep track of the myriad details when you get to the set.

This step is more simple, slightly tedious work. You will go through your script again, marking the key elements of each scene. You can underline these elements with colored pencils or highlight them with colored markers. Pick a different color for each of the following categories:

- Cast — speaking roles
- Extras or stunt performers
- Action props — cars, planes, go-carts, horses, etc.
- Props
- Wardrobe
- Special effects, animation, special camera gear
- Atmosphere — raining, foggy, sunrise (These are all difficult to achieve on a limited budget with limited time. Your script should have avoided these items or used them only as scenes that can be shot by the second unit. Day and night by themselves are going to pose enough problems for you.)

You already have scene headings that designate interior or exterior, location, day or night, and length of scene, so there's no need to mark these items.

At the same time you are marking these items, you can be filling out the information on the actual script breakdown pages. A breakdown page lists all these pertinent details about each scene. When they are all done, put them in a three-ring binder for your unit production manager. On the set when the shooting schedule calls for doing scene 16a, the unit production manager will flip to the breakdown page for that scene and be able to see that the yellow sweatshirt is needed. All in all, a useful organizational tool, and there was at least one occasion when it would have saved us some clothing confusion.

Here's what a script breakdown page should look like:

Page # __1__

Scene Breakdown

Production Title __"Beyond Bob"__

Scene #	Script Page #	Length In Pages
1	1	1/8

Location / Set	Sequence	Time Period
Cliff near river	Bob hang gliding	10 years ago

Day or Night	Interior or Exterior	Season
Day	Interior	Summer

Scene Synopsis

Bob drives up in his car with hang glider tied on top. He removes hang glider and gets tools from trunk. We see "Honk if you love Bob" bumper sticker.

Cast	Extras / Stunt Performers
Bob — Michael Levin	None

Action Props (Vehicles, Etc.) & Animals	Props
Bob's car (without rust) Hang glider	Tools Bumper sticker Ropes to tie on hang glider

Wardrobe (Cast and Extras)	Special Effects, Animation, Special Camera Gear

Bob's costume:
     Letter Jacket
     T-shirt
     Jeans
     Tennis shoes
	Second-Unit Camera (MOS)

Atmosphere (Rain, Fog, Etc.)	Set Construction
Early morning sun	None

Scene breakdown page

In addition to filling out the script breakdown pages, some people total the number of pages (in 1/8ths) for which major elements are needed: cast, locations, day, night, props, wardrobe, etc. It was less work for us to do this in a later step. The only reason to do it now is if you need to know how long you'll be using some specialty wardrobe. Wardrobe won't show up on the production-scheduling items that are next.

Step 3: Making the strips and the production board

This is nothing like cruising the strip — it's much more fun. Here's where you begin to put every single scene of your movie on little strips of tag board, so they can be sorted into a production schedule. The first thing you could do is waste $100 to $150 buying a commercially produced production board and strips. Unless you are being paid more than $50 an hour during your free time, don't do it. You can make your own for about $20 in materials (which you may be able to scrounge) and two hours' time.

Yes, it's arts-and-crafts time, class. The materials you need are 15 full-page plastic sheet protectors (top-loading); a ruler; a fine-point permanent pen; double-faced adhesive tape; lightweight, white tag board stock; a paper cutter (optional); a pen knife and straight edge; and enough dimes to make a few photocopies.

Tag stock 11 inches wide

A. Cut the tag stock into 11-inch widths. Keep it as long as possible to save time in the next step. You have enough tag stock if you can make about 14 pages that are 8 1/2 inches x 11 inches.

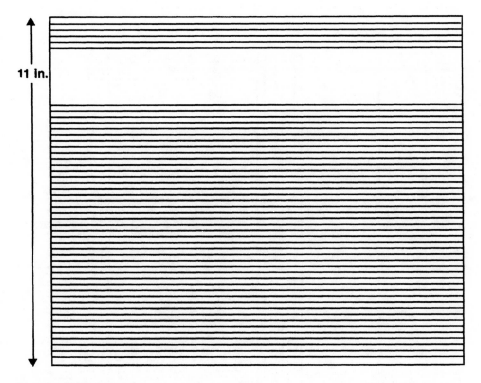

Lines marked on tag stock

B. Next you need to mark lines on the sheets of tag stock as shown in the illustration. Starting from the top, measure down and draw five lines 3/16 inch apart. Next measure down two inches from the last line, and draw the next line. Then continue drawing lines that are 3/16 inch apart for the rest of the page. This will be about 40 more lines.

Cutting strips from lined tag stock

C. As shown in the illustration, cut off one strip from your tag stock that is 1 1/2 inches wide and 11 inches long. This will become the header for your production-board pages. Now cut up the rest of your tag stock into strips that are 1/4 inch wide and 11 inches long. These will be your scene strips. You can use a penknife and straightedge to do this, or you can use a paper cutter. Either way, this task is a little mind-numbing, so don't daydream and trim off any appendages. You'll end up with a big pile of little strips.

Breakdown Page #	
Day or Night	
Location or Studio	
Exterior or Interior	
# of Pages	

"Resident Alien"	
Dir. J. Gaspard	
Prod. D. Newton	
Prod. Mgr. K. Erickson	

Scene #	
Cal	1
Leslie	2
Allen	3
Davis	4
Jack	5
Bunson	6
Verner	7
Joyce	8
Doris	9
Deputy	10
Tish	11
Naom	12
Reporters	13
Action Props Cal's Truck	14
Leslie's Car	15
Jack's 4x4	16
Davis' Sedan	17
Locations Motel Ext.	18
Roof Ext.	19
Leslie's Apt.	20
Cal's Apt.	21
Allen's Apt.	22
Newton's Land	23
Sheriff's Office	24
Laundry Rm	25
Vacant Lot	26
Bathroom	27
UFO Detector	A
UFO Debris	B
Alien Spacesuit	C
Geiger Counter	D
Metal Detector	E
45° Effects Box	F
Second Unit shot	G
Miniature-Animation	H
Monster Head	I

Filling out the header strip

D. It's time to create the header for each page of your production board. (Actually, this should be called a "sider," because it goes on the left side of the page.) You'll make this by labeling major elements of your movie on the 1 1/2-inch x 11-inch strip you just made. These elements will then be used to break down the scenes in your script. Start out by labeling the top five slots as follows (see illustration):

- Breakdown Page Number
- Day or Night
- Location or Studio
- Exterior or Interior
- Number of Pages

The next slot on the header is a wide one. On the scene strips, this will be used for scene descriptions. On the header strip, however, use this area to list the title of your production and the names of the director, producer, and unit production manager. That way if you lose your production schedule on a bus, the person who finds it will know who is in deep trouble.

The next narrow slot should be labeled as follows:

- Scene Number

Follow this slot with the important scene elements from the next list. These slots should be numbered from top to bottom on the right-hand side of the header strip. To the left of each number, write the name of one of the important scene elements. Don't repeat any numbers, because they will be used as shorthand identifiers for each individual item. Fill in these slots with the following:

- All Character Names
- Extras (this is just one slot)

117

• All Action Props (cars, motorcycles, hang gliders, etc.)
• All Locations

The next list of items should be identified with letters from top to bottom on the right-hand side of the header strip. Write the name of the item to the left of the letter.

• All Specialty Props
• All Special Effects, Animation, or Special Camera Gear

If you found yourself uncertain about what to list under some of the categories on the header strip, you may want to go back and do *Step 2: Script Breakdown Pages*. As you mark the key elements of the script, keep a list of every new item, and use that list to fill out the header strip.

Now you have the completed header strip for your production boards. Make about 15 photocopies, cut them out, and use double-faced tape to attach them to tag stock the same size as the header strip. If you're really into wasting time, write 15 more of these header strips by hand instead.

To finish your low-cost production board, use the double-faced tape to attach a header strip inside each plastic sheet protector along the left-hand side. Save a couple of header strips for holding alongside the scene strips as you fill them out. Now that you've completed your production board, you're ready to move on to making the scene strips that will fill the board.

Breakdown Page #	41
Day or Night	D
Location or Studio	L
Exterior or Interior	I
# of Pages	⁴/₈

"Resident Alien" Dir. J. Gaspard Prod. D. Newton Prod. Mgr. K. Erickson	Leslie looks at Cal's books

Scene #	90	
Cal	1	1
Leslie	2	2
Allen	3	
Davis	4	
Jack	5	
Bunson	6	
Verner	7	
Joyce	8	
Doris	9	
Deputy	10	
Tish	11	
Naom	12	
Reporters	13	
Action Props Cal's Truck	14	
Leslie's Car	15	
Jack's 4x4	16	
Davis' Sedan	17	
Locations Motel Ext.	18	
Roof Ext.	19	
Leslie's Apt.	20	
Cal's Apt.	21	21
Allen's Apt.	22	
Newton's Land	23	
Sheriff's Office	24	
Laundry Rm	25	
Vacant Lot	26	
Bathroom	27	
UFO Detector	A	A
UFO Debris	B	B
Alien Spacesuit	C	
Geiger Counter	D	
Metal Detector	E	
45° Effects Box	F	
Second Unit shot	G	
Miniature-Animation	H	
Monster Head	I	

Scene strip next to header strip

E. The tag stock strips in the pile you made are ultimately going to represent every scene of your movie, so pick up your script and get ready to write. This is another good group activity for the leaders of your production. Just make sure everyone is filling out the scene strips the same way, and make sure you don't skip any pages or miss any scenes that cross multiple pages. (And for you punsters, yes, you do need a scene strip for a strip scene.)

Hold a scene strip next to the header strip, and you'll see that the top five slots on each strip represent the information that's in each scene heading and in the information that you marked on your script. For the Breakdown Page Number on your scene strip, write in the script page where the scene begins. Write in "D" or "N" for Day or Night, "L" or "S" for Location or Studio, and "I" or "E" for Interior or Exterior. (For our productions, the only shots that weren't location were credits and special-effects shots that we did in a studio.) Next, write in the page length that you've written down by each scene heading on your script, such as "3/8." Don't forget to fill out scene strips for those hidden scenes you've found too.

As you're filling out these strips, you'll want to color code them with a highlight marker to make the upcoming sorting easier. Pick four different colors to represent day-exterior, day-interior, night-exterior, and night-interior. Common practice is to do day-interior as white (uncolored), night-interior as blue, day-exterior as yellow, and night-exterior as green. Just use the appropriate marker to color the long slot where you'll be writing the scene description.

119

Next move to the long slot, and write a short phrase that describes the main content of the scene, something like "Cal wakes up" or "Davis' car drives up to motel." Then write in the scene number in the next slot down.

Now that you've gotten the basic scene setup coded onto your strip, you need to identify its component parts. Follow down the strip and mark the number of each character who appears in the scene in the appropriate slot on the strip. Use the number rather than just a check mark, so you can tell at a glance that character #3 is in the scene. This is also the reason not to repeat any numbers. When we had a scene where a character was only present as an off-scene voice, we still wrote in the character's number and added a V.O. for Voice Over or O.S. for Off Screen so we were sure to record this dialogue. Many times you'll want the same room ambiance for the off-scene voice, so you'll want to record it at the same time as, or immediately after, you shoot the scene.

Continue on down the strip, listing the appropriate number or letter for extras, action props, locations, specialty props, special effects, animation, or special camera gear needed for that particular scene. When you get to the bottom of the first scene strip, move on to the next 200 or so strips you have to do. It's not gene splicing, but you have to concentrate and envision the scene and how it's going to be shot.

When you finish going through the entire script, you'll have a pile of tag-stock strips that looks like shredder residue at the CIA. The next step is to make some sense of these color- and number-coded strips. (Timesaving tip: If you share your dwelling with a pet or child or roommate who likes to chew cardboard, lock the door.)

Step 4: Sorting the strips
Here's where the hours of tedious coding start to pay off and those enigmatic steps are recognized for their brilliant usefulness. You're going to sort through your strips several times, so clear some table space or shovel the debris of life from the living room floor.
o

Begin by sorting your big pile of strips into smaller piles for each shooting location you will be using. Because you have a separate number for each location, you will be able to just glance at a strip and see if it has a number 20, representing "Leslie's apartment." After doing this sorting, you should have a pile for each location and one additional pile for studio shots. Already that mass of scenes to shoot should be starting to look more manageable.

Next, sort the scene strips for each location into three piles: Interiors (both day and night), Exteriors-Day, and Exteriors-Night. Moving outside to do exterior shots will require several changes in camera and lighting setup as well as time to move the equipment, cast, and crew, so you will want to group these scenes for your location together. For scheduling, you'll need to know how much of your exterior shooting has to be done before the sun goes down and what scenes can't be started until after sundown, so day and night exteriors are separated. We didn't separate the interior scenes into day and night on *Resident Alien* because we avoided showing windows and modified our lighting to create either circumstance. If you want to or need to show windows with day or night outside, as we did with *Beyond Bob* and *Grown Men*, you should sort for Interior-Day and Interior-Night also.

Now that you have each location separated and divided up by lighting and equipment changes, your next step will be to figure out the most efficient shooting schedule. Now is a good time to put the strips into the production board pages that you've made (the plastic sheet protectors). Later you'll put a strip of double-faced tape inside the top of the plastic sheet protector to hold the strips in place, but for now you want to be able to shift them around. Just lay the sheet flat so things don't slide around. Start putting the strips in the production board pages, grouping them by Location and Interior, Exterior-Day, and Exterior-Night. You can turn over a blank scene strip to use as a divider between sections.

Step 5: Laying out the shooting days
This is the point where your director and unit production manager must be involved if they haven't been so far. You want to organize the shots in your production schedule so that:

1) you don't waste time setting up scenes or moving equipment,
2) you move efficiently from one location to the next,
3) cast members aren't sitting around for long periods waiting to do scenes,
4) you help the cast give the best performances possible,

121

5) you get the necessary number of pages done each day,
6) you accommodate any outside scheduling issues.

It's time for some examples.

SCHEDULING FOR SCENE SETUP: For our film *Resident Alien*, we used a single motel room to represent the three different motel rooms that were about half of our shooting schedule. It made sense to set up shop at this motel room and shoot all of the scenes there before moving on, so we spent two entire weekends shooting at this location. In redressing the room for the three different settings it represented, we started with the setting that required the most changes to the room. We shot every scene that occurred in that setup before we changed the look of the room. Each subsequent redressing of the room removed more props and furniture until we got to the final redressing in which the room was virtually bare.

SCHEDULING FOR LOCATION: *Resident Alien* called for a variety of short outdoor scenes at different locations, some of them 50 miles apart. To avoid wasting a lot of production time driving to locations, we shot major scenes that were closest to these locations for most of the day. Then toward the end of the production day, we'd hit the road with the cast and crew to pick up these short scenes. That way, when we finished we were already packed up for the day and ready to go to the next day's shooting location.

SCHEDULING FOR ACTORS: On *Beyond Bob* we scheduled our shooting so that we started the day with all the scenes using just one of our principal actors, letting the other actors sleep late. We did scenes that called for six actors toward the middle of the day, and then shifted to scenes involving a different principal actor at the end of the day. This way, the majority of the actors could complete their scenes and leave earlier, allowing them to get more rest in a weekend of 14-hour shooting days. (The crew was fried, but they didn't have to look good on camera.)

If it works in the scheduling, it's nice to shoot scenes in their actual order as much as possible. Try not to have performers jump from a tense, angry scene directly into a humorously romantic moment.

Also consider the time for makeup changes between scenes. It's hard to go from a bed-head look to knock-dead glamorous in a few minutes' time. Generally, wardrobe changes can be quick, so the only ones we considered much during scheduling were those requiring elaborate costumes or major makeup changes.

SCHEDULING TO STAY ON SCHEDULE: You'll need to consider how many pages of script you have to shoot each day. This is easy to calculate. If you have a 90-page script in standard screenplay format and you know that you'll be shooting on four weekends (eight days) and four Friday evenings (figure 1/4 day each), you have to shoot 90 pages in nine days. You need to plan for at least 12 pages of shooting per day so you don't get squeezed at the end if production gets delayed. Just count up the page lengths on the scene strips to see how many pages you're placing in each day's schedule. Be sure to consider how many are night shots and how many are day shots, so you don't schedule yourself to do 14 hours of night exteriors on the heels of a full day of daylight shooting.

Set a fast pace early on so the crew and cast know how quickly they must work. Hollywood productions average two pages per day, so you're going to be working in a very fast lane doing 11 or 12. It's best to make the scenes early in your production schedule some of the easier ones. This lets your cast and crew get used to working as a team at a breakneck pace before they face the more challenging scenes.

SCHEDULING AROUND OTHER SCHEDULES: If you have problems with an actor availability, a prop vehicle, a location, or even a time of day (such as sunset), be sure to consider this when setting up the shots you'll do each day. For example, on *Grown Men* we had one extended sequence that took place at night and ended with the rising sun visible out the window. Although a sunset stood in for sunrise, we had to schedule that event, just like the arrival of lunch or an important prop.

As you're probably understanding, setting up the actual shooting schedule is going to require trial and error. Just take a stab at it, and have your director, unit production manager, and producer look it over and make changes based on problems they see. We set up our shooting schedule in an evening. We also hit some weather problems during production, so we had to move some shots to different days in the production schedule. Using a production board, this was an easy matter of moving a few scene strips to another page.

123

	Leslie looks at Cal's books	Leslie and Cal discuss UFO's	Leslie's come on to Cal	Cal and Leslie on Phone	First view Cal's Apt. Leslie Bursts in	Leslie's bandaged hand dial phone	Cal's POV - Alien attack	Leslie's POV - Alien Approaches	Cal bursts through door	Alien POV - Attacking Cal	Cal on Phone - L & A enter	Cal's Apt - Manuscript	Cal, Leslie, Allen in Cal's Apt.	Allen on Road before UFO	UFO over Allen - Still cut out - Still Photo	Allen greets Naom & Tish	Allen with Naom & Tish	Allen, Tish, Naom leave	Allen's arrive	Faces for Allen's dream
Breakdown Page #	41	42	44	54	1	17	53	53	53	53	63	67	76	89	89	90	90	92	89	54
Day or Night	D	D	D	N	D	D	N	N	N	N	D	D	D	N	N	N	N	N	N	N
Location or Studio	L	L	L	L	L	L	L	L	L	L	L	L	L	L	S	L	L	L	L	L
Exterior or Interior	I	I	I	I	I	I	I	I	I	I	I	I	I	E	E	E	E	E	E	I
# of Pages	1⅛	9/8	1⅜	2⅜	1⅝	7/8	3/8	3/8	9/8	3/8	1⅜	1⅛	4/8	⅛	⅛	4/8	3/8	⅛	⅛	⅛
Scene #	90	91	94	118	2	39	106	106	106	106	121	127	151	128	175	178	180	182	176	110
Cal — 1	1	1	1	1	1				1	1	1	1	1							
Leslie — 2	2	2	2	2	2	2					2	2	2							
Allen — 3							3	3			3	3	3	3	3	3	3	3		
Davis — 4																				
Jack — 5																				
Bunson — 6																				
Verner — 7																				
Joyce — 8																				
Doris — 9																				
Deputy — 10																				
Tish — 11															11	11	11	11	11	
Naom — 12															12	12	12	12	12	
Reporters — 13																				
Action Props Cal's Truck — 14																				
Leslie's Car — 15																				
Jack's 4x4 — 16																				
Davis' Sedan — 17																				
Locations Motel Ext. — 18																				
Roof Ext. — 19																				
Leslie's Apt. — 20						20	20	20	20	20										
Cal's Apt. — 21	21	21	21	21	21						21	21	21							
Allen's Apt. — 22																				
Newton's Land — 23														23	23	23	23	23	23	23
Sheriff's Office — 24																				
Laundry Rm — 25																				
Vacant Lot — 26																				
Bathroom — 27																				
UFO Detector — A	A	A	A	A	A						A	A	A							
UFO Debris — B	B	B	B	B							B	B	B							
Alien Spacesuit — C																C	C	C	C	
Geiger Counter — D																				
Metal Detector — E																				
45° Effects Box — F																			F	
Second Unit Shot — G														(G)						
Miniature-Animation — H														(H)						
Monster Head — I							I	I												

"Resident Alien"
Dir. J. Gaspard
Prod. D. Newton
Prod. Mgr. K. Erickson
10/1/89

Production board page

Once you've settled on your schedule, put a strip of double-faced tape inside the top of the sheet protector to hold the scene strips in their order. Now you can take these pages and make photocopies for your production crew.

A production schedule obviously can't be done in complete isolation from your other preproduction tasks. To really set a schedule, you'll need to know where your locations are, when you can use vehicles and major props, who the cast members are, and when cast members are available. You can try to get these items figured out before you begin your production schedule, or you can set a tentative schedule and make modifications as these details are settled. We did a bit of both. We had found some locations and knew our cast's schedules, but we didn't arrange for some locations or vehicles until after we'd set a tentative schedule. Sometimes it's easier to get permission to use a prop or a vehicle if you can say specifically when you need it. This leads us to another task that you'll have to undertake sometime during preproduction — a treasure hunt.

Props, action props, locations, and assistance
The kind of treasure you're after is free, photogenic, and convenient. In the next chapters we'll describe how to find a cast and crew made up of diamonds in the rough. Right now your task is to find several hundred thousand dollars' worth of personal goods and real estate, just to borrow for a while. This work will have a lot of bearing on the final quality of your movie. A tolerant and gracious homeowner (John's sister) gave us full access to a beautiful suburban home as the major setting for our film *Beyond Bob*. This completely furnished, attractive, multiple-room location easily added $200,000 to the apparent production value of our finished film. And it didn't cost us a dime. You can get the same kind of screen value for vehicles, props, and wardrobe that you borrow. This is part of the reason distributors thought *Beyond Bob* cost $900,000 to make.

So where do you find these hidden treasures and how do you get permission to use them? Answer: Lots of places and by asking.

There's a theory that you are no more than six relationships removed from anyone in the world. This means that a client of an uncle of a girlfriend of the mailman of the dentist of your lead actress owns the lime-green Corvette you need to borrow. We found vehicles, houses, wardrobe, camera gear, specialty equipment for props and effects, artwork, and furniture just by asking the friends and relatives of our cast and crew.

Start by making a master list of all the locations, vehicles, wardrobe, and props that you need, and then put the word out. You'll be pleased and surprised how willing people are to help you find what you need to make your movie. Feature-length movies are the conjurations of modern-day wizards like you, and people want to catch hold of your cloak in hopes of feeling a bit of the magic. We even received unexpected help from other movie professionals who knew all about the tricks behind the magic. Your vision of your finished movie has the power to bring to you the people and the resources you'll need to finish the project. So spread your vision around and let people know that they can be part of it by loaning you the things you need.

The people affected by your magical vision are not just friends and family. Complete strangers who happen to own businesses that are perfect locations for your shooting will succumb to your spell. Just say the magic words, "We're making a movie, and your business would be an ideal setting." Our experience is that businesspeople don't agree to help with a movie because of the potential publicity. They agree because they personally want to be connected with a feature-length movie. In Hollywood, moviemaking magic is so common that it's lost much of its power. Elsewhere in the country it still fascinates the crowds. Most people are thrilled to be associated with a movie, as long as it's not too much trouble.

If you've been a good neighbor in your local production community and helped out other people with their projects, you'll have a much wider group from whom you can ask favors. Many moviemakers own props and have access to locations that will be useful to you. Similarly, you have access to things and places that can help in someone else's movie. A well-connected group of local moviemakers may have at their beck and call resources that rival that of a small movie studio. So get on the team.

Other willing participants are local artists, ranging from musicians to clothing designers to painters. Their work can give your movie a piquant local flavor and a unique look. Showcasing their talent won't hurt the artists, and it may actually help them succeed with their own dreams. Look around for interesting additions to your project and offer the chance to participate.

When searching for exterior shooting locations, don't overlook public areas, such as parks, wilderness areas, and the local scenic vistas. Bigger movie productions pay lots of money to shoot on locations that are in your neighborhood. These are free, and if you shoot quickly, you can avoid any permits or location releases. Now, if you need to be at one of these sites for an extended period of time with lots of cast, crew, or equipment, you'd better seek formal permission. It's awkward to have your entire day of planned shooting halted by a park ranger with a demigod complex. Don't forget that you need a location release for using any property that isn't public land.

If you need help finding or getting permission to use a particular local vista, your state or city film office may be able to help. While you're out searching for that pink adobe bungalow for a location and scavenging for that brass seaman's compass for a prop, there is also technical work to be started.

Choosing a look

This is the point where you'll want to start talking to your director of photography about the production and how you're going to achieve the look you want for your digital movie. As you learn more about locations, the director and director of photography should be discussing the types of shots they want to do, especially if they involve specialized equipment. This is the time to determine the look you want for your movie, because there won't be time for this to evolve on the set. You need to know before you roll tape what kind of images you are trying to achieve and what techniques will be used to create them. Viewing other movies and looking at their techniques is a good way to get ideas and select the look for your production. Movies on video are great because you can stop and study how particular images were achieved.

Recognize that you have to create your look with 1/100th the money and 1/6th the time of almost any movie you watch. So consider what time, resources, and money you can commit to creating the look you want. It may be enough to create the visual tone of your production in a few key scenes and use a simpler and faster-to-shoot style for the remaining shots. Often an audience's memory of a movie is linked to a few monumental scenes. *The Wizard Of Oz* has hundreds of gorgeous scenes, but most people's memories gravitate to a few: the tornado; the Munchkins; meeting the Scarecrow, Tin Man, and Lion; the audience with Oz; the flying monkeys; melting the Witch; and unveiling the Wizard. You can't possibly rival the overall production values of a film like this, but you can create a half dozen memorable scenes that will stick in your audience's heads.

For example, in our film *Resident Alien*, we knew that we needed to make the crucial collision and climax scenes the visual high points in the production. Even though we were unable to achieve much style in 90% of the scenes we shot, we took extra pains to make sure these key points in the story set the visual tone for the movie. They also had our most elaborate special effects. The result is that most people recall these, our best scenes, when they think of our movie, not the lackluster images our budget forced us to accept for much of the production.

Technical preparation
In addition to planning the look of your movie, you need to do considerable technical planning. It's no good to get to the location and find that you can't use your lights because you need two-prong adapters for the electrical cords. As you find and get approval to use your locations, do location inspections. If you wish, you can draw a diagram of each room, its windows, doors, and electrical outlets to help you plan your shots on paper. If the number of locations is small, which will probably be the case for your production, you can just do a walk-through with the director and the camera and lighting crew. They can see the conditions they will be working in and decide what equipment will be needed to adapt to it.

For example, if half the living room you're shooting in is floor-to-ceiling glass windows, you're going to have a hard time avoiding showing the out-of-doors. This means you'll probably need to shoot day scenes during daylight and night scenes at night. It also means that you'll have to color-correct the windows with large gels (expensive!) or balance the lights with daylight gels (less expensive). You'll need more lights and electricity to compete with a bright sun, so you'll have to figure out if you have enough electrical circuits to handle the load. This is the kind of thinking you need to do on the walk-through.

The most important item to locate and examine for every indoor location is the circuit box. Find out if it has circuit breakers or fuses. If it has fuses, note the type and size so you can buy some extras. It's almost guaranteed that you'll blow a breaker or fuse somewhere during your shoot, so you want to be able to find the circuit box and reset it as quickly as possible.

Other things to look at while visiting the location are room modifications that will be needed, where your crew is going to work, and where meals will be prepared and served. Make sure the owners of the location are comfortable with any changes you wish to make, such as moving the furniture around, temporarily removing a light fixture, laying down dolly track, bringing in furniture and equipment, and demolishing the odd wall here and there. Keep in mind that you are allowed to work at this site only because of the owner's generosity. Make their wishes and concerns a priority and be willing to change your plans to make sure they are happy. If they aren't happy, they can pull the plug on you during the middle of shooting. And common decency demands that you treat their property with care and respect. If you can't work within their restrictions, it's better to learn that early and find a different location. As we've said before, one of our guiding principles is that we don't leave behind any owners of locations we've used who wouldn't allow us to come back.

Besides looking for where you're going to shoot your scenes, consider the other work areas you'll need. Where will the hair and makeup supervisor work? It can't be on the set. Find a laundry room, bathroom, kitchen, or utility room with a sink for them to set up their stool and makeup and to plug in the 47 hair curlers, fluffers, and whippers they need. Make sure it's a room with a door, so they won't interfere with sound recording.

Where will the cast change costumes? A bathroom, spare bedroom, or office space will do. If you have a lot of wardrobe, the dressing room should be near the room or hallway space where wardrobe is stored.

You'll also need to find accommodations for the creature comforts (even if you're not doing a monster movie). Input and output are two major issues. Where will you prepare, deliver, and eat food? What bathroom facilities are available? The kinds of meals you can provide for your cast and crew will be controlled by the kitchen equipment available. If you don't have running water, electricity, a refrigerator, and a microwave oven or stove available, you'll be in camping-food mode: coolers, water jugs, camp stove, grill, sandwiches, and such. If you have electricity, you can bring electric fry pans, crock pots, and coffee pots to create a mobile kitchen.

Limitations in the bathroom area are much more problematic. You need to find something nearby, especially at lunch time. If your location is in a building, this can usually be arranged. If you're going to remote locations, you'd better give some thought to this issue. If the best you can come up with is a pit stop behind a bush, you'd better make sure the people you select for cast and crew can work under those conditions. Otherwise you'll have some very unhappy campers complicating your shooting days.

When you're working indoors, you need to find a place to store actors when they are not being used. You'll be keeping crew people working pretty much nonstop, but the actors are going to have breaks in their work. The last thing you need on a busy set are people who have time to chat. It erodes the work ethic you need, they get in the way, and their talking and horseplay ruin takes. You need to find a reasonably comfortable "green room" for the actors to spend their time away from the set. It doesn't have to be fancy. An unused patio area, a recreation room, or a television room will do. Just a place where they can relax and talk or read while waiting for their next scene. Having a specific room will also help you know where to find them when it's time for their scenes. We suspect that the Hollywood tradition of the star's trailer is not just for pampering the star; it's also to keep them from roaming. (A producer of early Marx Brothers films actually chained them in their trailers to keep them from wandering away, or so the legend goes.)

On the technical front, there are a few more tasks to complete. You need to talk about the locations and the scenes that will be shot at each with your sound recordist so that she or he understands the sound-recording situations that will be encountered. You will realize that even the quietest location becomes much noisier when you actually want to record sounds in that spot. You easily ignore that airplane passing overhead as part of your daily routine, but it becomes a challenge when you start recording sound.

The sound recordist doesn't necessarily need to walk through the locations, though this can be helpful. The main thing the recordist needs to know is what equipment will be available and how many people will be speaking in each scene. Sound equipment is pretty lightweight and portable, so the sound is usually the last consideration on the set... to the perpetual annoyance of sound recordists. That's what they get for being flexible.

With all of the technical crew, make sure they understand how to operate borrowed, rented, or purchased equipment. Get a copy of the operating manual for them to read, or get the owner of the equipment to give a quick lesson on operating it. Try to get the crew a little hands-on experience (for free) before they get on the set. Even with this, do a little looking over their shoulders on the set. Ask to hear a little sound playback and have a peek through the camera lens after a shot is framed and focused. Asking the crewpeople to explain their equipment to you is a subtle way to check their technical proficiency without insulting them. If you think someone is unclear about what they are doing, ask more questions and keep checking their work.

Another important part of preproduction is making lists — and lots of them. Most of this obligation falls to the unit production manager, but if the director and producer duplicate this effort, there's less chance that something critical will be overlooked. Each weekend will be the equivalent of a separate production from the logistics viewpoint, so lists should be done separately for each weekend of shooting. You'll be picking up rental equipment each weekend and checking that every item on your equipment list is included and in working condition. You'll be packing up supply boxes each weekend and making sure the necessary production supplies are inside. Wardrobe will have to be organized and transported each weekend. Props will have to be gathered and delivered to the locations. And each weekend, food will have to be arranged for and served on the set. The only way you'll keep this all organized is with lists for equipment, production supplies, wardrobe, props, and food. Hopefully, your makeup and hair supervisor has a list for his or her supplies too.

The director, producer, and unit production manager should have lists with the names, addresses, and phone numbers of all the members of the cast and crew, just in case someone oversleeps. We also gave these lists to all the principal cast and crew members so they could call each other for help if necessary. You'll also want to carry a stack of forms: shot-log sheets, talent release forms, group release forms, and location releases. It's a pain to run out of these forms when you need them, so make sure you have plenty on hand at all times. We've included samples of these forms in the appendix; however, with your computer, you can customize these forms, make legible lists, and create other useful production documents.

The other documents you'll want are the business version of nagging. For instance, make maps to each location for everyone. We simply photocopied the appropriate sections of a street map and highlighted the main travel routes. You can also print out maps and directions from map resources on the Web. We also included the address and phone number at the site in case someone got hopelessly lost. If you have cast or crew members who are always losing stuff, pin the maps to their shirts. If you have a schedule that has the cast or crew changing a lot from day to day, you might consider doing a call sheet that lists who is needed for each day of the shoot. Give this out before the start of the production weekend. In our case, the major cast members and all the crew were needed every day, so our production manager just told the supporting characters when to show up. We only had a problem with them not arriving on time about four times in three movies.

A useful memo for the cast and crew is one explaining the conditions they will experience on the shoot and a recommended list of personal supplies to keep them comfortable. Because we were working indoors and outdoors in variable weather, our recommended supply list included hat, long pants, shorts, socks, tennis shoes, sunglasses, sunscreen, insect repellent, jug or other water container, and rain jacket. We advised people to avoid bringing along valuables to reduce the chance of losing them. We also let people know that there would be food and drinks provided on the set. In general, try to anticipate problems and annoyances that will make your production company unhappy, distracted, or uncomfortable.

And don't get cocky. Just because everything goes smoothly one weekend, don't assume the next one will. Use your lists. We slacked off for a minute when checking the list of rental equipment, and we ended up using a spare light stand as a makeshift microphone boom pole all weekend. About the only thing you can do to reduce some of your checking and double-checking is to write the contents on the outside of the production supply boxes (spare fuses, black plastic, duct tape, clothes pins, spare batteries, etc.), and then repack and replenish them at the end of each production weekend. On the following weekend, we always checked these boxes before loading them and then made sure they got loaded.

Don't assume anything has been done unless you've seen it with your own eyes, and just to be safe, make sure no one has undone it when you weren't looking. Your major tasks in preproduction are planning, finding, planning, listing, planning, nagging, planning, checking, planning, double-checking, planning, shopping, planning, and waking up in the middle of the night to write down something you left off the list. If at any point you feel like you've gotten it all organized and ready, get nervous. You're probably forgetting something.

We still haven't talked about one of the biggest preproduction jobs — selecting the cast and crew for your digital movie. That's next.

CASTING THE CAST
(To Be or Not to Be for Free)

Unless you're working on an Andy Warhol-type movie (an eight-hour static shot of a skyscraper, two hours watching butter melt, or 90 minutes of your computer's screen saver), odds are your movie is going to be populated by characters that need to be brought to life by actors.

So, with both the script and the budget in good shape, it's time to tackle one of the truly enjoyable parts of the process: casting your movie. This is the occasionally magical time when you'll see your story's characters start to come to life before your eyes.

There's a truism that says that casting is 90% of a movie's success. For ultra-low-budget movies, this figure may be on the low side. Odds are, you can't afford huge production values. Instead, you must have well-drawn, involving characters who are beautifully interpreted by skillful actors.

And where will these skillful actors come from? How will you pick the best and the brightest? And how will you get them to work for minimum wage or just meals? Read on.

Finding actors

If you live in one of the major movie or theater centers in the country (New York, Los Angeles, Chicago, Minneapolis/St. Paul, Seattle, San Francisco, Orlando, and so on), you may find yourself with no shortage of excellent actors. If you live elsewhere — and let's face it, most of the best people do — there are still excellent actors to be found; you may just have to dig a little deeper.

Talent agencies

Talent agencies may seem like a logical starting point, and in some cases, they are. However, a talent agent's primary mission in life is to earn money from their clients' *paid* work. This may explain why they're not returning your calls.

Plus, because your ultra-low-budget movie will be non-union, those agents who work with the unions, such as the American Federation of

Television and Radio Actors (AFTRA) for television and the Screen Actors Guild (SAG) for feature-length movies, may be reluctant to work with you. While both unions have created low-budget options for their members, these costs are still way outside your budget range.

With some luck, though, you may find one or two far-sighted talent agents in your area who see the value of getting their actors in a movie — any movie, short of a skin flick — and who don't mind bending the rules a bit to do it. Good actors can learn a tremendous amount about their craft while working on a movie. Smart talent agents recognize that fact and do their best to get their clients in front of the camera.

However, in order to get talent agents on your side, you have to persuade them that your project has merit, is going somewhere, or at the very least will be completed.

A good starting point is your script. Don't be shy about sharing your script with talent agents who are willing to look at it. They generally know the best actors in your area, and the more they know about your project, the better their talent recommendations will be.

It won't hurt to give agents some references if they're unfamiliar with you or your work. Good agents protect their clients and want to be sure that they're sending them out on reputable assignments.

The agent may also want a look at your contract or release form. They'll be making sure that their actor isn't signing on for more than intended, and they're looking to see what wages or future share of profits you're offering. After all, they get ten percent of it.

These are all reasonable requests, and will help to get the talent agent on your side and excited about your project. If no talent agents are available in your area, don't lose hope. There are other sources of actors available to you.

Local theaters
If you aren't already seeing a lot of plays in your community, put this book down right now and go see a play.

Okay. Are you back? How was it? Did you have good seats?

The point here is that you should be seeing local performers perform. A lot. You should know who's who in your area, and who does what, and how well they do it. Local theaters — both community theaters and professional theaters — allow you to see a wide range of performers in an equally wide range of plays. They help you to see who has "star quality," who knows how to move well, who seems naturally funny, and who shouldn't quit their day job just yet.

With this information, you'll be in a good position to invite actors to audition for your movie. You'll already be familiar with their work, their style, and at least some of their skills. In casting, that's half the battle.

Open auditions (a.k.a. cattle calls)
Cattle calls are about as fun as they sound, which is not very. They're insane and noisy and exhausting for everyone involved. But they can be a good way to discover unknown talent.

A cattle call involves bringing in a herd of actors (usually through an announcement in the newspaper), making them mill about for a while in a tight space, then releasing them into the audition arena (one at a time or in pairs), and having them read short scenes from the script.

Finding the right actors in a cattle call is like finding your spouse-to-be in a singles bar. It does happen, but you may have to dance with a lot of duds to find a winner.

The disadvantage of cattle calls is that there has been no prescreening. Using talent agents or going to theaters to find actors is an excellent winnowing process, because you're looking at a pool of talent that has at least some experience in the business. Cattle calls, on the other hand, throw you into a much larger pool, filled with actors who have a widely varying range of skills and experiences.

It's a sink-or-swim experience, and it's an easy place to drown.

In an audition, you want everyone to get a fair shot. That means adequate time to prepare for the audition and adequate time to perform the audition. When you have 50 people in the lobby and you only have the room at the community center for two hours, nobody wins.

135

The solution? Start your open audition through the mail. Ask people to send in pictures and resumes first, well in advance of the audition date. Wade through the material and get a good sense of who should audition for which parts. Then schedule the auditions so that each actor has adequate time to do their stuff as well as enough time for you to mix and match actors in different combinations.

Prescreening, while time-consuming, can turn the chaos of a cattle call into a well-organized and, with any luck, fruitful casting session.

Auditioning actors
When it comes time to audition the actors (whether you're getting them from agencies, local theaters, or an open audition), there are a few things you're going to need to make the day successful.

A place to audition
This doesn't have to be anything fancy. It can be the rehearsal space at a local theater, a classroom at a nearby school, or even someone's nicely furnished basement. Some people hold their auditions in conference rooms or suites at local hotels; as long as you get the space for free, more power to you.

There is one requirement, however. You will need two spaces that are adjoining or at least relatively close together: a room for the actors to check in and wait, and a room for the actual auditions. These must be two separate spaces. The people waiting to audition should not be watching the auditions. This may seem like nitpicking, but how would you like to have a job interview with the competition sitting around watching? Get the two rooms and give the actors their best chance to do well.

A traffic manager
This can be anyone — your mom, your brother, a friend. Anyone except you.

You have too much to do to spend time checking people in, giving them scenes to study, pairing up actors, and handling all the other business of the auditions. This is not your job.

There's an advantage to having someone from your production team handle this task. (We used our production manager.) Afterwards, you can get reports on how the actors were to work with when they didn't have on their best audition face. We also got interesting insights into who had good chemistry in the waiting room.

So find someone to handle this chore or get a couple of people to share it. It will keep your auditions running more smoothly, and it will keep you where you need to be — in the other room, watching auditions.

Sides
Sides are simply scenes from the script that have been photocopied and given to the actors to study and read for the audition. The term comes from the Shakespearean age, when actors were given only their own lines for a show, plus the cues that precede their lines. This was to prevent the actors from stealing the play and producing it on their own. Since they only had their "side" of any dialogue scene, they were unlikely to be able to swipe the whole play. And that's where the term "sides" came into use. (And, while we're discussing theater history, "sides" were rolled up and given to the actors at the rehearsal, which is where we get the expression "an actor's roll [role].")

There should be at least one good side, or scene, for each of the characters you're trying to cast. Each scene should be two to three pages long; anything longer won't tell you much more about the actor and will slow down the proceedings; anything shorter doesn't really give the actor a chance to get up to speed.

Take some care in choosing which scenes you want to use for the auditions. You'll want to pick a pivotal scene for each character — a scene that is dramatic or funny or telling and that really gives the actor something to play. The scene should have a good mix of talking (dialogue and short speeches) as well as opportunities for the actor to simply listen and react to another character.

You should also try to pick scenes that have a small number of characters, preferably two. This will allow you to audition two people at once and get a sense of how they'll play together. Any more than two turns the audition into a crowd scene and usually doesn't give each actor enough to do.

Often people will ask actors to read with someone from the production staff, but we prefer to let actors audition with other actors. It provides a better balance and allows for more spontaneity between the performers.

Finally, be sure to make enough copies of each of the sides so that there are enough to go around. Plan on having one for each person auditioning and some extra copies.

A schedule-conflict sheet

In addition to providing you with a picture and resume, you should ask each actor to fill out a schedule-conflict sheet at the audition. This document reiterates the planned shooting dates for the movie, with spaces for the actor to fill in his or her name and any work commitments or other conflicts they have with the production schedule.

Conflicts are a good thing to discover up front, particularly if a performer is available only for a few days of your shooting schedule. There's nothing worse than finding the perfect actor to play your lead, and then discovering that she'll be touring with *Nunsense!* for half of your shoot.

Video camera and operator

Videotape all the auditions. As with the traffic manager's role, you shouldn't act as your own video operator. Your focus should be on the auditions.

Rather than using a locked-down wide shot, instruct the camera operator to zoom in on the talent in order to get a better idea of how they'll look in your movie.

Review the tape before making any final selections, because people come across differently on camera than they do in person. We've been surprised to see seemingly vibrant people lie lifeless on tape, while performances we thought were lackluster absolutely sizzled on the TV screen. You'll be amazed to see how the camera really loves some people.

Finally, it's a good idea to hang onto this audition videotape well into production, in case you need to cast a replacement for a part.

The audition

Auditions can be tremendous fun. You'll get to see some wonderful actors; you'll start to see the characters come to life; and you'll begin to move one step closer to making your vision a reality.

However, for actors, auditions can be a real pain. They want to do a good job, and they want an opportunity to really shine, yet time after time producers and directors sabotage the process. This is very frustrating for actors, because the audition is their entrance exam. If they don't pass, they don't get to move to the next level.

With that in mind, we humbly offer the following rules to make auditions work for you and for the actors.

The Ten Commandments of Auditions

I.   *Thou shalt not be rude.*

Put yourself in the actor's Doc Martens. You've got a two-page scene from a movie you know very little about. You're about to go into a room full of complete strangers and prance around, doing your best to breathe life into a scene. Then, in the midst of your best efforts, you see the director or producer yawn, whisper, start to dig into their lunch, or worse yet, doze off.

Wouldn't exactly encourage you, would it?

During the audition, actors are using all of their skills to demonstrate their level of talent. The very least you can do is be polite. And if you can't be polite because it's the right thing to do, be polite because in the end it will save you money. "How?" you ask, your ears suddenly perking up. Here's how: If you like what the actor does, you're going to ask them to work for almost nothing. And if you were polite during their audition, they just might do it.

So don't do anything during their audition — talk, eat, whisper, sleep or anything else — except glue your eyes and your total attention to their performance. A little politeness goes a long way, and it can net you a great performance for a price you can afford.

Another important politeness tip is to introduce the actors to everyone in the room so that they know for whom they're performing. As one actor told us, "I like to have an idea of who's who in the room, so I know which people to suck up to."

Who can begrudge them that? So make introductions before you start making magic.

II.　　*Thou shalt put actors at ease.*

Auditions can make actors nervous. Why? Because it's their one shot. If they don't impress you in the first two minutes, the odds are against their working on your movie. At least, that's the way they look at it. As a consequence, many actors, even experienced performers, come into an audition a tad nervous. Hyped up. Scared to death.

In order to get the best performance out of them, it's up to you to put them at ease. Talk with them for a couple of minutes before they read. Ask them what they've been working on lately. Ask them about their past experiences. Ask them if they have any questions about the script or the production. Go over their schedule-conflict sheet and confirm any problem dates.

Then, after they've had a few moments to relax and just be themselves, ask them to be someone else for a couple of minutes, and let them read from the script.

III.　　*Thou shalt not close thy mind.*

Let's say that you wrote a great part in your script for Jim Carrey or Meryl Streep. (Probably not the same part, but who knows? That Meryl's one talented gal.) And let's say that for some reason — a mix-up, a time conflict, or lack of bus fare — neither Jim nor Meryl shows up at the audition.

What do you do? You open your mind, that's what. You'll be doing a disservice to your movie and the acting community if you don't.

The odds are against someone walking in who is a dead ringer for the character you pictured in your mind. The purpose of the audition is to find the actors who are best-suited for the parts, not to find people who merely look like what you had in mind or who can imitate a well-known personality.

For example, we once came across this audition notice in the newspaper: *"Actors for student movie needed. Black male, 23 yrs, 6', fit, short hair; white female, 28 yrs, 5'10", slim, long red hair; black male, 40 yrs, 6', strong, natural hair; white male, 35 yrs, 6', short hair. Unpaid."*

Wow. That's not a casting notice, that's a police report. The odds of finding good actors who fit these exacting specifications are extremely slim. Plus, by requesting such exact types, the moviemakers are ignoring hundreds of talented performers whose height or hair length don't fit these unnecessary standards.

Keeping an open mind also means considering actors for different parts than the one for which they audition. When you're watching auditions, remember all the roles you need to fill, not just the one that's currently being read.

However, if you decide to ask an actor to read for a different part, give them a few minutes alone to go through the new material. Asking them to read it cold isn't fair or productive.

IV.   *Thou shalt not discriminate on the basis of race or gender.*

There are a lot of things you can't afford at your budget level, and one of them is to let good actors get away. This can happen if you're too narrow in your casting search and you ignore entire populations swimming in the talent pool.

In very few instances, such as when it's a plot point in the story, is race an issue in casting. If you're remaking *Guess Who's Coming To Dinner?*, then race becomes a consideration. Otherwise, you're simply looking for the best actors, and their race should be of no consequence.

You can also overlook great candidates for your cast if you make stereotypical casting choices based solely on gender. The kindly old doctor in your movie doesn't necessarily have to be male; the helpful young nurse doesn't necessarily have to be female. Not all lawyers are men, and not all teachers are women. The person installing the phone can easily be a woman, while the owner of the perfume shop could be a cranky old man. In fact, now that we think about it, the perfume shop owner might be a lot more interesting if he's a cranky old man.

On an early feature John produced, several auditions were held to cast the part of a tough, no-nonsense cop. The auditions were fruitless — until someone suggested that they try casting the part with a woman. The perfect actress walked into the next audition and walked out with the part. And not one line of dialogue was altered in the script. In fact, it improved several scenes, such as the one where she followed the police captain into the men's room to finish an argument. It added to the scene, and to the movie, and it wouldn't have happened if the casting had been narrow-minded.

V.   *Thou shalt offer direction.*

Actors may be many things, but they're not mind readers. (Although many mind readers are darned good actors, but we digress.) All that most actors know about the part they're auditioning for is what they read on the page — unless you tell them more, which is what direction is all about.

If time permits, we usually let the actors perform the scene once without direction. This gives us a chance to see where their instincts take them. Seeing them work without direction reveals a lot about their natural skills (and the clarity of our scriptwriting).

Then we offer direction and try it again. At this point we're not looking at their instincts; we're looking to see how well they can take direction. Of course, this presumes that the directions you've given are good ones. We never tell an actor how to read a line. If you want someone who can imitate your every word, hire a parrot. Instead, we suggest the intention behind the line or the action and then let the actor interpret it as best they can.

For example, "Although you don't say it in the dialogue, in this scene you're angry at your wife for forgetting your birthday," or "Right now, your character has not slept for 36 hours, but he's trying to cover it up." These are more helpful directions than telling an actor to say one word louder than another.

In some rare instances, the first read will be perfect without direction. The actor will say every word right, every intention will be clear, and every motion will be poetry. You'll be amazed. You'll be ready to sign the contract and send everybody else home.

Not so fast.

Never hire an actor just because they read all the words right the first time. Instead, take some time and experiment with them. See if they can take direction. Ask them to play the scene in a less obvious way. If it's a romantic scene, have them play it for laughs. If it's an argument, tell them to make it into a seduction.

Remember, you're not looking for someone who can read just this one scene well. You're looking for flexible actors who can take direction. You want to see how they read with other people. Do they listen and respond to other actors in the scene, or are they acting in a vacuum?

If you still love everything the actor does after that (and after reviewing the videotape), then bring out the contract and break out the champagne — assuming it was donated in exchange for screen credit.

VI.   *Thou shalt look for simplicity.*

There's a technical term for the type of acting you probably don't want in your movie. It's called "Big-Face Acting." (All right, maybe that's not the technical term, but it's what we call it.) It's the kind of acting that plays to the balcony and works great if your audience is a hundred feet away and squinting.

Stay away from Big-Face Acting. On second thought, don't just stay away, run away from it.

The best way to avoid hiring Big-Face Actors is to videotape all the auditions. Then, after the auditions and before you offer anyone a role, review the tape and compare it to the notes you took while watching the actors live. You may be surprised. Some of the performers who looked great in person, from ten feet away, will seem overblown and unrealistic on tape. That's Big-Face Acting. However, other actors who didn't seem to be doing much of anything at all during the audition may come across as more compelling and interesting on tape. That's movie acting. Those are the ones you hire.

VII.   *Thou shalt give them a chance to do it their way.*

After you've given the actors direction and they've done it your way, ask them if they want to try it again and do something different. Some actors will jump at this opportunity, with good reason.

At this point in the process, they've done it for you twice: once just on instinct (the way they think you want it) and once with your direction (the way you think you want it). This third shot lets them combine the two approaches or try something entirely off the wall. They can take the scene right to the edge or even over the edge. They can give it a twist that you had never considered.

These "whatever you like" readings of the scene can be terrific. They give you and the actor a chance to really have fun with the scene and start to see all the possibilities. It's these "off the wall" readings that often give you a sense of whether or not you can bond with the actor and trust them to bring the character to life on screen.

Usually the approaches used during these readings don't make it into the movie, but they can be a great creative springboard for getting deeper into scenes and bringing them to life in unique and memorable ways.

VIII.   *Thou shalt take blame.*

It's happened to everyone at one point or another, and it's nothing to be ashamed about.

You'll have 20 actors read the same scene, and none of them will make it work. Your natural instinct will be to blame the actors. "If we had some decent actors in this town, this scene would be working. It's not the script. It's those darn actors."

No. It's the script. It needs more work.

However, don't think of this as a negative; this is simply part of the process. It's far better to realize script problems during auditions and rehearsals rather than during shooting or, worse yet, during editing.

So make notes during the auditions about which lines are consistently duds and which moments consistently don't work. Since you'll only be using a few scenes for auditions, problems with these scenes should spur you to give your entire script serious, objective scrutiny. If you're too in love with the script to see its warts, get help from people who will call a wart a wart, and listen to their advice.

IX.   *Thou shalt use as many actors as you reasonably can.*

This commandment doesn't mean we want you to turn your three-character story into *It's A Mad, Mad, Mad, Mad World*. It does mean that if somebody really good has auditioned for a role and they don't get it, you should consider them for other, smaller parts in the movie. As we've said earlier, actors live by their credits, and even a tiny walk-on part in a small, regional movie has value.

On every movie we've worked on, we've found great supporting players by offering roles to people who tested for the leads and for one reason or another didn't get it. So when you find good actors, give them parts in your movie. It gives them screen time, work in front of a camera, and a couple of minutes of footage for their reel. And it gives you performers who really want to be part of your project — and who turn tiny roles into small, sparkling gems. Everybody wins.

X.   *Thou shalt not lie.*

We don't need to tell you that lying is bad. You're an adult; someone must have mentioned it to you by now.

But often otherwise mature adults, such as movie directors and producers, will tell "little white lies" and even "big ugly lies" during the audition process in order to entice skillful actors to ply their trade in the moviemaker's latest opus.

Be warned: Lying will come back and bite you on the butt. Every time. And your reputation as just another low-life moviemaker will be posted on verbal bulletin boards throughout the acting community for years to come.

Don't lie about money.
We were very clear with the actors we auditioned, and even clearer in the release forms they signed.

We told them if they would get paid or not. We told them when they would get paid. We told them, in no uncertain terms, that the only money they could reasonably expect to see from the project was any "signing fee" or stipend we paid up front. The rest was wishful thinking.

So don't turn wishful thinking into promises you can't keep. It may get you through this project, but people will be less inclined to work with you later when they find out that you were lying earlier.

Don't lie about the nature of the movie.
If the movie involves nudity, the actors need to know this before you cast them — and not on the set just before you yell "Action!" If the movie will use graphic language or be explicit in its portrayal of sex or violence, the actors also need to know this before they commit to doing the movie.

Lying to the actors the very first time you meet them is not going to enable them to trust you where you need trust the most — on the set. So be honest about what kind of movie you're making, and start building that trust early.

Don't lie about the prospects for the movie.
Like all of us, actors are hopeful people. In fact, they're often more hopeful than the rest of us. Theirs is a business built on hope.

With that in mind, it's a good idea to muzzle your bounding hopes for the project and try to pull it back into the realm of the possible (or at least the probable) when you're talking to the actors.

Don't tell them that the movie will be released by a major studio. The odds are against it. You might get a limited theatrical release. You might make it to cable. It could go to home video. But a major studio release? Probably not.

Don't tell the actors that the movie will make them famous. The odds are against it. What your movie will give the actors is some experience working in movies and in a role larger than they would be offered if a big Hollywood film came to town. It will look good on their resume. It will look good on their reel. But it won't make them famous, yet. Sorry.

Don't lie about the budget. Don't talk about luxurious Winnebago trailers and fabulous costumes and multiple retakes. The actors need to know from the start that this is an ultra-low-budget project. They need to know all the project's limitations, so they can begin planning how to effectively use their talents under these circumstances.

Of course, there are lots of things you can tell the actors. You can tell them that this is going to be an educational experience, that it will help them grow as a performer, and that they will gain valuable acting credentials. You can tell them that you hope this will be the greatest movie in the history of time. That you hope it will revolutionize the movie industry. That you hope it will change the world as we know it. That's your dream, and it's good to share it.

But don't say that the movie will open in New York and L.A. in time for Academy Award consideration, before going national in 2,500 theaters. Talking excitedly about your dream is fine. Lying is not. Be sure you know the difference.

Casting the cast
Now that the auditioning is over, it's time to officially cast the movie. With any luck, you'll have a problem: Too many good actors, not enough parts. This is a good problem to have. A few pointers:

- •Don't cast look-alikes. We don't mean celebrity look-alikes, we mean actors who resemble each other. Unlike a Hollywood movie with big-name, recognizable actors, your movie will be filled with unknown faces. Don't confuse the audience by casting unknown faces that look similar. If you are forced to cast actors with similar builds, hair color and features, then be sure to distinguish them with unique costumes and hair styles.

- •Offer roles to your first choices first, before informing other actors that they didn't get cast. You need to offer the parts to these actors, and have them accept the roles before you let the other contenders go. Once all the parts are cast — and accepted — you can then start calling the contenders and breaking the news to them.

- •Thank the contenders, but don't go into details about why they weren't cast. Don't tell them that they were too tall or too short or too fat or that their nose was the wrong size. Don't critique their acting (unless it's a compliment and unless you really mean it). If you were impressed with their work, tell them that you'll keep them in mind for other movies and that you'll hang onto their picture and resume (and then really do it).

147

The results of a successful audition, the principal cast of Resident Alien. *Pictured, l to r; Mark Patrick Gleason, Nesba Crenshaw, Patrick Coyle.*

Asking people to "work for free"

Years ago, John worked as a writer on a trailer for a proposed low-budget feature. Early on, the producers decided to pay the crew and not to pay the cast. Their reasoning was that the crew would be working for the duration of the four-day shoot, while most of the actors would only be working for a day or two.

This saved them money. They thought it was a good idea. It wasn't.

The problem with their approach was that it sent a message to the cast. The message said, "We don't think your time and skills are worth as much as those of the kid holding the light stand." This was a bad message to send.

Did it hurt the movie? Probably. Did it hurt the chances of the producers putting together another project? Definitely. Because the word was out that those guys aren't just cheap; they don't care about the actors.

Well, we're happy to report that the word is out on us as well. We're cheap. We're known for it. Maybe even renowned for it. But we're also known for caring about our actors. For treating them fairly and honestly.

And for paying a paltry pittance. Of course, we don't pay the crew any more than that. We pay ourselves even less. We're nothing if not fair. Maintaining equity such as this is a key component in making your project work. It makes it a project fueled by hope, not by mere money.

Initially you'll probably feel guilty about not being able to pay the cast or crew what they are worth. Trust us. You'll get over it, and we're not being cynical when we say that. You may not be handing out paychecks each week, but the fact is that you're offering everyone involved in the project a professional study course that will look great on their resume.

Think about it. There are thousands upon thousands of actors and would-be actors in the world. How many of them ever get to act in a feature? Or, for that matter, play a leading role in a feature? Very few. But you're in a position to offer that to people, and that really is something of value. So don't sell yourself short, because you're giving these actors a great opportunity. As long as you warn them about what they're getting into, you should have a happy set and a productive shoot.

CORRALLING THE CREW
(ASSEMBLING THE DREAM TEAM)

Production Diary: During the last two weekends, the director of photography has been impersonating Dr. Strangelove behind the camera, the sound recordist and boom operator wore bathrobes and hair nets after being teased about taking naps between shots, the production manager stood on a picnic table operating lights to simulate a UFO landing, and we all worked 14 hours a day. Situation normal.

A little crazed, willing to leap conventional job delineations in a single bound, dedicated to the project — that's the description of a super crewperson for your movie. This type of crewmember is critical to the success of your production. Finding these people is just as important as finding the right actors for your cast. Without them, the actor's brilliant performances can be lost in a muddle of unusable videotape. Fortunately, there are many people eager to fill this bill.

Some of the steps you'll take to find these wonderful people are similar to the ones for getting a great cast, but it is a different process that is best approached separately.

Finding crewpeople
Before you begin your quest, you need to know what the holy grail looks like. Who do you need for your crew? The essential crew positions have already been identified in your budget:

- Unit Production Manager/Script Supervisor
- Production Assistant
- Director of Photography/Videographer
- Sound Recordist
- Lighting Gaffer/Boom Operator
- Makeup-and-Hair Supervisor

A screenwriter is also essential to your production, and we've discussed how to select one in the script chapter.

Some crewmembers don't need to be brought onto the project until postproduction. We'll talk about selecting people for the following

151

positions in the postproduction chapter:

- Composer/Music Supervisor/Songwriter
- Session Musicians
- Video, Sound, and Music Editor

Some crew positions are optional and will depend on the nature of your specific project:

- Assistant Unit Production Manager
- Art Director
- Wardrobe Supervisor
- Singers
- Stunt Coordinator
- Special-Effects Coordinator
- Model Builder
- Set-Construction Coordinator
- Animal Wrangler

We haven't mentioned director or producer in these lists because most people who are foolish enough to produce a feature-length movie for a song (or merely a verse) are just crazy enough to direct or produce it themselves. Just in case you've retained a sliver of good sense and want to get someone else to direct and produce your movie, we'll give you some guidelines after we talk about the rest of the production crew.

So where do you find a crew that's strong of back and keen of mind? We found our people largely by word of mouth. We spoke to people who had worked on short films and videos and other low-budget features in our area. Most of them were happy to recommend good people with whom they'd worked. When we called these prospective crewpeople, they often suggested friends and acquaintances for other crew positions. We also watched local productions and contacted people who had done good work on them. Generally, working video and film professionals were afraid of doing a project that broke so many of the rules, so the best recommendations were for people who were just starting in the business. You may find people who are trying to advance to the next level in their professional careers and will join you to get experience they can't get in their day jobs. You can also place ads on the bulletin boards at local colleges and film schools, on the Internet or in the newsletter of the closest Independent Feature Project chapter. The state or city film office in your area may also have job listings for movie crews. Even equipment rental houses may be able to tell you who's looking for the kind of opportunity you're offering.

Cast your net widely to get names of many possible crewmembers. Don't be bashful or apologetic because you can't offer high-buck salaries. The type of experience you are providing is rarely available to fledgling movie crewmembers. You're taking a chance doing this production in order to fulfill your dream. They will happily join you in realizing your dream because their own dreams are attached to yours.

This is a good point to remind you to put on your blinders. We mean the good kind — the ones that don't see color, gender, age, or body type when looking at a candidate, only abilities. There are many good people looking for jobs on movie productions who get these biases thrown in their faces daily. You can use that to your advantage by scooping up those candidates with great skills who have been rejected for irrelevant reasons.

The first positions that you should be trying to fill for your crew are the unit production manager/script supervisor, the director of photography/videographer, and the sound recordist. These are your key crewmembers, and they should have some input about who will be their helpers — the production assistant and the lighting gaffer/boom operator. In several instances on our productions, the key crewpeople recommended people whom they had worked with before and who turned out to be great additions to the team. So you can save yourself some work by starting with these three key positions. If they don't have any suggestions, then it's a good idea to have them involved in interviewing the other job applicants.

Once you have a list of potential candidates, you're ready to start panning for the gold.

Interviewing the crew
Your first contact with crewpeople will probably be a phone call. "Uh, I'm (your name), and I'm making a low-budget digital movie. I got your name from (an acquaintance, someone they worked for, their response

to your ad, the editing-room wall at a film school). Are you interested in working as a (mouthwatering crew position) on our production? By the way, there's no pay, the hours are long, and we work on weekends." If they don't hang up laughing derisively, they will probably ask what type of movie, what format, and what your goals and dreams are for the production. Sell your project to them. As far as you know, they are going to win an Academy Award for their next movie, and it could be yours. You need their interest to find out if they are right for your movie. They'll only consider joining you because your dream is catching, so tell them enough to capture their imagination.

If they are interested, ask them to send you a list of work experience, some references (unless they've already been referred to you), and an availability schedule. For the sound recordist and director of photography, ask for samples of their work. You need to know that these crewpeople can deliver results. Be sure to ask what their role was in the sample they send you. For example, if a director of photography candidate only loaned a camcorder to the video production you're viewing, you have no idea if he or she can even focus a lens.

Once you have sized up the candidates from their resumes, references, work samples, and a little bit of conversation on the phone, you're ready to arrange for interviews. Be sure to look at two or more candidates for each position. That way, the people you ultimately select will give their best work to keep this plum assignment, knowing there are challengers out there just waiting for them to stumble. You'll also get a feel for the range of candidates available to you.

Your interviews don't need to be elaborate. They can be done at the kitchen table. You can also do them by phone, though you'll usually get a better sense of someone's personality by talking face to face. Keep it informal, and start by telling them honestly about your production. It's a waste of time to give the impression that this is a bigger production than it actually is. Crewpeople will find out the truth as soon as the discussion turns to technical needs and you point out that you can't afford more than three rolls of gaffer's tape. Don't forget to mention hard work, long hours, minuscule budget, small crew, unconventional techniques, little or no pay, non-union, and slim chances of the final movie being a financial success. If they're going to be scared off, now's the time for it to happen.

After laying out the grisly truth of your project and your commitment to it, let them do some talking about their education, experience, goals, dreams, ideas, and why they're right for your crew. You should be listening for the characteristics and attitudes of a good crewmember. This list applies to postproduction crew as well as production crew:

Desired characteristics and attitudes
- Good humor
- Can-do, problem-solving attitude
- Enthusiasm and respect for your project and ideas to make it even better
- Good work ethic
- Willingness to help with other aspects of the project (loan props, paint sets, find equipment for free, etc.)
- Technical proficiency and basic skills needed for their duties or the ability to learn them fast
- Cooperative, willing to follow directions
- Aware of the challenge, but not afraid to try
- Good vibes — you should have a good feeling about this person and be genuinely excited to work with them.
- Actively trying to improve their skills by volunteering on other projects, working on their own movies, or taking classes
- Owns equipment and uses it. These people are serious about their avocation and could bring equipment they are familiar with to your production.
- Has connections and is willing to call in favors to enhance the project
- Antiestablishment, let's-make-an-end-run, who-says-we-can't-do-it attitude

Granted, it will be rare to find every one of these characteristics in every crewperson, but try to find the people who best match this list and you'll end up with a dynamite crew.

Specialized skills or attitudes
In addition to these general characteristics, you'll be looking for some specific skills and attitudes in the positions of unit production manager, director of photography, and stunt coordinator.

Unit Production Manager/Script Supervisor

As we stated in the chapter on preproduction, you want this person to be very organized and conscious of details. If a candidate for this job shows up late for the interview saying they lost the address, keep looking. This is the one person who has to double-check every step of the project, so make sure she or he is up to the job. You also want a take-charge kind of person, not someone who doesn't move without direction.

This person will be helped by the production assistant. Together they will make sure camera tapes are labeled before being put in the camcorder and are securely stored when taken out. They'll slate scenes. They will keep an accurate log of the shots and will make sure the cast is wearing the proper costumes and hairstyles. They'll check that the right props are on the set, they'll make sure lunch is ready, and they'll keep track of continuity between shots. Obviously, the unit production manager is a busy and important crewmember, so make a careful choice for this position. And pick an able production assistant too.

Director of Photography/Videographer

This person will be your image expert, so the candidate for this job must have a vision of how the movie can or should look and the ability to make it happen. This may not match the producer's and director's vision initially, but if this person can see how to create different looks for the movie, then you have a starting point for some serious visual discussions. A person who can only create gothic-horror lighting is only useful for that type of movie. You want someone who's familiar with the sorcery that can be performed using lights and lenses and filters, someone who relishes the challenge of making art from nothing, someone with ideas on how to create a big look with no money or time. If you can't find such a person, then you at least want someone who can properly compose, focus, and light a shot.

We found that this position became the leader of the production crew, setting the mood and the work pace for the others. Sure, the director is in charge, but if the director of photography is always grousing about the working conditions, you'll have a surly, disgruntled crew. We've been blessed with good-humored directors of photography, and, with rare exceptions, we've had happy crews even when working long hours in overheated, crowded motel rooms, when circling a skating rink for 20 hours straight, and when shooting on a roof all night in 40-degree temperatures. The people we've used as directors of photography on our movies have had a "we can do that" attitude for every challenge, and that made our crews invincible in the face of technical challenges. They didn't know it was impossible, and we'd be the last people to tell them.

Just a word on experience: People who want to be your director of photography may have a variety of film and video experience, some of it helpful, some of it not. The trick is to tell the difference. Working on industrial and training films and videos may not adequately prepare a person to be director of photography on a feature-length movie. If they have shot only corporate meetings and done classroom-style training productions, they may not be experienced in how to create a mood with lighting and how to compose a shot for beauty and effect. On the other hand, if they have done productions that use dramatic segments or movie techniques, they may be ready to soar with your project. Look for examples of their work that show they know how to enhance the tone and meaning of your script. If you don't see evidence of this skill, don't consider adding them to your team unless you're convinced they will educate themselves a lot before you start production, including doing actual test shots to establish a look for your movie.

Stunt Coordinator

You may have no need for this position on your project, but if you do, you don't want a devil-may-care risk-taker. In fact, the stunt coordinator should be the most cautious and safety-conscious member of your crew. The right person for this job is someone with a magician's mentality. How can we trick people into believing a stunt is dangerous as heck... without risking anyone's safety? We know of would-be stunt performers who just like the idea of jumping from moving cars for real. Unless you want your production known for its toll in human lives, steer clear of these gonzo types.

🎥🎥🎥

Once you've found your top one or two candidates for each position, it's a good idea to have a second interview to check your perceptions and to see if they are still interested. (Polite people may not tell you that they think you're crazy, at least not while you're in the same room. Crazy

157

people have been known to snap, you know.) This interview can be done by phone if you wish. This is a good time to talk about how this person would approach the production tasks ahead if you add them to the crew. Be especially impressed by those who have started preparing for the job. They've done research, they've gotten connections for low-cost equipment rentals, they've learned how to use the equipment, and they've come up with good ideas that will help the production. These are the go-getters you need.

Choosing the crew

After a couple of conversations with your prime candidates you should be getting a feel for their personalities and getting some vibes about each person. We've learned to pay a lot of attention to vibes. It's that nagging sixth sense that a person will be a problem, that vague uneasiness about the person that belies their skills and what they say. Pay attention to these gut reactions. Sure, they could just be that burrito from lunch, but we've found our vibes about people to be pretty reliable. We also get good vibes about people, that euphoric sense that this person will do great things for your movie, and some of those people have become friends who have worked on many of our projects.

Just as when you select your cast, call your first choices for crewmembers first and get their acceptance before you turn down anyone. If your first choice declines to join you, you can ask your second choice. If you're lucky enough to have two great candidates for a position, consider putting one of them in an assisting position if there's one available. You're likely to create a work team that will have even more good ideas to add to your production. Now, don't expect to have a list of experienced people for every position. A small production like yours may not have any experienced people who are interested in working on it. Don't be disappointed. There are many wannabes out there who want a chance to work on any kind of professional production. Every experienced professional had a first production, and often it was a low-budget project much like yours. Sure, they didn't know everything they needed to know that first time, but they knew enough and learned enough to do a respectable job, and it led to more productions. One filmmaker we know worked with a director of photography who went on to win an Academy Award for shooting *Schindler's List*. There are lots of talented people out there looking for their first break.

If you don't have a list of experienced crewpeople to choose from, you have to be on the lookout for promising people. That describes many of the crewpeople we've had on our productions. They were people who had worked on movies in lesser jobs and were ready to move up. And some of them had never worked on a movie before.

There are lots of diamonds out there languishing in the rough. You just need to recognize them and give them a chance. You won't be sorry, because they will give you their very best work — to your mutual benefit. So consider giving the director of photography position to that production assistant who's graduating from film school or the sound recordist position to that boom operator.

Selecting a director and producer
It's likely that you have decided to be the producer or director of your digital movie. Retaining control of the project is why most of us decide to make independent movies in the first place. If you happen to be a screenwriter in search of a production company, then you may need to find a producer and director.

Finding a producer won't be that hard. Finding one that's right for your project may take a little more effort. You need someone with experience developing budgets for movies and someone who can pinch a penny until it bends. Many people in the audio-visual production business know how to do these things. Because most of them have planned video productions, they should be equipped to create a realistic budget for your digital movie. You need someone who will be the guardian of the budget and will calmly and insistently say "no" when the budget doesn't allow for that camera boom. A good producer will then come up with three ways that you can do just as good a shot for no extra money.

Producing is a job that can be learned. In fact, you can do it yourself after having read this book. Dale's experience had been in budgeting and shooting videos for government projects (contrary to popular belief, most government projects are decidedly low-buck). By going to producers' telephone school, he learned enough to serve as producer on feature-length movies.

What's producers' telephone school? Basically, you call people who know the business — say, a video retailer — and try to get a price for a digital video camcorder for your budget. You'll sound like a moron during the phone call when they ask, "Do you want single CCD or three CCD?" and you don't know the difference. Your cheeks will be red as you ask them to tell you the difference and they patronizingly do. You hang up and note how glad you are that you did this by phone. You go back for your next lesson by calling another retailer and asking for their price on a 3-CCD digital video camcorder. Those cheeks of yours start heating up again when they ask if you want DV, DVCAM, or DVCPRO. You swallow your pride again and ask them to explain these formats and tell you what models are available. More patronizing education. You hang up, let your cheeks and pride recover, and then call retailer number three. This time you ask for the price on a Sony 3-CCD DV DCR-TRV900 camcorder. In three easy lessons, you know what you're talking about.

Actually, most businesses that supply production equipment and services are happy to give you an education about their services. They know a potential customer when they hear one. Some reading and some discussions with knowledgeable people can give a would-be producer enough information to do an adequate job. (There are a number of useful magazines that are sent free to production professionals like you. Check the appendix.) If you can get someone with experience, you're likely to get better than adequate. Dale's experience producing videos and his own movies meant he could offer many cost-cutting ideas that a less-experienced producer might have missed. If your producer is inexperienced, try to talk over your plans and budget with other producers who have done low-budget projects. You'll get suggestions that will help you control costs on your movie.

If you're not going to direct your project, you'll have the much harder task of finding the right director. The director has fingers in every one of the production's pies; it is his or her vision that will guide the project. And that's the challenge: Is it the same vision you have? If your director is seeing how to get laughs from the scene that is your dramatic pinnacle, you've got a double-vision problem, and the two of you won't be seeing eye-to-eye throughout the project. You may even be at each other's throats before you're finished. This is not a good way to work. This is the reason many independent movies have screenwriter/director listed in the credits. It can be very difficult to find someone who respects and shares your vision.

Selecting a director is a type of marriage. You have to have a similar vision if you are going to be able to work as a team to realize that goal. That doesn't mean that there won't be disagreements in this marriage, but it does mean that there's a shared respect for the vision you're trying to achieve. If so, your arguments will only be about the best way to achieve that vision.

Obviously, good vibes are essential when selecting a director. Some lengthy discussions about movies in general and your project in particular will help you figure out if your director candidate is the one. Don't decide until you're sure you've found a person you can trust to take charge of your baby.

Your best choice is also going to be someone who has managed big production projects before, because a feature-length movie has almost endless details that must be remembered while directing. It's usually best if your director has had experience getting actors to do dramatic performances for the camera. Experience directing training videos and industrial films is useful but different. If you decide to use a director who lacks this experience (maybe yourself), there are a number of good books on the art of directing which are listed in the bibliography. The director should read them. It would also be good to practice directing some scenes on video before production starts. This will help the director see what the results on the screen look like.

First-time directors can do a good job if they've done their homework. (Orson Welles on *Citizen Kane* is an example.) Sometimes they even bring a fresh vision to the screen because they haven't been trained to think in conventional ways.

Letting your crew do its best
Once you've selected your crewpeople, encourage them to make suggestions and give ideas on how to improve the production. This can be hard. You've probably been living with this dream for a long time, and it's hard to let go and share it. It can be even harder to let other people change your dream. Be brave. One of the most important lessons we've learned while making our movies is that dreams grow stronger and more beautiful when other people add to them.

We found that every actor and every crewmember brought a little bit of themselves to the dream and added to it. The screenplay that we started with was only the seed, and each person who came to the production made it grow into something better. The actors brought depth to the characters that hadn't existed on the printed page. The director created compelling scenes that crackled with energy. The camera crew created images that strengthened the messages of the story. The editor created pacing that propelled the story forward. The composer amplified the emotional content of scenes with music. In the end, our movies were much more than they started out to be on paper because we let others embellish our dream.

PRODUCTION
(LIGHTS, CAMERA, CHAOS!)

When most people imagine making movies, what they're actually picturing is just one element of that process — production. They envision beautiful actors and actresses in costumes, huge lights, dollies, cranes, cameras, and egomaniacal directors with monocles and megaphones, yelling "Action!" and "Cut!"

In reality, the production phase is just one element of the overall moviemaking process, though a vital one. Making a digital feature doesn't begin when you yell "action" for the first time on the first day of production or end when you yell "cut" after the last scene is shot. However, if you do your job correctly during the production phase, you can save yourself time, money, and headaches during the subsequent phases.

With that in mind, we've assembled the following production notes to help the director and producer through the production process. This list is by no means exhaustive — the circumstances surrounding your own production are bound to be as unique as the movie you're making — but there are certain common elements and concerns that have a tendency to pop up in all productions.

Training
No, we're not recommending film school. Why spend $15,000 a year to go to a film school (where you'll be lucky to make a couple of short movies), when you can create your own feature-length movie using less than one year's tuition? (And without having to take 12 credits of a foreign language.)

No, by training we mean getting in shape, physically and mentally. Make no mistake, directing is a grueling undertaking. Some people have compared the experience to running a marathon. Of course, this is ludicrous because a marathon is over in a measly 26 miles while you've got an arduous eight, ten, or 20 days of production to survive. Take it from us, your average marathon runner would be begging for mercy after the first half day of shooting. You must be made of stronger stuff. The best advice we've ever heard about directing was to "wear comfortable shoes." Directing requires intense concentration and stamina. You'll need to be on your feet most of the day and on your toes at all times.

Taking care of yourself before production (eating well, exercising often) is important; taking even better care of yourself during production is just as vital. This means eating regularly and well (not junk food) during the day and getting as much sleep as you can reasonably get each night.

We also recommend staying away from artificial stimulants like sugar and caffeine because while they will make your highs higher, they will also make your lows lower. And there's nothing worse than finding yourself staring at the ceiling at 3 a.m., your brain cells screaming with a Mountain Dew buzz, while you curse your inability to sleep and your 5 a.m. alarm setting.

It's also a good idea to get off your feet at least once during the day. You can call it meditating, you can call it power napping, you can call it whatever you want — just do it. It will clear your head and increase your energy for the rest of the day. This break isn't just for the director and the producer, either. In all likelihood, your director of photography will be on her or his feet just as long (particularly since this person is also acting as camera operator). With setting up the lights, shooting the scenes, tearing down the lights, and preparing for the next setup, your director of photography rarely gets a chance for a break throughout the shooting day. So find a way to give the director of photography a break whenever you can. This may slow you down for a few moments, but it will pay you back with more energy throughout the day and better results.

20 (thousand) questions

As a movie director, you will be asked more questions and will make more decisions during preproduction and production than you have throughout your entire life. Director Edward Zwick (*Glory, Legends Of The Fall*) has said that each day of production involves so many decisions that "I open a menu and try to think about what to order for dinner, and I'm ready to burst into tears."

You will quickly find that the questions are constant and they all demand answers: "Do you want him to wear the white shirt or the off-white shirt?" "When you say 'close-up,' how close do you mean?" "Do you want to break for lunch now or in ten minutes?" "Are we going to see that wall or not?" "Is the car needed in this scene?" "What do you want to do next, scene 112 or scene 4?" "Do you want to do a retake?" "Does it matter that he moved?" "Are there any other shots you need or should we send the actor home?" "Are you going to intercut on this shot?" "Are we doing a reverse?" And the question you dread the most, "How did you get this job, anyway?"

You will be expected to have the answers to these and 19,988 other questions on the tip of your tongue at all times during production. In most cases, if you've done your homework (such as knowing the script inside and out), the answers will be within easy reach.

However, in some cases, your mind will be blank, and you simply won't have an answer. That's when it's best to fall back on those three infamous words that some people find difficult, if not impossible, to say: "I don't know."

There is no shame in not knowing, particularly if you follow up immediately with, "What do you think?" Keep in mind that the person asking the question is usually someone you hired for their knowledge and skill. They may already have the perfect answer to the question they've raised.

Another good answer, after "I don't know," is "What are my options?" This gives you choices, which are always easier to deal with. The truth is, as a director, you may not always have the answer. But if someone gives you a choice, you will always have opinions.

Just because you don't have all the answers, though, doesn't mean you aren't in charge. The director is the captain of this ship, and this concept must be communicated throughout the staff. This doesn't mean you have to run your set like you're Mussolini on a bad hair day. But it does mean that all suggestions and instructions should flow through the director — and this includes comments from the producer. The entire cast and crew should look to one person for direction, and if you're the director, that person is you. This is especially important on a fast-paced production like yours. You can't afford the miscommunication and confusion that result when more than one person is giving instructions.

The big lie

You may remember that a couple chapters back we told you lying was a bad thing.

Well, we were lying.

There is one occasion on an ultra-low-budget production when lying is not only permitted, it is required. That's when it comes time to "psyche up" the cast and the crew. To do this you must lie. Just this once. Actually, twice.

Here's how it works: Before you start your first day of shooting, take the members of the crew aside, sit them down, and give them a pep talk. It goes something like this, "Listen folks, you're the best. I know you can do this. With your help, we're going to make this the greatest movie of all time…"

(So far, it's just hyperbole, which is always acceptable. Here comes the lie.)

"The thing is, though… well, it's the cast. A lot of them are pretty new to moviemaking, and some of them are going to screw up. So all of you on the crew, who are more experienced, have to work extra hard to make sure that you don't make any mistakes, because the cast is bound to. So when they get it right, we don't want to miss it for technical reasons." Thus ends Lie Number 1.

For Lie Number 2, you sit the cast members down, give them the hyperbolic spiel, and then say (here comes the lie), "The thing is, though… well, it's the crew. A lot of them are pretty new to moviemaking, and some of them are going to screw up. So all of you in the cast, who are more experienced, have to work extra hard to make sure that you don't make any mistakes, because the crew is bound to. So when they get it right, we don't want to miss it for performance reasons."

With two little lies you have psyched up both the cast and the crew, built up their egos, and persuaded them that the success or failure of the movie rests in their capable hands — which is true. Of course, once you've finished this, you have to go back to telling the truth full time. Or at least until you start dealing with distributors.

Read-through and rehearsals
The odds are that your movie will be shot out of sequence; that is, all the scenes that take place in one location will be shot at the same time, regardless of where they appear in the story.

While this is great for your schedule, it puts an extra strain on your actors, who must be able — on nearly a moment's notice — to accurately portray their character at any given point in the story.

In a play, actors have the luxury of following the arc of their characters' emotional, psychological, and physical changes from beginning to end, both during rehearsals and in performance. No such luxury exists on a movie set, where actors are routinely required to play widely disparate scenes in quick succession, such as a violent argument followed immediately by a tender love scene.

For example, one segment in *Grown Men* involves a budding romance between a young woman who works in a blood bank and a victim of panic attacks who collapses while he's donating blood. For scheduling and lighting reasons, we had to keep jumping back and forth while we shot, first shooting portions of the early, relaxed scenes between the two characters and then jumping quickly to moments from the intense, dramatic and emotionally exhausting scenes, and then back to the relaxed scenes — often in the space of just a few minutes.

A thorough read-through and comprehensive rehearsals made these dramatic leaps possible.

The read-through
A complete read-through of the script is an invaluable exercise for the cast and crew as well as for you. What were once just words on paper come to life during the read-through, and everyone gets a chance to see how the story develops from beginning to end.

Because of the fractured nature of movie production, this is possibly the only time the cast and crew will hear the entire story from start to finish until the night they take their seats at the movie's preview. As such, it's a good idea to gather everyone together for this event. If that's not logistically possible, then the principal cast members and all the department heads should be required to attend (production management, sound, camera, and hair and makeup). Knowledge is power, and the more knowledgeable everyone is about the movie, the more powerful the end result will be.

As with every other facet of your production, the read-through doesn't require any extravagance. Schedule a decent block of time (three to four hours), secure a space big enough to hold everybody (a good-sized living room will often do), provide some food and beverages (bargain soda and homemade cookies), and then start reading from page one.

You may want to tape record or videotape the proceedings so that you can refer back to moments that caught your attention, either positively or negatively. Otherwise, just sit back, shut your eyes, and listen, imagining the movie while you hear the dialogue and directions. (It's a good idea if someone other than the producer or director reads the directions so that they can concentrate on just listening.)

At the end of the read-through, you can solicit comments from the group: what worked, what didn't, which parts seemed confusing, and so on. If time permits, you can also go back and have the cast reread troublesome scenes to help you locate problems and get some ideas for solutions.

The read-through is a very valuable tool because it provides you with yet another opportunity to make changes and adjustments to the script before the meter starts ticking.

Rehearsals
The best feature of our shooting schedule for *Grown Men* (where there were often three to four months between segments) was that it provided plenty of rehearsal time and recovery time. We'd shoot like demons for a couple weekends, then have a couple months to regroup, recover and rehearse scenes for the next segment.

Unlike the read-through, which was a sit-down affair, the rehearsals allow you to put the scenes and the actors on their feet. Rehearsing is, without question, one of the best parts of the production process, because it allows you to do all kinds of experimenting and to take all sorts of risks without spending a dime.

You'll need an empty space for rehearsing, a location where the owners and the neighbors won't mind if you get a bit noisy or work a little late. Chairs for sitting and for use as props are a must, and a bathroom is always a nice perk.

We scheduled rehearsals using the same approach as scheduling the production. If an actor had three scenes to be shot over the course of the upcoming weekend, all three of those scenes would be rehearsed on the same night. This way the actor didn't have to sit around waiting to rehearse.

For each scene, we let the actors do it once without direction to see where their instincts took them, just like in the audition. Then we gave them direction and started to refine the blocking (the movements within the scene). As we worked on the blocking, we started thinking about our shots, noting how we were going to cover the scene. Will it need a master shot showing all the characters together? What sort of shots can we do to get the most out of the scene, to make it as visually interesting and effective as possible?

We recommend moving around while you're watching the actors rehearse, observing them from all sides to help find the most cinematic way to execute the scene. If you plant yourself in front of them and watch their actions like a play, you're more likely to shoot the scene like a play, which, although a workmanlike approach, is hardly an effective use of your visual tools. So, just as you've put the actors on their feet during rehearsal, you should stay on your feet as well, circling the action and beginning to make some decisions about how each scene will be shot.

Well-rehearsed actors are a godsend that allow you to accomplish a lot using very little of your precious production time. For example, one of the segments in *Grown Men* had over 20 pages of dialogue that we had to shoot in two locations over three days. (Remember, due to some outstanding equipment deals, we were able to shoot this movie at a more leisurely pace than normal.) In order to minimize relighting, many of the scenes were shot out of sequence, meaning that we'd shoot one actor's shot on one day, and then do the reverse shot of the other actor later on the next day.

All the scenes played beautifully and came off without a hitch. The actors knew the scenes backward and forward, and they could pick up at any point in any scene at a moment's notice. They knew the lines and they knew the pace, all because the scene had been thoroughly and rigorously rehearsed.

Of course, you do need to walk that fine line between being adequately rehearsed and over-rehearsed. You don't want the scenes to sound rote or become flat. The key is to rehearse each scene enough so that you and the actors are comfortable, but not so much that it loses its freshness.

Shot lists
Using your notes from the rehearsal, you can assemble your shot list for each scene. The shot list tells you and your director of photography how you're going to cover each scene. This can be a list of shots ("Two-shot of Daniel and Mary, Mary's point of view of the boxes, single shots of Daniel and Mary as they enter") or crude storyboard drawings that detail each angle.

Keep in mind that every shot is another setup that will require lighting (or relighting), which takes time. The more shots you have, the more time it will take to shoot the scene. And with the clock always ticking (sometimes louder than others), you may run out of time before you run out of shots. So always do the key shots first, and then plan on grabbing the remaining shots as your schedule permits.

Long takes
Of course, no one ever said you have to shoot masters and close-ups and then intercut them. You always have the option to compose your scenes as long, continuous takes with the actors moving artfully within the frame.

Cinema history is filled with revered examples of this technique, from Orson Welles' fluid opening shot in *Touch Of Evil* (which was parodied in Robert Altman's *The Player*) to Jim Jarmusch's achingly static camera in *Stranger Than Paradise*. Mike Nichols pulled off some remarkable long takes in *Carnal Knowledge*, and directors as diverse as Alan Arkin and Michelangelo Antonioni have made them work in movies as diverse as *Little Murders* and *The Passenger*. Even Woody Allen has used this approach, to greater and lesser effect, in many of his movies.

There are, however, drawbacks to this technique. The first is that if it isn't staged properly, it can become visually boring. If that's your point, then fine. Otherwise, the trick to making a long take work is to keep the frame energized by moving the camera, moving the actors, or presenting a very dramatic moment so that you hold the audience's interest without turning the shot into a videotaped stage play.

The second drawback is that long takes are risky. A long take requires that the actors and the crew get it right — absolutely, flawlessly right — from the beginning of the take right down to the very last frame. If someone blows it in the last few seconds, you've got to start all over again. If someone blows it on the second take, you start from the beginning yet again. And again. And again.

Long takes are also risky because they give you no options in the editing room. Often a long, continuous take will seem great while you're shooting it, but when it's edited into the movie, it will slow the pace or even bring the movie to a dead stop. If you haven't shot any additional shots (known as "coverage") of the scene, you'll be left with no options, which is always a bad place to be.

On the positive side, if you have performers who can do a scene perfectly and a crew who can execute a camera move flawlessly, long takes can save a lot of time and tape during your production schedule. It's just a question of weighing the risks and the advantages.

Abandoning your shot list
Of course, the best-laid plans occasionally go awry. You may find when you're on location that the scene you rehearsed and storyboarded so meticulously simply can't be shot the way you intended. You may have lost your original location. There may be technical problems. Or you may simply have run out of time. Whatever the reason, you are now faced with a serious problem that needs a speedy solution.

The best solution that we've found is to go back to the basics. Ask yourself what your original intention was. What ideas were you trying to convey with the shots you planned? Rather than forcing your shots into a room or a schedule that can't hold them, you need to rethink your plan, using your original intentions but finding a new way to reach your goal.

171

Often you'll find that the best solution is the simplest. Of course, the simplest solution is sometimes the hardest one to discover. It may not be the one that will make future movie students "ooh" and "ahh," but if it gets the job done and keeps you on schedule, it's the right solution.

For one segment of *Grown Men*, we'd planned on doing an elaborate dolly shot around a bed, showing a couple as they moved closer and closer to reconciliation. It would show the passage of time, dissolving four times as the dolly moved around the bed, each time showing the couple in different pajamas and bedding, getting closer and closer together.

Nice idea, but when the time came to shoot it, we found that the room was too small to make it work. However, what the room lacked in floor space, it made up in height, sporting a nice, tall ceiling.

Going back to the basic idea behind the scene, we composed four high-angle shots, from four points in the room, where we could see the couple in bed as they moved closer together. Different bedding (and dissolves) showed the passage of time, and we were able to make our visual point, despite not being able to do our original shot. And, in the end, the scene was better for it.

Continuity
The key to continuity at this budget level is to keep a keen eye on the big things and make sure that they match from shot to shot. Try to make the small details match too, but don't sweat it if you miss.

For example, if you have a character exiting one room wearing a blue shirt and entering an adjacent room wearing a red shirt, you have a big continuity problem that you need to correct. That same character exiting one room wearing earrings and entering another without them is less of a problem, unless the earrings are the size of hubcaps.

In general, the continuity issue is the domain of your unit production manager, assuming it gets past the actor. (Most actors are remarkably adept at remembering which costume goes with what scene.) To prevent these potential snafus from happening in the first place, the unit production manager needs to take a Polaroid photo of each of the actors during their final costume fittings or the first time they wear each costume during production. Each photo should show the actor wearing one of their costumes for the movie. If the actor has six costume changes during the course of the movie, the production manager will have six Polaroid photos of them. On the bottom of each photo should be noted the scene numbers in which the costume appears. This technique can also be used with special makeup or hair styles. It then becomes a simple matter to check the photo against what the actor is wearing before each scene to ensure that continuity is being maintained.

It should be noted here that your production is missing one important crew person — the script supervisor. This is the person who makes sure the lines in the script are said correctly and that continuity — at least the major stuff — matches from shot to shot and from scene to scene. Our unit production manager performed this function during takes. She read along with the script as the actors said the lines, and she noted details like which hand the actor used to hold the carving knife. Script supervisors on big productions keep very detailed notes, but your project will probably be simple enough that the unit production manager and the actors can keep track of continuity issues, though it's a good idea to have everyone on the cast and crew watching.

Touchups
We mentioned this before, but it's worth repeating: Tell your hair and makeup person to keep touchups to a minimum. Primping and fluffing the actors before each shot wastes time and generally makes no appreciable difference on tape.

That's not to say that the makeup people shouldn't be alert to makeup problems and be prepared to jump in and correct them. You simply must establish up front what you consider to be a problem and what you can live with.

You may not even have a full-time makeup person. Instead, the make-up-and-hair supervisor may stop by in the morning, do the makeup for your key actors, and then disappear for the rest of the day. If this is your situation, it's a good idea to get this part-time makeup person to create makeup kits for the key actors. Each kit can be as simple as a baggie filled with the materials each actor will need to repair his or her own makeup throughout the day. Because different actors may be using

A very quick touchup on the set of Grown Men. *Pictured, l to r; Actress Susan Vee, Unit Production Manager Nicola Muoio, and Executive Producer (and Boom Operator) Dale Newton. (Photo courtesy of Granite Productions, Unlimited.)*

radically different shades or types of makeup, creating these individual kits makes it easier to keep all the makeup elements straight and in a place where the actors can find them.

Where to begin... and where to end
On your first actual day of production you may find yourself filled with feelings of trepidation and anxiety. Consequently, we recommend that you lessen your burden a bit and start your shoot with something simple. And that you start off quickly.

Starting quickly establishes a quick pace for the production, and it establishes the director as a take-charge sort of person. Starting simply gives everyone a chance to get up to speed with a scene or a shot that is not too taxing or difficult.

On some productions, because of the logistics of locations or the availability of actors, you have to start your first day with a dramatically intense or technically complicated scene. In such cases, there's nothing you can do but dive in and do your best. But as a rule of thumb, don't start with the hardest scene.

If possible, it's also a good idea to save scenes that aren't pivotal for the last few hours of your last day of principal photography. These are scenes that advance the characters without necessarily driving the plot. If you begin to run over schedule on your last day, you can eliminate these final scenes without doing serious damage to your movie. Of course, it's best to have every scene advance both the characters and the plot; however, there are usually a few minor scenes that can be deleted without irrevocably damaging the logic of the story line.

The geography lesson
The beginning of the movie is where your audience becomes acclimated to your characters, the tone of your story, and the environment in which your story takes place. Part of your job is letting them know who's who, what the relationships are, and where the story is set so that they aren't asking these questions later.

As the storyteller, you want the audience to laugh when you want them to laugh, be moved when you tell them to be, and be confused only when it serves your purposes. To that end, it's best to perform a sort of "geography lesson" early in the movie. As the characters are introduced and the situation is established, you also want to tell the audience where everything is located.

In *Beyond Bob*, it was important to establish that the primary location was a lake home situated in the middle of nowhere. This was done with establishing shots at the beginning of the movie and then reinforced visually during early interior scenes by placing characters in front of windows that overlooked the forest surrounding the house. (The "forest" was actually several artificial Christmas trees strategically placed to block out the other homes in the suburban housing tract that was our primary location.)

These early scenes were also used to establish where each room was in relation to the others, geographically laying the groundwork for later sequences. The shots explained where the kitchen was in relation to the living room, where the deck was in relation to the den, and so on.

175

You need to keep this concept of the "geography lesson" in mind while you're planning your shots, particularly when you're shooting out of sequence. Scenes that take place early in the story — but perhaps late in the shooting schedule — need to present the "lay of the land" more than scenes that take place in those same locations later in the story.

For example, the scenes we just described from *Beyond Bob*, showing the windows and the trees outside, were terribly time-consuming to set up and shoot: The light from the outside had to be color-balanced with the light from the inside; there were only certain times during the day when the light was right; and the trees and the shots had to be positioned with great care to avoid revealing our actual location.

As a consequence, the only time you see out the windows in the movie is at the beginning of the story. Once the location had been established, the windows were either not shown or the shades were drawn. The audience, however, still believed that the story was taking place in a lake home surrounded by trees because this had been established earlier.

Directors vs. producers
If you've ever sat through the closing credits of a Hollywood feature, you've probably realized just how many people it takes to make a big-buck movie happen. From the Assistants to the Assistant Director to the Good, Better, and Best Boys, there's a big crowd of folks on the average movie set. That's one of the reasons those movies are so expensive.

Of course, your budget is much smaller, and consequently, you will be dealing with fewer people. But don't kid yourself, you will need to deal with them. Part of your job as producer or director is managing the people working on the movie to get the most out of them without killing them.

One of the ideas you'll need to communicate right away is the concept that this is a professional production (the absence of paychecks aside), and everyone is expected to act professionally. That means that you can have fun on the set, but when it comes time to crack the whip and get the work done, everybody does their part.

Consequently, you'll need to decide who is going to be in charge of cracking that whip. Our approach has been a variation of the good-cop/bad-cop method, adapted for our purposes as good-director/bad-producer. This means that the producer is the person who ultimately says no — as in, "No, we can't afford that prop," "No, you can't keep shooting," "No, you can't have a helicopter," and our favorite, "No, you can't have a percentage of the gross." This technique allows the director to maintain her or his rapport with the crew and cast.

Of course, making a movie is a high-pressure situation, and conflicts are undoubtedly going to arise. After long hours of intense work, nerves may become frayed and tempers may flare. As producer or director, it's your job to keep those conflicts to a minimum.

One way to do that is to hire charming, funny people who can keep the atmosphere light on the set. We've been graced with some terrifically funny cast- and crewmembers who have helped to keep spirits up and make the long hours move much faster. From joke-telling competitions to dueling impersonations, these folks kept their coworkers smiling and the production moving smoothly.

Despite all the jokes and the fun, you may encounter a situation in which a crew- or castmember is simply not working out. They may be a constant complainer, a malcontent, or simply incompetent. Whatever they are, they are trouble, and they can do serious damage to morale and to the movie.

Just as no one likes to be dumped, there are few people who enjoy the act of dumping someone else. But in some situations it must be done, and for the sake of your movie, it must be done quickly and cleanly. We had a situation with a crewmember on one of our movies who was not only verbally disruptive but who also blatantly and repeatedly disregarded our instructions. Although everyone was essentially working in a volunteer situation, there wasn't room for unprofessional and damaging behavior. So the crewmember was asked to leave and not return. The person received credit for work done, but it's the last time that person will be working for us.

Tough to do? You bet, particularly when you're in the midst of a complicated shoot and you're losing a key crewmember. But that's when you have to do it. Waiting and prolonging the inevitable only exacerbates the problem.

Sound advice

Although you're working in a visual medium, don't ignore your sound engineer and boom operator during the planning process for each scene. They need to know as soon as you do what sorts of shots you're planning, so they can find the best and most efficient way to record each scene. Ultra-wide shots, characters moving within the frame, moving shots, and master shots with characters talking to each other across a wide space can be real headaches for your sound team. So the sooner you let them know what you're planning, the more likely they'll be able to figure out how to record the best sound.

A basic rule of thumb about recording sound is that if you're in a pinch and the sound is bad but the picture's okay, move on. You can fix the sound later. This is generally true. Bad sound is much easier to fix than a bad picture. However, that doesn't give you carte blanche to record bad sound. You'll want to record the cleanest sound you possibly can while on location. That's the primary concern of your sound engineer on location — getting clean dialogue. Beware of the sound engineer who makes your track sound like a finished, mixed soundtrack. You don't want that. You want dialogue — spotless, pristine dialogue that's so clean you could eat off it. That way you don't lose any of your sound-mixing options for editing.

A point to keep in mind is that with digital sound, you never want to have the meter on the camera peak at the top of the scale. At that point, the sound turns into an unusable crackle. It is better to run the sound levels a little too low rather than too high. When you get into editing, it is possible to raise the levels as much as needed without introducing tape hiss, because the recording is digital.

Sound effects are definitely a secondary issue. It's much simpler and often better to add them in post. For example, in *Grown Men*, there are a number of scenes with characters sitting and talking in busy locations (restaurants, offices, bars, a blood bank). For each of these scenes, it was much simpler to shoot them without any ambient sound effects and add them later.

The same is true of any scenes with specific sounds, such as crowd noises, doors opening and closing, phones ringing, doorbells, crickets, babies crying, and so on. Save yourself the trouble, and add the sound effects later. You may want to record the effects as wild sound while you're on location, but it simplifies the editing enormously if you record them separately from the scene itself.

The background extras are quiet during shooting; the sound of a restaurant full of people will be added in postproduction. A scene from Grown Men. *Pictured, l to r; Michael Paul Levin and Nancy Crocker. (Photo courtesy of Granite Productions, Unlimited.)*

On a related note, make sure that your sound engineer records plenty of "room tone" from each location. Room tone is best defined as the sound you hear in a room when you don't hear anything at all. Stop reading and listen. What do you hear? The sound of the refrigerator in the next room, the sound of traffic outside, or the "presence" of an empty room. That's room tone. Your editor will need plenty of this ambient sound to help cover dialogue edits, so don't leave a location without having everyone stand very still while the sound engineer records two minutes of ambience. This is also a good time for silent prayer; the quieter the better. (For the ultimate view of what happens while room tone is being recorded, rent the best movie on the subject of low-budget moviemaking, *Living In Oblivion*.)

You've been framed

You may have modest expectations for your movie, hoping it will play at some festivals, get posted for downloading on the Net, maybe get sold to cable television, and perhaps even end up in your local video store in the Manager's Choice section. These are noble ambitions, but we recommend that you aim just a little higher, if only during production.

179

137:1 Ratio 16mm Film
Frame Format

1.33:1 Ratio Television
Format

185:1 Ratio Wide-
Screen Format in U.S.A.
(35mm blowup)

1.66:1 Ratio Wide-
Screen Format in
Europe
(35mm blowup)

All Four Formats

Film and television frames

There's always the slim chance that your movie may end up as a 35mm theatrical release. Don't count on it, don't bank on it, and certainly don't borrow against it, but be prepared for it just in case. That preparation includes framing all your shots so that they'll look decent if your movie gets blown up to 35mm wide-screen format. If you don't, all of your wide shots will cut off your actors at the forehead and ankles and your close-ups will take on the look of a dermatological examination.

Our advice is to play it "TV safe." The diagram on the next page compares the two most common wide-screen theatrical formats and a standard 16mm or 35mm film frame with the "TV safe" frame of the digital video you'll be shooting. As you can see, if you frame your action a little tighter than the "TV safe" area, you'll also ensure that you don't exceed the limits of the wide-screen format.

Feeding the masses

There is one thing you can provide your people that's more important than the opportunity to express themselves artistically, and that's food. Hot, healthy food, and plenty of it. People will put up with almost anything on a movie set, from long hours to lousy conditions, if the food is good and plentiful. Or even just plentiful.

Regular meal breaks are an important part of your production schedule, as is the easy availability of snacks and drinks. Good food doesn't have to be costly. In fact, nonprofit productions are often able to persuade local restaurants to donate food. On *Grown Men*, we had a couple local restaurants that regularly donated box lunches to our cause. So by all means get good, varied food. It shows your cast and crew that you care.

Extra! Extra!
In order to make your movie look like it takes place in the real world (not necessarily the existing world, but a real world nonetheless), you will discover the occasional need to populate your movie with people other than your primary actors. This population can be drawn from your family, your friends, friends of your friends, friends of your family, and even strangers off the street. These are your extras.

There are three key things to remember about extras. The first is that you don't want them to look at the camera. Ever. For most of them, their previous movie experience (if any) was probably in home videos, in which the on-camera participants are often encouraged to mug and wave at the camera. You must stop them from doing this. Nothing ruins a perfectly good scene faster than some yutz in the lower right corner of the frame who's making goo-goo eyes at the lens. So instruct, order, and threaten them not to look at, around, or near the camera. If they're members of your family, they'll just think you're being bossy and mean.

The second point is to be sure to get release forms from *everyone* who shows up to be an extra. Whether they actually end up in the movie or not isn't the issue. You need signed release forms from all the people who might appear in the finished movie, or they don't step in front of your camera.

And finally, organize any shooting that involves extras for the maximum value over a minimal amount of time. In other words, do whatever you can to avoid feeding them. Offering extras beverages is only fair (we recommend inexpensive bulk drinks, such as lemonade, as opposed to individual cans), but unless you're heir to a food-service business, nothing will chew up your food budget faster than trying to feed ten, twenty, or fifty extra mouths.

181

On all of our features, we've always scheduled scenes with extras to take place before or after a food break. Even when it means getting two different sets of extras (one group for before lunch and one group for after), it's still cheaper than trying to feed your cast, your crew, and 20 good-hearted extras with large appetites.

Photo opportunity

One of the first things most distributors will ask about your movie (right after, "Do you have any name actors, any violence, any sex, or any name actors having violent sex?") is whether or not you have production stills.

Production stills are very important to distributors. They are a vital part of their publicity campaign, and they're hard to create once the movie has wrapped and the actors, costumes, props, and locations have dispersed. Consequently, having decent production stills will make your movie more attractive to potential distributors. Of course, if they hate your movie, it seems unlikely that they'll distribute it just because you have great production stills. But stranger things have happened.

Most Hollywood movies employ a full-time photographer who uses a special camera box to take silent photos as scenes are being shot. Since these photographers are there all day, every day, covering every scene, they burn through a lot of film. As a result, the distributor usually has a treasure trove of photos from which to choose.

You can get some good stills for a minimum outlay of time and money by having a photographer join you (preferably for free or for the cost of film and developing) for a particularly photogenic day of production. Or you can set up a later date to shoot staged publicity stills. Be sure to get a creative release from the photographer so you own copyright on the photos.

You can shoot digital photos for virtually nothing if you have a decent digital still camera. If you go this route, be sure to shoot at the highest quality level the camera will allow. It makes for big files, but you may need that level of quality when you hit distribution. If you are staging publicity photos, you may be able to shoot digital stills with your DV camcorder, if it has a "photo" setting, as many do.

If money is really tight (and when isn't it?), shoot 35mm photos, but don't process them until later. Process only one roll to make sure there were no technical problems. Keep the rest of the unprocessed film in a safe, cool, dry place until a distributor asks about production stills. If they're interested enough in your movie to distribute it, they'll welcome the opportunity to pay for the processing of your production stills.

A rare good publicity shot captured on the set of Beyond Bob. *(Pictured, l to r; Patrick Coyle, Michael Paul Levin, Peter Moore, Leslie Ball, Julie Briskman Hall, Dan Rowles, and Kathryn O'Malley.)*

Action and stunts

We can't emphasize enough the need for planning and safety in anything you shoot that could even vaguely be considered an action scene or a stunt. While we don't expect that you'll be creating *The Matrix 7* or *Die Hard 39* on your budget, you're bound to encounter one or two sequences that could potentially be dangerous. Scenes that involve explosions, moving cars, or even a fistfight are all potentially dangerous scenes and must be approached and executed with the utmost care. When in doubt, bring in an expert.

The opening scene of *Beyond Bob* called for Bob to assemble a hang glider, strap it on, hold his finger out to check the wind, and then step off a high cliff and glide away across the sky. So we shot our actor doing all those things, up to the point of stepping off the cliff. For that we brought in our hang gliding expert, dressed him in Bob's costume, and shot him as he stepped off a frighteningly steep cliff and floated away. Our expert has been hang gliding for years, so his performance, which was breathtaking to us, was just another day of flying to him.

To further ensure the actor's safety, the shots of assembling and strapping on the hang glider were photographed far from anything that even vaguely resembled a cliff. We didn't want to take the chance of a big gust of wind blowing away one of our primary actors.

Fight scenes are another area for concern. Something as seemingly simple as throwing a punch can injure participants who aren't trained in stage

183

combat. Even the simplest fight scene should be choreographed like a tight dance number, with no surprises and little margin for error. On *Grown Men*, we had a shot of a bar bouncer throwing a customer out of the bar. To ensure everyone's safety, and at the same time to make it look as real as possible, we brought in a stage combat expert to help with the shot. If someone in your cast isn't trained in stage combat, it's well worth the effort to seek out an expert who will help stage the scene and keep it safe. The end result will be well-staged, believable, and injury-free.

Finally, there are many things that happen behind the camera that aren't stunts but are potentially dangerous as well. In most of our movies, we've had instances in which skylights needed to be covered to block out sunlight, and we had one instance when several lawn chairs needed to be placed on the peak of a two-story house. To ensure the safety of the crew in these situations, we came up with a novel solution: We made the producer (Dale) do it.

While he may not have been the most qualified person for the job, there were certain things we knew about him that made him our first and best choice. He had insurance. He wouldn't sue us if he were injured. And if, God forbid, he fell off the roof, shooting could continue unabated.

Seriously, we feel that's it's often best to do these dangerous tasks yourself. You're in no position to cover someone else's medical bills, nor can you foot the cost of a lawsuit. This doesn't mean that you should approach these tasks cavalierly; however, you can trust the person doing it, and you can handle the consequences if something goes wrong.

Intimate scenes
Unless your day job involves shooting photo layouts for Victoria's Secret catalogs, you may find it awkward doing scenes that involve partial and total nudity or intimate moments. These scenes can be as difficult and as tense as staging a stunt or action scene, with the added pressure of having naked people around.

Your first concern in these scenes should be the comfort and security of your actors. While they may have learned to overcome shyness about baring their souls, baring physical parts is an entirely different matter and should not be treated lightly. To begin with, they must know up front what is expected; trying to coax someone into disrobing on the set is not only unreasonable, it's unprofessional. It's also not kosher to ask them to disrobe under the pretext that you "won't show anything."

The set should be cleared of any unnecessary personnel, and you should be prepared to be very stringent when you define "unnecessary." In many cases, the remaining crew can simply be the videographer, the director, the sound recordist (if you're recording sound), and the unit production manager. For some reason, nude scenes attract a crowd like a fire sale, so make sure your unit production manager clears the set and keeps it clear. Be both diligent and vigilant about protecting the actors' privacy during these scenes.

It will probably make the actors more comfortable and will better prepare the crew if you rehearse the scene once or twice with the actors fully clothed. Keep checking with the actors throughout the process to see how comfortable they are with what's happening and what you can do to make it easier for them.

Before we shot a sequence of one character running naked from a lake in *Beyond Bob*, the actor broke the tension by saying to the crew, "We're all adults here. We've all seen 'Willie' before." That's the sort of attitude that you should pass on to your cast and crew. They are all adults. They've all seen Willie before. So just shoot the scene and move on.

Viewing dailies
In the old days, you shot the film, sent it off to the lab, and then the next day watched the previous day's work. Hence the term "dailies."

Nowadays, after you shoot a scene, you have the option of playing it back instantly. And repeatedly.

Avoid this option.

Watching each take, or even an occasional take, while on the set will burn up production time like you won't believe, and work will stop on the set as everyone comes to watch too. While it's always a good idea to do some spot-checking during the day (to ensure that you're actually recording images on tape), your time is needed for shooting more footage rather than watching what you've shot.

That's not to say that you shouldn't watch what you've shot. We recommend it, but not while you're on the set. Instead, schedule some time off the set to review your material before you start shooting again. Some people restrict attendance at these viewing sessions to those on a need-to-know basis (director of photography, camera operator, unit production manager, hair-and-makeup supervisor, producer, director — basically, everyone but the actors). Their thinking is that they don't want the actors to freak out when they see themselves on-screen, fearing that it will change the actor's approach and ruin their performance. Or something. This strikes us as a bit silly. As much as anyone else on the shoot, the actors need a chance to evaluate their work while in the process, when it can do some good, rather than at the premiere, when it's impossible to change things.

On our projects, everyone is invited and encouraged to attend these screenings. Our reasoning is that once people get over the shock of seeing themselves on-screen, they begin to realize that they are involved in making a real movie. This has proved to be the case, especially with the more experienced actors who were somewhat skeptical about our low-buck approach. Our sessions of watching "weeklies" turned into a great support group and morale booster, with everyone cheering on each other's work.

After all the effort — the proverbial blood, sweat, and tears — they were beginning to see the fruits of their labors up on the screen. Viewing the weeklies after the final shoot, they laughed and cried and said how sad they were to be "done with the movie." However, for the director and producer, it's only the beginning and far from the end.

SPECIAL EFFECTS
(PLEASE PASS THE CONSTRUCTION PAPER.)

The goal of movie special effects is to convince the audience they saw something that really wasn't there. We did one step better than that. We convinced seasoned Hollywood distributors that they were seeing $50,000 of special effects when we actually had spent about $1,000. That's fifty dollars of production value on the screen for each dollar spent. Hollywood producers fantasize about ratios like this when they look at their budgets. Ironically, some of the most visually exciting shots were produced for nothing but the cost to run the camera (and a healthy chunk of our spare time), and some of our most expensive special effects went unnoticed, which is the goal of all but the big showy effects, like UFO crashes.

A certain amount of special effects is needed just to make routine movie magic, such as a blender that blasts orange juice into an actor's face, an establishing shot of a building that doesn't exist, or the illusion that day is night and night is day. Some special effects are essential to create a fantasy world called for by a screenplay, such as a UFO encounter or a ghostly manifestation. And most important for all you ultra-low-budgeteers, special effects are used to save on expensive production costs and to let you show images that you can't really afford to go shoot. And if these weren't reasons enough, special effects are a blast to do, and it's fun to trick the audience.

You may not realize that just about the whole realm of special effects production is available to you. The reason is that most special effects techniques were developed between 1896 and 1933 using technical resources that are within the reach of today's low-budget moviemakers. Also, today's computer special effects, which rely almost exclusively on these seminal techniques, are largely available to you as part of the video-editing software you'll be using on your nonlinear editing system. If you add photo-retouching software, such as Adobe Photoshop LE, there is little you can't achieve, except 3D animation. And you can buy software for that too.

This means that by investing more time and using older techniques and new desktop-video software, you can achieve lots of special effects comparable to Hollywood's. We'll tell you about ours to give you some ideas on how to do your own.

Miniatures
Miniatures saved us a bundle of money and days of production time. Shots that would have been too difficult or costly to shoot for real were created in Dale's basement for mere dollars. An example of a mundane but completely effective shot is from *Beyond Bob*. The script called for a night shot of a stoplight hanging on cables over a secluded rural intersection. The changing lights on this traffic signal were integral to one of the movie's funniest scenes; however, this type of traffic light arrangement is relatively rare. We only located one in our area, and shooting it posed some significant problems. First, it was hanging 20 feet in the air, making a face-on close-up challenging. It also hung at a relatively dark intersection with no electrical outlets within reach. Consequently, lighting the exterior of this traffic signal would require powerful lights and an electrical generator. Very expensive for ten seconds of footage in the finished movie. So we used a miniature instead.

Dale built a 1/4 scale miniature of the stoplight out of cardboard, mailing tubes, aluminum foil to reflect heat, a $3 can of highway-yellow paint, spare lamp parts, and some colored overhead transparencies. The miniature was shot in Dale's basement using utility floodlights with photoflood bulbs for lighting. The end result is a shot so convincing that no one has ever suspected that it wasn't real. Sure, it took a day's work to create, but almost no cash. Renting the equipment to shoot this for real could have cost hundreds of dollars. Time we had, money we didn't.

We also used miniatures built with inexpensive hobby-store materials to create a night shot of a military air base. Cheap plastic jet models were lit by lights shining through hidden holes in the cardboard runway. In the foreground, a miniature chain-link fence made from wire mesh completed the illusion for another shot we couldn't afford to light. The key to using these miniatures effectively was keeping their on-screen time brief and making them night shots. Convincing daylight miniatures are much harder to create.

We also used quite a number of miniature signs when real ones didn't exist or conveyed the wrong impression. These signs were usually small so we could take advantage of paste-on letters or computer-generated typefaces on 8 1/2 x 11-inch sheets of paper. For example, Skatedium roller rink is a major setting in *Beyond Bob*, but the rink's name only appeared on an uninspiring soft-drink sign. We built our own sign, starting with a piece of white tag board about 8 x 6 inches. We scored it with a knife and damaged the edges to create the look of painted sheets of plywood. Colored adhesive vinyl letters provided the words "Roller Rink," and some salvaged plastic letters from a lobby informational sign were glued on as the "giant" plastic letters spelling "Skatedium." We added a tacky "giant" skate painted on tag board "plywood" to complete the look. A few nail heads with rust stains dripping from them were drawn in using colored pencils, and a gray crayon was used to give the black plastic letters a weathered look. A sprig of juniper branch intruding into the corner of the shot created a convincing billboard that helps convey the feel of the setting. Cost was zero thanks to Dale's pack-rat pile of supplies. We used a similar approach to create the sign for a rural sheriff's office. We shaved bark from one-inch tree branches and stained them dark brown to create a convincing frame for this rustic sign.

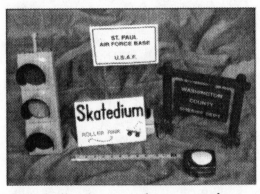

Miniature signs from Beyond Bob *and* Resident Alien.

Miniatures seem to work best when they are simple. More detail is not necessarily better. Just look at professional matte paintings. These are paintings that replace a portion of the movie frame to put in a visual element that isn't really there, such as a castle on a hill. You'll be amazed how impressionistic these paintings are.

The matte painting that was used for one of the closing scenes for Alfred Hitchcock's *The Birds* shows a huge landscape covered with roosting white birds. On the actual matte painting, only a few of the painted birds even look like birds. The rest are nothing more than white streaks of paint. However, the short shot in the finished movie is totally effective, because you expect to see birds. We created a foreground wheat field

189

for one miniature by just making random streaks on a strip of cardboard with yellow, brown, and tan crayons.

You can test your miniatures by shooting test footage and making adjustments to parts that don't look realistic. When shooting miniatures, be sure to use the same camera angle you would use if you were shooting the real thing.

Photographs can help you put people in your miniatures. In *Resident Alien*, we have a wide shot of a character looking up at a hovering UFO. The person is standing still, thanks to a special-effects-conscious script. We took a still photograph of our character in the actual setting. Minnefex, a special-effects company which offered its services to the movie, built a miniature of the real setting and suspended a UFO over it. The actor's photo was enlarged to the proper size on a photocopier, hand colored, cut out, and placed in the miniature setting. The result is a shot worth thousands in street value in the movie capitol. If you don't have a handy special-effects company to build miniature settings, contact the model-railroad crowd in your area. With a few adjustments, their skills adapt well to movie production. Also, there are many good library books on miniature construction (again, usually aimed at model railroaders).

Mini-sets
Many times you need a shot that doesn't require an entire set. Mini-sets that can convey a sense of a larger location can be easily created, and the audience fills in the rest at no extra charge.

In *Resident Alien*, we needed interior shots of a mysterious spaceship showing an unseen person's hand adjusting the ship's controls. There was no need for the entire spacecraft interior, so a control panel was built from painted cardboard (one of Dale's favorite building materials, because it's usually free, reasonably durable, and can be easily shaped). A few lights, plastic parts, colored gels, and a hand wearing a spray-painted rubber glove created the control panel set piece. The distant wall of the spacecraft in the background is actually a nearby mini-set constructed of spray-painted egg cartons and cardboard packing material. A little mood lighting created an effective, short scene in the spacecraft. To see how far you can go with sheets of cardboard, check out the extraordinary corrugated-cardboard spaceship sets in the movie *Plan 10 From Outer Space* by Trent Harris. Masterful painting makes them one of the highlights of the movie.

We've also used realistic mini-sets to save the time of doing special effects during full production. For *Resident Alien*, we needed a scene of someone putting bare wires into an electrical outlet, creating sparks. The scene was shot during production without this close-up shot. Later we bought a piece of art board that roughly matched the look of the location's walls and attached it to a scrap of sheetrock wall board. We cut a hole and installed a real wall outlet that was wired to an extension cord. Using this mini-set, the character's costume, and Dale's hand, the second unit did this insert shot several times to get the proper sparks, without danger to the actors or wasting expensive time with the full production company.

Replacement shots and continuity tricks

Mistakes are going to happen when you're shooting up to 80 setups a day. Perhaps there's a close-up you should have done for dramatic emphasis or you accidentally crossed "the line" so your shot is from the wrong camera angle. At this pace of production, you're long gone from the location by the time you review the footage all together, and you can't afford to take the whole production company back for a reshoot. What do you do? If the shot is of minor importance, you live with what you've got. Those are the breaks in the low-budget biz. But sometimes it's an important shot. In that case, you assign the shot to the second unit. For us, that was the director and producer wearing different hats. You take the DV camcorder you bought and shoot replacement shots quickly, efficiently, and cheaply.

Here's an example. We shot a scene of a character falling asleep at a tape recorder while holding a cup of coffee. In the medium shot, the coffee spilling in the character's lap just looked silly, and we had no close shot. So we took the same cup, a similar shirt, and a different person, and reshot the cup spilling in close-up. This improved the suspense of the gradually tipping cup, and when we cut to a shot of the tape recorder's VU meter as we heard the character yell, the scene became funny as intended. The replacement shot worked great, and it cost us just an hour of time.

Continuity tricks can make the audience believe they are seeing two things together that in reality were never in the same vicinity. An actor on the pitcher's mound can throw a fastball to a batter at home plate who is performing months later at a different ball field. Careful use of props for continuity can connect the performances.

191

We pulled off this kind of trick when we couldn't get a sheriff's vehicle and a performer we needed to an out-of-town motel location during the *Resident Alien* shoot. The scene called for the actor to drive up in the vehicle and have a conversation with a passenger while parked in front of the motel. The motel had a front awning supported by white wooden posts. These posts had been seen in earlier shots of the motel, so we just painted a board white and stood it within the frame where a motel post would be. The sheriff's vehicle pulled up to a post 60 miles from the motel, but you'd never guess it from watching the movie.

It is truly amazing what an audience will believe it saw when it is expecting something. This makes continuity tricks even easier. In the opening title sequence of *Beyond Bob*, a character repeatedly walks past a photo on a dresser. With each pass, we jump closer to the photo. However, only the first two passes were shot with the actor in silhouette passing the actual photo. We then cut to an enlargement of the photo, which was shot at another time, to allow us to see close-ups of the people in the photo. The actor's body still appears to pass the photo, but it is actually Dale's hand inside the sleeve of a black sweatshirt. Because the first two shots established an expectation, no one has ever seen anything but the actor.

Tricks like these can save flawed shots and can do much to simplify scheduling problems during production.

On *Grown Men* we had a schedule with long breaks between the shooting of each segment of the story. Rough edits were prepared during the breaks in order to identify any problem shots that needed to be redone as part of the next segment's shoot. This way, we fixed problem scenes without adding to our production dates.

Poor-person's process shots

Let's do a definition first so no one feels left out. Process shots are ones in which a nonexistent background is created behind performers or an object, such as a window. This can be done using any of several optical, rear-projection, or digital-effects techniques. An extremely common example is the shot of people riding in the car. Many times the view out the car's rear window is a process shot, and the actors are actually sitting on a soundstage. The image behind them was shot at a different time. In film, these shots are called "matte" shots. In video, they are called "chroma keys" or "green screens" and are usually shot in front of a background color that is not part of flesh tones, such as green or blue. Most video-editing software can do a simple version of this. More expensive software can do it better, but it's still a challenge to make it look convincing, and this software is a bit pricey for your ultra-low budget.

However, (You're starting to expect this, aren't you?) you can afford a poor-person's process shot, and the results are often very good. The riding-in-the-car shot is a little hard to fake in daylight, so you'll probably shoot it for real and do what we did — scrunch the camera into the rear seat or the passenger's seat and give the camera operator a neck rub when the shot's over. Nighttime is a different story. For a night shot, you can just drape the windows that are visible in the background with a black cloth. While the actors take their imaginary ride, just have someone occasionally push down on the bumper to create a little road bounce. You can add to this by panning a light that's spotted to its narrowest beam across the car from front to back to simulate passing headlights. Adding sound effects of passing cars in postproduction will complete this illusion.

You can create the illusion of flying during day or night using a similar technique. Just frame your shot so there is a featureless sky with no clouds in the background. You can fly through the air or have an airplane plummet to its doom, and the background view looks okay. We did this with a hang-glider shot. The glider was suspended by a rope from a tree, and the actor was strapped to a board on sawhorses. The pilot's cocoon hid the board. Using a low-angle shot, all we needed to give the illusion of flight was a wind-direction cloth tied on the glider within the frame. We blew the cloth with a leaf blower. This kind of minor but significant detail doesn't really register consciously with the audience, but it creates subconscious supporting data that helps make the shot convincing.

That significant detail helped us do another process shot that is common in movies but difficult for us independent moviemakers. We wanted a clean cutaway shot of some actors appearing on a television screen. We didn't want picture roll and other TV artifacts that result from shooting a video image on TV. Instead of using a pricey technical approach, our solution was to get the front frame of a TV and put clear plastic across the screen area. The actors' performances were shot live through this facade. We just lined them up with the camera looking through the frame. A little bit of light was allowed to reflect on the clear plastic to create that significant detail that says "Hey, this is a real TV." The result looked better than the usual matte or chroma-key shot, where an image is inserted onto the TV screen. There was no annoying blue halo around the edges of the screen image, and you could see reflections on the "picture tube."

We also used a very simple version of a "matte" shot to remove a dock we didn't want in a night scene at a lake shore. The sky, land, and water were essentially black except for the pool of light where our shot would take place. Unfortunately, a nearby dock was also catching the light. To eliminate it, we simply hung a piece of black construction paper in front of the lens so it blacked out the offending dock, making it look like more black lake water. Because the paper was very close to the lens, the edges were out of focus, creating a "soft matte" that was invisible in the final shot.

Specialty costumes

If you're doing a realistic story set in modern times, your costumes will largely come out of the closets of the people connected with your production. Our first movie, *Resident Alien*, was a science-fiction comedy romance, so some unusual costumes were pretty much mandatory for the genre. Knowing this, Dale wrote in scenes requiring a monster costume and space suits.

We used one technique to make all of these costumes, in part because the script called for them to be reminiscent of each other. The basic space suit was lightweight long underwear from a surplus clothing store. We added foam rubber accessories — breastplate, brief, helmet, footwear — and then spray-painted the whole thing with metallic paint. The paint does tend to rub off slowly, but it was quick, looked good, and lasted long enough to get the shots.

Foam rubber is easy to use for these types of soft costumes. Just cut out the shapes you want from sheets of foam that are 1/2- to 1-inch thick, depending on how thick you want the final costume. You don't have to have seamstress skills to design with foam rubber, though it is helpful. Just hold the sheet of foam rubber up to the person you are fitting, and tuck and pinch it into the shapes you want. Wherever you have to pinch the material together, mark the edges that come together with a marking pen, and then cut out the excess in between with a scissors. In sewing terms, you have created a "dart." Usually the 1/2-inch foam rubber works best for this type of fitting.

To assemble the costume, spread carpenter's contact cement (the nasty-smelling solvent-based type works best) on the edges where the foam rubber will butt together. You don't need to overlap the foam unless that's the look you want. Gluing the edges together will create a seamless look. Let the glue dry to the touch on both edges, and just squeeze these edges of the butt joints together. Voila! Instant seam. If you have the pieces all cut, you can assemble an entire costume in about a half hour.

For larger shapes that need a support structure, such as space suit helmets and monster heads, corrugated cardboard is our material of choice. It's light, easily cut, easily glued, and usually free. The support structure we used was designed much like the keel and ribs of a wooden boat. The foam rubber is like the outside skin of the ship.

Before you spend time making your real support structure, test your design with a small-scale version that you can quickly cut out of tag board. (Old potato chip or cereal boxes from the recycling bin work nicely.) After your support structure is completed, fit pieces of foam rubber over it, cut the pieces, and glue them together with contact cement over the structure.

The beauty of these lightweight and soft materials is that you can easily modify the final shape to better fit the performer, and you can spray-paint or airbrush the entire rig when you're done. One word of caution: Sunlight and air tend to deteriorate foam rubber and make it crumbly. We've stored our headgear in plastic bags, and many years later it is still usable.

Producer Dale Newton (right) makes some final adjustments to foam rubber costumes on the set of Resident Alien.

195

Mechanical and electrical effects can also be added to costumes. When we needed a glove with glowing lights in it, we used a painted rubber glove and poked miniature Christmas-tree lights through holes in the palm. Wire for the lights traveled down the glove, up the sleeve, and out the back of the costume to the power source. (Be sure this kind of wiring is well-insulated to protect the performer; we had to convince our actor that it was safe. It's best to use DC battery power rather than AC power to minimize the risk of dangerous shock.) The finished hand glowed nicely on the screen, and in the medium shot we used, the lights weren't visible until lit.

Specialty props

We've used many specialty props to add spice to our movies and to achieve specific effects. One simple specialty prop was a branch that a pigeon had to walk on for a key shot in *Beyond Bob*. Unfortunately, after we had made arrangements to use a racing pigeon as our performer, we learned that racing pigeons are trained not to land in trees, only at their home roosts. So we had a trained bird to use, but it didn't like sitting on branches. Our solution was a specialty prop. We used a real tree branch that was attached to a stand. Along the branch, we drilled holes out of view and filled them with corn. The pigeon was enticed out onto our branch by the line of corn, and it eventually did a nice little performance for our shot.

Beyond Bob also required a couple of ghostly floating effects. In the movie, we used black string to lift up objects that the ghost was moving. Generally, the biggest giveaway for these kinds of "wire" shots are the wires that the audience looks for overhead, so we put our wires out to the sides. We stretched two black strings between two wooden handles, and we attached the strings behind a tree branch that the ghost was "carrying." Out of camera range on each side of the branch, two people held the wooden handles. With this arrangement, they were able to fly the stick and give it movements, much like you would do with a marionette.

In the story, the invisible ghost uses the same branch to write in the sand. We did it with some careful postproduction editing and a different technique. We drilled a hole in the end of the branch so it would fit onto a large nail. That nail stuck out of a wooden handle and protruded through the letter "S", which had been cut into the top of a box, like a stencil. By burying the box under a thin layer of sand, we could move the handle and make the stick appear to write a letter "S" in the sand by itself.

Also for *Beyond Bob*, we couldn't get permission from a major game manufacturer to use a game board that "mystically" spells out answers to questions. (Hint: The game's name rhymes with "squeegee gourd.") This forced us to come up with our own connection to the spirit world, and the results were much more fun. Our spirit board looked like an Oriental roulette wheel with the alphabet and the words "yes" and "no" printed around the edge of the wheel. A dragon-shaped ticker hit nails around the edge of the wheel as it spun. When the wheel stopped, it pointed to an answer or the next letter in the answer. The entire board sat on a cloth, giving the impression that there was no way of manipulating it from below. Actually, a slit in the cloth allowed us to slide a trigger cable up under the wheel. This cable lifted a Velcro pad up to hit another Velcro pad on the underside of the wheel. We just moved the pad on the wheel to match the letter we wanted it to stop on. All this was invisible to the camera, and it allowed us to show a continuous shot of the actors spinning the wheel and it stopping on the desired letter. Very convincing, very simple, very cheap.

The spirit board created for Beyond Bob.

In *Resident Alien* we needed to show a rigid chunk of UFO debris become pliable when an electrical charge was applied to it. The debris itself was easy; two prop pieces were used. A rigid one was made from auto-body putty, and a pliable one was made from foam rubber. We painted and decorated them to be identical. The rest of the trick is in planning the sequence in which electricity is applied to the debris. We designed the natural points where edits would occur — such as going to a close-up of poking the electrified debris — as the points where we would switch the props. As long as all the edit points seemed to be naturally motivated by the other actions in the scene, the audience didn't realize that we were using them to switch the props. In fact, audiences are so used to this kind of editing, many of them don't even realize an edit has been made. Just ask a non-moviemaker to tell you how many shots are in a fast-paced soft-drink commercial, and they will usually guess about ten. What they actually watched may have been 50 edits. You can use this obliviousness to editing to help your specialty props create some surprising effects.

A more mundane type of specialty prop was a jail-cell door. We needed one to create the right atmosphere for a small-town sheriff's office, and we couldn't arrange to use any real jail cells. So we made our own cell door by drilling holes through 2 x 2-inch boards and inserting an electrical conduit for the bars. A few screws to hold them in place, a wooden box for the lock, and a coat of black spray paint created a convincing cell door that we just slid into a regular doorway. Interestingly, while visiting the set of a television western for which he was writing, John spotted a jail-cell door constructed the same way. The lesson is that specialty props don't have to be elaborate to be effective.

We've also used vinyl adhesive sheets to good effect. In *Beyond Bob*, a car needed to be aged ten years. We considered starting with a rusty car and paying for it to be repaired to a ten-years-earlier look, but that was too expensive. Instead, we painted brown rust on pieces of clear adhesive plastic and applied them to the car's fenders, wheel wells, hood, and trunk. This easily knocked a couple grand off the resale value — temporarily. (The car later rusted in the spots we had predicted.)

Paste-on letters and decals cut from colored adhesive sheets also helped us transform a family car into a convincing police vehicle.

Animation and in-camera effects
Optical-film-printer effects and digital computer effects are the standard techniques for creating many special-effect shots in the movie industry. However, many times an effect that is achieved completely in the camera is more believable than all but the most expensive lab tricks. Digital computer effects can lose almost-indiscernible bits of reality — a bit of haze here, a shadow or reflection there. While it's hard to put your finger on the specific loss, something in the audience's subconscious sees

what's lacking and spills the beans to the conscious mind. Because in-camera effects and animations really occur before the lens, they retain more of these intangible trappings of reality. In the early days of film, most special effects were done in the camera, and it has worked well for us too. Watch the original *King Kong*, which has animation by Willis O'Brien and special effects that primarily were done in the camera. While the animation is a bit choppy by today's standards, hundreds of other special-effects shots still look great. Many times, animation, split screens, rear projections on miniature sets, and glass mattes (scene elements painted on a pane of glass positioned in front of the camera) were all used within the same scene, creating stunningly realistic special effects. The use of more than one technique can distract and confuse the audience's subconscious minds, preventing them from figuring out any of the tricks.

Some in-camera effects are time-consuming and elaborate, others are laughably simple. Here's a simple one that we did:

We wanted to show space travelers being transported by a beam of light from their ship to the ground. To accomplish this effect, we relied on a technique that was pioneered in a 19th-century magic trick called "Pepper's Ghost," which was used to conjure up an apparition. It's a simple effect that uses a thin pane of glass placed in front of the viewer (or camera) at a 45-degree angle. The diagram on the following page will show how it is set up. You've probably seen this effect if you've ever opened one of those casement windows with a hinge on the side. On a bright day, you'll see an image reflected in the glass from the left or right of the window.

Superimposing an image with a 45-degree-angle glass

We created a light beam that delivered our space travelers by installing the 45-degree-angle glass in a medium-sized cardboard box that was painted black inside. The front and the back of the box were open so the camera could look though the 45-degree-angled glass. One side of the box was also open but covered with a piece of black construction paper. The shape of the light beam had been cut out of the paper, and the hole was covered with some Rosco tough spun (tissue paper would have worked too). We put a light with a dimmer behind the paper cutout. Then we covered the cutout with a piece of cardboard hinged with tape to the bottom of the box. We started the shot seeing only the empty location. By slowly lowering the hinged piece of cardboard, the light beam was revealed from top to bottom, so it appeared to drop down from the sky. The light beam's image reflected in the 45-degree-angled glass was brighter than the night location, so the beam couldn't be seen through. At this point, we stopped the camera and brought in the actors to stand behind the beam. The camera was started again, and we dimmed the beam's light source, revealing the actors. We shortened the shot in editing, but other than that, the effect was done completely in camera.

We used simple single-frame animation to help achieve some shots that were beyond our technical expertise to do for real. Because it's always a struggle to make animations look realistic, using computer tools is not particularly a disadvantage here. Let us give you an example of an animated effect we did when we worked on film and tell you how we'd do it today. We wanted a night shot of a military jet landing behind a military air-base sign. The sign didn't really exist, so we made a simple miniature and placed it in front of a night sky that consisted of aluminum foil that was spray-painted black and then attached to a glass window. (We know you can buy expensive black aluminum foil, but you didn't really expect us to do that, did you?) A light source and some Rosco tough spun to diffuse the light were placed behind the glass. Small holes poked in the aluminum foil created a starry night sky. Because we were working on film at that time, we shot a first pass of the sign against a star field background one frame at a time. We animated a black cutout of the jet across the background to create an unexposed hole in the star field so no stars would show through the jet. Then we wound the film back and did a double exposure to animate a flat painting of a jet across the darkened sky and behind the now-blacked-out sign in the foreground. Of course we had to use the camera's frame counter and keep an accurate log of what happened in each frame. The result was a jet flying in front of a star field and behind a sign in the foreground.

One of the big problems with animation is that it looks too sharp. Real motion images are slightly blurred in individual frames. The big special-effects companies use special motorized equipment to slightly move models during single-frame exposures to create this blur. For our jet, we just painted it with blurry streaks coming off the trailing edge of the image, so each frame already had this blur. The final shot isn't perfect, but because it's short, because it's a night shot, and because there is a jet-landing sound effect to match it, no one has noticed it wasn't a real jet landing behind a real sign.

Thanks to computer tools, we would no longer do this shot hunched over an animation setup for hours. Today, we would be hunched over our computer screen for hours as we used our video-editing software (such as Adobe Premiere or Apple Final Cut Pro) and photo-retouching software (such as Adobe Photoshop LE) to do the same trick.

We would start with still-frame images of the sign, the starry sky, and the jet (scanned photos or digital photos). If we could take a still photo of a real jet, then we'd blur it using software tools. Otherwise we would use the original painted artwork. Using the photo-retouching software, we'd use the stars as a full background layer. Then we would cut the sign and jet from their backgrounds and make each of them separate layers of the image, with the sign being the front layer. We'd do any adjustment of brightness, contrast, color, etc. to make sure all the base elements worked together before we moved on. If you decide to change an image after you're done with your animation frames, you may be talking hundreds of corrections.

Next we would create and save a sequence of frames (30 for each second of video, of course) in which we gradually would change the position of the jet in the middle layer to move it along its flight path. Each image would have the jet in a slightly different spot. When all of these images were done, we'd import them into the video-editing software as a single video clip. (Be sure to check that your program can do this before you create hundreds of animation frames.) After adding a jet sound effect, you'd have a shot you couldn't have gotten otherwise. And thanks to the wonders of computer technology, you wouldn't have an animator's backache... though you might be going a little bit blind in one eye.

If you want help doing cartoon-style flat animation, you can use a technique called rotoscoping. Shoot video of real things moving, capture it in your editing system, and export it as a sequence of still images. (Again, check the manual to make sure you can do this on your system.) Then, using the layers of your photo-retouching program, you can draw your animation on top of the live-action images to get realistic motion. Then delete the live-action layer, and import your animation as a video clip. For the title sequence of a video, Dale used this method to animate a stylized image of a deer running. Some of you have already realized that this method allows you to combine animation with live-action performances. Think of the possibilities.

You'd take a different approach if you needed three-dimensional animation, such as a flesh-eating Martian spider sneaking up on an unsuspecting author as he toils at his computer. (Yikes!... Take that, arachnid!) For this kind of scene you would use an animation puppet that can be posed, just as you would with conventional 3-D animation. Instead of using a film camera to capture the frames, you could use either a digital still camera or use the photo function that's included with many DV camcorders. If there is a remote-control trigger, use that to avoid shaking the camera. Some camcorders actually record a few seconds of any still you shoot, so you'd need to capture still frames from this video using your editing software, and then put them together in editing. A word of warning: Live-action video on a DV camcorder is often recorded differently (interlaced-scan video) than digital stills on a camcorder (progressive-scan video), so live-action footage and animated stills of the same shot may not match when put side by side. For images from a digital still camera, you'd use the same approach, except that you could just import the image files rather than capturing them. Of course, there are many kinds of 3-D animation software available too. But in addition to the money and time it would take to buy and master this software, it takes a ton of skill and computer processing power to create realistic-looking objects and put them in a believable digital world. It's a lot less trouble to create creatures and objects in the real world and animate them.

Conventional cell animation or cutout animation can also be done. Just use a digital still camera or a camcorder with a photo function instead of the usual film camera on the animation stand, and then combine the stills in editing.

Titles

Titles can make or break the first impression an audience or a buyer has of your movie. It's very important to do them professionally, and thanks to computer-based editing, they are a snap these days. However, there are a few points to keep in mind.

Look at some television titles and then look at the titles on a feature film. You'll notice a difference. Wide-screen movie titles tend to be smaller text and often don't fill the entire screen unless they are scrolling. They would be overwhelmingly large if they filled the big screen. TV titles tend to fill the entire screen so you can read them off your 19-inch box across the living room. You want your audience to mentally put your production in the movie category, not the sitcom category, so make your titles look like theatrical ones. Also, not using the entire frame will help you protect your titles for the possibility of a theatrical release in wide-screen format.

It's always nice to select a typeface that conveys the spirit of your movie. If you can't find one that does this, go for a simple block style that won't clash with your movie's content.

Most editing software comes with capabilities that allow you to do stunning opening titles. While it may take more effort to produce them on the editing software you can afford, long hours can deliver just about anything you can think of for opening credits. The low-budget German film *Run Lola Run* has one of the most unique titles seen recently. An overhead shot follows a soccer ball as it's kicked straight up over a crowd. As the shot moves upward, it reveals that the people in the crowd are grouped so that they spell out the title. Very cool.

The film *Four Weddings and a Funeral* uses another title technique that is stylish and easily done. The titles were inspired by the film's subject matter. Title cards were done as wedding invitations and were shot as part of a tabletop arrangement of wedding paraphernalia. This approach could be easily adapted to many movies. The titles for a children's story could be scrawled in colored chalk on the sidewalk along with kids' drawings. Titles for a college drama could be written as notes in the margins of textbooks. A movie about the tribulations of waitressing could have titles written on restaurant order slips that are clipped to an order carousel and rotated into view. You get the idea. These types of titles can be simple to do and can really help your title sequence come to life.

Camera rigs and effects gear

It's very likely that your script will call for some type of special gear to create an effect or special camera rigs to create certain shots. Some of what was once specialty gear, such as camera dollies and wind machines, is now considered routine equipment. Sadly, this equipment is often too expensive for ultra-low-budget producers to rent, and it's too cumbersome to fit our hit-and-run shooting schedules. Of course we've come up with some inexpensive alternatives.

We built our own low-cost, easy-to-move dolly after seeing one advertised in a filmmaking magazine. The basic concept was to use light PVC pipe as the dolly track and to attach special wheels to a sheet of plywood to make the dolly. The commercial version cost $500. We built our own for $80. It can only roll in a straight line, and for sound shots, you need to put talcum powder on the PVC pipe to stop squeaks, but it adds a lot of production value by creating some very acceptable dolly shots. The heart of the dolly is the wheel sets that hug the PVC tracks. We made our plywood sheet smaller and hinged so it would fit in our car trunks, but you can add these wheel sets to just about any platform. We cut hardwood on a table saw to create the angled base for standard cart wheels with their own brackets. We made four sets with two wheels each and just bolted them to the plywood base. See the diagram below for creating your own wheel sets.

For the actual dolly track, you can use 10' lengths of PVC pipe. We improved ours by cutting the PVC pipe into 3-ft. lengths and using connectors that fit inside the pipe to allow the pieces to butt together. This allowed us to carry 24 feet of track in a car. We added some threaded metal rods with wing nuts as spacers to hold the tracks at the same width as the dolly's wheels. The completed dolly and track can be assembled in less than 15 minutes, it can be easily picked up and carried around the location, and it all fits in a car trunk.

A low-buck but effective camera dolly

Dolly wheel assembly

On *Resident Alien*, we needed a wind machine to simulate the concussion from an explosion. Our solution was a leaf blower, which is a ridiculous use of technology for removing leaves but a great portable wind machine for a limited area. We simply aimed it at the actors' faces, turned it on, and we had an explosion concussion that would blow the rug off a Hair Club member.

We've also seen other slick home-built equipment, such as a skateboard with a tripod head mounted on it for those "I feel so low" dolly shots and simple camera stabilizing gear for handheld shots. Just look through the equipment advertisements in an *American Cinematographer* magazine to see some of the latest low-cost camera systems. If you're a bit handy and willing to trade chrome and aluminum for wood and PVC pipe, you can build your own versions of these wonders for tens of dollars. True, they won't be quite as streamlined or attractive, but who are you to be so picky?

In addition to this general-use equipment, you may need something very specific for a scene in your movie. The first step to designing this type of equipment is freeing yourself from any thoughts of how professional it has to look. The only thing that matters is what the result is on the screen. For *Beyond Bob*, we needed a blender that sprayed orange juice on one of our actors. The actual blender wouldn't throw it effectively, so we built an orange-juice squirter. It was made entirely of scrap parts in a half hour. A nozzle of pinched-off copper pipe was stuck in the end of a plastic tube that led to a piston made from two plastic pipes, one inside the other. We taped the nozzle behind the blender, filled the piston with juice, and squeezed the piston together to douse the actor. It was primitive and ugly, but highly effective. You can achieve all kinds of effects with simple apparatuses like this. Just remember, it only has to work for the shot, and it doesn't matter how cobbled together it is.

We've also created some equipment that helped us speed up production and trim costs. For example, in *Beyond Bob's* opening sequence we needed to show a car repeatedly passing highway signs that are in the same position in the frame. To compose the shots identically, we attached a thin board under the camera that extended in front of the camera lens, out of view. To this we bolted a small square of clear plastic that sat in front of the lens. For the first shot of the sequence, we marked the plastic to show the position of the sign and the roadway. We removed the plastic square and did the first shot. Then we composed each subsequent shot using the plastic square, removing it before shooting. The shots matched beautifully.

The moral: Don't be embarrassed by any equipment that works.

Chemistry and science effects
You can create a variety of interesting effects using simple kitchen and bathroom chemistry. Dale once poured vinegar mixed with food coloring over baking soda to create a sink drain that frothed up with colorful bubbles — a no-cost effect that worked well on camera.

A chip of dry ice or seltzer tablets and water inside a small container like a 35mm film canister, can create mini-explosions. The ever-popular dry ice is also great for making boiling brews and mist effects. Mousetraps attached to fishing line can jerk objects so they look like they've been shot.

A word of caution: Be sure you know the effect of chemicals you plan to mix together. If you whip up a batch of ammonia mixed with chlorine bleach, you will become the star of your own snuff movie. Remember that the carbon dioxide given off by dry ice is not breathable, so use it with proper ventilation. Be careful. There are a number of good books on effects for theater and movies that will give you tested, safe ideas. If you're thinking about creating that *Star Wars* explosion, read on to the next section.

Don't-try-this-at-home effects

During our first film, we were very fortunate to be approached by a relatively young special-effects company called Minnefex. The two owners offered to do our spaceship and explosion effects for cost. Most of the time they were creating effects for television commercials — fun things like break-away bags of charcoal briquettes — and they wanted to do some challenging dramatic-movie shots. We struck a deal, and they delivered some great special-effects shots with spaceships, explosions, and miniature sets.

Minnefex co-owner Dave Weiberg puts some finishing touches on a spaceship model for Resident Alien.

The point is that the people who do special effects professionally rarely get to do the really interesting jobs that first attracted them to the business. Most of them have a closet full of *Famous Monsters of Filmland* magazines somewhere. (Our special effects guys now have John's collection as a thank-you for their hard work.) This means that many of them will do whatever possible to help you with your digital movie, just to get a chance to do the neat stuff. So if you need to do some of the dangerous tricks like explosions, ask some of the professionals. They may be willing to do it for fun. That's a lot better than hoping you won't lose a hand while you learn the art of miniature pyrotechnics.

As you can see from our examples, there are many types of movie magic that are available to you on a low-budget production, especially if you have a script that is designed to make good use of simple, well-placed effects. If, as you've read through our examples, you came up with better ways to do the effects we described, you're on the right track. Once again, creativity and ingenuity will greatly enhance your production values where money can't.

POSTPRODUCTION
(THE LIGHT AT THE END OF THE TUNNEL:
COMPLETION OR ONCOMING TRAIN?)

Whew! It's finally in the can (actually, on tape, but you know what we mean). You've made it through production in one piece, and the hard part's over, right? Sorry. You're probably beginning to suspect they're all hard parts. How astute of you. Postproduction now lies before you, and it can be just as grueling and exhausting as production, but in a different way. If production was like boot camp, postproduction is like months of cross-country marching that slowly (and sometimes painfully) moves you toward completion or makes you go AWOL.

Of course, there is some fun along the way. Editing is equal parts pleasure and pain. The process allows you to finesse and perfect your movie, but at the same time, it magnifies all of its inadequacies. Your rough cut will let you see your movie as you've never seen it before, all together and in one continuous piece. Adding sound effects and music will take the movie to the next level. But we're getting ahead of ourselves. Suffice it to say that the end is in sight, but it's only visible with high-powered binoculars.

The postproduction process consists of a number of occasionally overlapping phases: editing the rough cut and the fine cut; sound-effects editing; dialogue looping; music scoring; sound mixing; and then creating the final master tape.

Editing
Finding your editor
In outlining how to find and work with an editor, we're making the big assumption that you're not planning to edit the movie yourself. At this budget level, it's a very common practice for the director to wear a couple of hats, sometimes a whole hat rack. Director-writer, director-composer, director-actor — you can find plenty of examples of these combinations working and even working quite successfully. The same can be true of director-editor.

And with the advent of so many different (and affordable) digital editing options available to you, you may think that there's no reason to turn your movie over to anyone else for this final phase. And you may be right.

That said, we'd like to champion the idea of bringing on an editor. Not just any editor, of course. You need to find someone who can work with you as a partner to shape the movie and get the most out of the footage you've worked so hard to shoot. As with everyone else who's been involved in the project, an editor will bring something extra to the table. He or she can take what was shot and get the most out of it, often finding things in the material that may have slipped past the director.

That's because the editor brings a fresh set of eyes to the movie, another perspective that is entirely divorced from the travails of the production process. Good editors don't care how hard a shot was to get; they only care about making each cut and each scene work the best way possible, regardless of what went into shooting the footage. A good editor partners with the director, helping find the great movie trapped within the raw footage.

So how do you find this partner? The same way you've found everyone else: through the grapevine, word of mouth, networking. Put the word out in your production community and get a sense of who's good, who's great, and, most important, who's interested. Editing a feature-length movie is a major undertaking, roughly equivalent to a second full-time job, so you need to find someone who is as committed to the project as you are... if such a thing is possible.

An editor who owns an editing system is a plus, but that alone isn't sufficient reason to sign them on. What you're really looking for is someone with a philosophy similar to your own. When it comes right down to it, editing is as much about philosophy as it is about technique. Talk with candidates about what movies they like. Find out who their favorite editors are and why. Start to get a sense as to whether or not you "click" with this person. You're going to be spending a lot of long hours with them, so rapport is required.

Looking at their past work is helpful but also problematic, because the best editing is seamless. If it's done right, you won't recognize how an editor may have saved a scene. Conversely, a beautiful and dramatic montage on their demo reel might be cut exactly as the director storyboarded, with little input from the editor.

Looking at some of their past projects will begin to give you a sense of their work; however, the best editor for your project may not have much appropriate material to show you. Instead you may be looking at samples that include documentaries, industrials, news stories, and student films. Some potential editors may have no dramatic examples on their reels. So how do you know if they'll be right for your movie? Again, it comes down to philosophy and rapport. Like everyone else who's signed on so far, the editor may be looking at this project as a way to take a step up the ladder and learn more about their craft. If they're committed to the movie and you feel a philosophical connection, you may have found your partner.

One advantage of computer-based editing is that you can let the editor cut a scene or two as an example of their work. If you don't care for the results, both you and the editor have only wasted a handful of hours. And if you like their work, then you're already on your way.

Editing equipment
If you find an editor you like and can work with and they already own (or have access to) a digital editing system, then your choice of system is already made, and you can move on. Good for you.

Don't feel you need to invest in a new system if your editor's system (or your system) is not strictly state-of-the-art. There's always a price tag attached to state-of-the-art gear, and this could be your only chance to substantially reduce your movie budget. There are advantages (mostly financial) to being a step or two *behind* the times. At this point in the process, when money is tighter than ever, it may be best to sacrifice the newest toys for the cheapest toys. As long as they can get the job done.

If you are in the market to buy, lease, or rent a system, be warned: There are a lot of different systems out there, ranging from home-movie-style editors that come bundled with low-end computer systems (such as the iMovie software with the iMac DV) to the highest of the high-end systems, favored by postproduction houses and other professionals. You can drop a lot of money on systems that do much more than you'll ever need.

The key here is research. Read everything you can on all the current (and not-so-current) systems, to determine which features you really need and which ones would just be fun to play with. There are a few points to keep in mind during this process:

- Does it fit in your production budget? If not, are you prepared to up the ante? Remember, the odds of the movie making a profit or even recouping its investment are slim. Don't burden yourself with unnecessary debt.
- Can you put the editing system on a paying basis? That is, are there video opportunities out there that would, over time, pay off the system? Whether you're shooting and editing wedding videos, producing low-budget videos for local companies, or renting the system to fellow moviemakers, a little effort can make your new system pay for itself in a short time, and then start turning a profit (which may be more than your movie will do). The time to start researching these opportunities is now.
- What's the learning curve on each system? A lower-end system that your editor is already proficient with may be the most practical move.
- What is your ultimate plan for the finished movie and how will this system help or hinder your plan? If the system is ultra-cheap but burns some bridges (for example, system output that's not lossless DV but a composite video format, or a system that doesn't maintain your original time code numbers for a future high-end edit), then it may make sense to spend a bit more and get what you need.

There are a lot of choices out there, with no absolute right or wrong answers. Do your homework and before you know it, you'll be into a new and exciting part of the process — editing the movie.

Working with your editor
Often the hardest part of working with an editor is simply letting him or her do the job. The urge to micromanage the process may be strong, but we recommend that you resist it. Leaning over your editor's shoulder critiquing every cut will drive both of you batty and one of you off the project.

Instead, sit with your editor and review all the footage for a given scene, talking about which elements you like and which you don't. Once you've reviewed the footage, let the editor go off and put the scene together using your comments as a starting point and adding his or her own creative "zing" to the process. Then review the work, offer suggestions for changes, and let the editor take another crack at it. Keep doing this until both of you are happy with a scene, and then move on to the next one.

We've found that this approach works well for both parties. It allows the director to come in and look at each scene fresh, without any baggage about

212

how difficult it was to edit. And it provides the editor with some creative license to work without someone watching and second-guessing each move.

Take it from us, you won't get the most benefit from the relationship if you simply look upon your editor as an order taker. Just as you have with the other creative people who have joined your project, you have to let editors stretch their creative muscles a bit. It will be good for your editor, and it will make your movie better.

The rough cut or first cut
Nowadays, with nonlinear editing systems, the differences between the rough cut and the final cut are not nearly as distinct as they used to be. Since most systems allow you to do many of the visual effects (dissolves, fades, and so on) and often have room for multiple soundtracks, the rough cut can look pretty fine indeed. On an $8,000 budget, you will produce your final cut on your edit system.

In the early stages of the rough cut, you often make a real switch in your thinking. You stop trying to make the movie you set out to make, and you begin to define the movie that you've made. All the pieces are there; it's up to you and your editor to assemble them in the most effective way. For some, it's a major overhaul, where the movie is literally remade in the editing room. (See Ralph Rosenblum's excellent account of the editing-room re-creations of *Annie Hall*, *A Thousand Clowns*, and *The Night They Raided Minsky's* in his book, *When The Shooting Stops... The Cutting Begins*.) For other movies, it's a question of juggling, moving things around, and deciding to add or subtract some elements. (See Charles Grodin's very droll description of the editing of *11 Harrowhouse* in *It Would Be So Nice If You Weren't Here*.)

Whether the surgery is major or minor, it's important that you keep an open mind and be willing to make the painful cuts in order to make a better movie. That said, it's just as important to make sure that you don't throw out good material that simply hasn't been perfected yet. A good example is the seance scene from *Beyond Bob*. From the beginning, this was always one of our favorite scenes. It had atmosphere, it had humor, and it also had a couple of powerful character moments. However, in the rough cut, the scene stunk.

The problem started with the sound and just got worse. On the night the scene was shot, there was a problem with dialogue recording that made half of it unusable. The rough assembly of the scene was painful to sit through as sound jumped from bad to indecipherable, making the scene nearly unwatchable. Even if it had perfect sound, it appeared that the scene was clearly a turkey headed for Thanksgiving. John was ready to toss it out and cut our losses. But Dale and the editor argued for it and eventually won out. The scene stayed, and repairs were made.

As it turned out, the only real problem was the sound, but it was such an overwhelming problem that it masked an otherwise good scene. In the end, with a number of the lines in the scene re-recorded by the actors and some terrifically creepy music added by our composer, the scene played great and is a high point of the movie.

The lesson here is to use your rough cut as an opportunity to take a cold, hard look at what's working and what's not working, and make decisions accordingly. At the same time, make sure you understand why the scene isn't working before you decide what to do about it.

This process of refining the movie — shortening and cutting scenes, moving sequences around, shaping each scene so it has the utmost impact — may take many weeks or months. For some movies, it takes years. But after all the pruning and preening, you will eventually arrive at a major destination, The Fine Cut.

The fine cut
There's no question that, left to their own devices, some directors and editors would never reach the fine-cut stage. They would instead spend the rest of their lives tweaking and futzing with the movie, making imperceptible changes here and there, completely unwilling to throw in the towel and call it done. Nonlinear editing only adds to this problem by making it possible to create multiple versions of every scene and forestalling the final decisions for eternity.

One of the best ways to determine if you've actually reached the fine cut is to screen the movie for a small group. The ideal audience is one that doesn't know anything about the story; however, by this point the only way you'll find anyone in your life who's unaware of all the minute details of your movie is to pull strangers in off the street. This is the approach we took with *Beyond Bob*.

With the help of our local Independent Feature Project chapter, we got the use of a local theater with a video projector and advertised a special "sneak preview of a locally produced movie."

To get an unbiased reaction from our showing, we held an earlier, invitation-only screening for cast, crew, family, and friends. This private screening ensured that these people wouldn't show up for the public screening and skew the audience reaction. Although a few of them stuck around for a second look at their work, their reactions didn't seem to affect the crowd.

After the screening, our test audience was asked to fill out comment cards, but this was of marginal value. Most of what we needed to know had been learned simply by watching and listening to the audience while they experienced the movie for the first time. And we learned a lot.

The screening was great because it gave us a better sense of which scenes moved too slowly (too many of them) and which ones moved too quickly (almost none). It also told us which jokes were drowned out by laughter from previous jokes (an enviable problem), which plot points were obscured by laughter, and which scenes got laughs we didn't intend. The screening helped us identify big problems, such as scenes that had to be shortened or eliminated, and little problems, such as sound that needed further repair or music that wasn't quite right yet.

Our showing was more elaborate than most. You can also get good results just by sitting several people in front of the computer.

Sound-effects editing

Throughout the picture-editing process, you (or your editor) will probably also be adding the different sound-effect tracks you'll need to give your soundtrack a full, "lived-in" sound. A sparse, hollow soundtrack is a dead giveaway that yours is an ultra-low-budget movie, but with a little work and ingenuity, you can spice up the track and give the entire project a bigger-budget sound for very little money.

Before you begin assembling your effects tracks, you need to decide if you're going to do the final sound mix in your editing system or take the project to a sound house for a final mix. For financial reasons it's going to be cheaper to do it yourself, but if you have access to professionals who will cut you a good rate (or better yet, do it for free), then by all means jump at the chance.

215

The system we used for editing *Grown Men* had up to 99 soundtracks available, which we never came close to using. However, as with the movies we cut on film, we did establish a pattern for the tracks, which made it easier to work on the system.

The first four tracks were used for dialogue. When the movie was just about finished, we also went in and removed all the sound effects from the dialogue tracks and moved them to the separate sound-effects tracks. These tracks also included sound effects that we added in postproduction and room ambience. We also duplicated any sound effects that were intermixed with the dialogue and put them on a separate track. This track was turned off unless needed to produce a music-and-effects-only soundtrack.

The next tracks were the music tracks, which we divided into source tracks (music that the characters could hear in the movie, such as a song played on a radio) and underscore, which is music that only the audience hears. Keeping them on separate tracks made it easier to cross-fade from source music to underscore.

This consistent approach made it easier to turn sound or music on and off as needed while working on the soundtrack. If we wanted to hear just the effects and music, we simply switched off the first four tracks. If we wanted to test how a sound effect played against the dialogue, we could easily switch off the music tracks. If we were putting in dialogue recorded in postproduction, we could toggle back and forth between the original and the new dialogue tracks to test the sync.

Finally, this system made it easy for us to create a foreign music-and-effects (M&E) version of our soundtrack should an overseas distributor want to buy the movie and add their own foreign-language dialogue.

Dialogue looping
While you're recording your sound effects and doing your foley work (creating effects to match actions in the movie, such as the sound of footsteps), you may also need to "loop" or rerecord lines of dialogue that were not recorded cleanly on location.

On *Grown Men* we had one entire scene — seven minutes long — which needed to be looped because the actress lost her voice on the day of shooting. Needless to say, this was not an ideal situation. However, we heeded our own advice: When the picture is good and you can't get good sound, shoot it anyway and fix it later. Which we did, with the help of a friend who had access to an actual Hollywood sound studio and the necessary automatic dialogue recording (ADR) equipment.

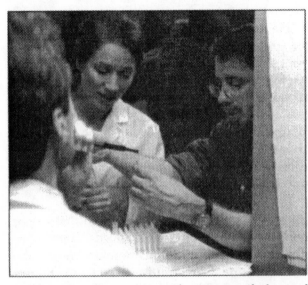

Due to losing her voice the day of shooting, actress Susan Vee had to loop all of her lines for this scene from Grown Men. *Pictured: Susan Vee, Director John Gaspard. (Photo courtesy of Granite Productions, Unlimited.)*

With this approach, the actor goes onto a recording stage where he or she watches the scene and hears the original sound on headsets. The system is set up so that the actor can watch and say the same line again and again until she or he is able to rerecord it perfectly in sync with the picture. (To see the ADR system in action, look at the climax of the film *Postcards From The Edge*, where actress Meryl Streep rerecords a scene for director Gene Hackman.)

You can create your own version of this system using your editing system. Create a repeating loop of the lines that need to be replaced. In the case of the *Grown Men* looping session, there were 50 separate lines that needed to be rerecorded. It took very little time to create a tape of all 50 lines; each line was repeated five times in a row to give the actor five opportunities to get it right. Record this looping audio and video on your DV camcorder, and then duplicate it on VHS tape for playback.

Then find the cheapest recording studio or in-home studio (likely one and the same) you can that has a recording deck of some kind. DAT is great. Reel-to-reel still works fine. Your DV camcorder does CD quality. The studio should also have a separate soundproof recording booth with a viewing window and a skilled engineer. Set up a VCR and monitor so that the actors

217

in the booth can see the television screen through the viewing window. (You don't want the monitor or the VCR in the sound booth because both make noise.) The sound from the picture on the VCR needs to be routed into the actors' headphones so they can use it as a reference. The VCR reference sound also needs to feed through the mixing board and into the recorder. This allows the engineer to lay down the reference sound onto the recording at the beginning of each take and then remove it just before the actors rerecord their lines or place it on a separate track. The actors, however, will hear all the reference sound to help them sync up their voices with the original track. Just keep rewinding and replaying the videotape until the actors get it right or close enough.

If there's no cheap recording studio in your area or no studio at all, then you'll just have to make your own for dialogue looping. Don't worry, this isn't time for carpentry. It's time for creative reinterpretation of your living space or any other space you have available.

A space without room tone will let you record clean dialogue that can be adjusted to fit any scene once the scene's room tone is added. (Remember, we said to record room tone at each location?) You'll want to find a room that doesn't get much outside noise from traffic, aircraft, neighbors, construction, nearby garage bands, and such. Check the room by recording some sound in it so you can hear those hums and rattles that you're mentally filtering out. Below-grade rooms (such as basements) and rooms with no windows (such as bathrooms and closets) are good candidates. Make sure they don't have loud plumbing or noisy appliances you can't turn off. If your home has a 1950s air-raid shelter buried in the backyard, you've got a good start on a makeshift studio and on first-strike survivability.

Next you'll have to deaden any hard surfaces that reflect sound. Fluffy rugs on the floor and heavy fabrics (towels, blankets, drapes from Tara or the Von Trapp household) hung on the walls will do the trick. You can usually skip the ceiling. You don't have to do an entire room. Just use the fabric to divide a corner off the main room. (And your parents thought that building blanket forts in the living room wasn't a useful skill.) If there's a large walk-in closet filled with clothes, you have a ready-made sound booth.

Just as you would at a sound studio, set up a TV and VCR to show the VHS tape of the dialogue loops. Run the sound to headphones for the actor.

Rent a decent desk microphone (not a shotgun microphone) and put it on a stand so the actor can say the lines while standing up. The cable from this microphone should go to your DV camcorder to record the new sound. You may need some adapter cables to get this all working.

Obviously the VCR and camcorder should be outside your sound booth. The TV is trickier, because it makes a good deal of electronic noise but has to be close enough for the actor to see lip movement and visual cues for the start of the lines. If you have a room divided by a French door, you can just put the TV outside of the glass. Otherwise you can get a cardboard box larger than the TV (so it doesn't overheat and burn you and the actor to cinders), and cut out a hole so just the screen shows through. Put the open back of the box outside of the sound room for ventilation, and then put thick blankets and pillows around the part of the box inside the sound booth to muffle the TV sounds. It may not look pretty, but your makeshift sound booth is ready to do the job.

One final note on looping: When you cut your replacement dialogue in with the existing location dialogue, you'll probably need to dirty up these new lines. Generally, the dialogue you record in a recording studio will sound a lot cleaner, so your looped lines might not mesh well with your original dialogue. By using the filters and equalization controls on your nonlinear editing system or by adding some sound effects to the entire scene (such as street noise), you should be able to balance these two different tracks. The end result will be a consistent-sounding track, and the audience will be none the wiser.

Music
Few things are as important to the success of your movie as music. Music can enhance the emotional content of a scene, build suspense, link a scene to previous scenes, reinforce comic or tragic moments, help set the time and the place, and much more. The right music score can improve a mediocre movie and can often save a weak scene. Conversely, a bad or inappropriate score can really drag down an otherwise good movie. So plan on putting a lot of effort into this part of the process. Even though it happens toward the end of the line, it is worthy of your complete attention.

It's also going to cost some money. How much depends on the amount of music your movie requires and how it is created and recorded. However, at this point in postproduction, your checking account has probably dipped into the low triple or double digits — or even lower. Because the creation of the music score usually comes near the end of production, it is the most vulnerable to budget cuts. This is unwise; "borrowing" against your music budget for other production elements will weaken your final product, perhaps immeasurably. So strive to keep money set aside for music, and then make sure that's where it ends up.

Using existing music

The odds are really against you having the money to put recognizable music into your movie. That's because, with the exception of the classical music of Mozart, Bach, Beethoven, Brahms, and that ilk, most recognizable music is not in the public domain. Even "Happy Birthday to You" is owned by someone, and it will cost money for you to use it, even if it's only hummed or sung a cappella.

Leslie Ball sings a song written especially for the movie in a scene from Beyond Bob.

If you do find music that's in the public domain, you can't just take it from your favorite record or CD; you must pay the people who recorded the music and the people who distributed the recording. This costs money, usually lots of money. And at this point in the production, you'll be lucky to have enough money to jingle in your pockets, let alone to get a jingle on your soundtrack. Your only option for using public-domain music is to have it recorded by your own musicians.

Some music publishers and record companies will allow you to use existing music on a "festival-only" basis, which means what it says: You can license the music for a small fee, but you can only show the movie at festivals. If you end up striking a distribution deal, you'll have to pay full rate for the music, which may end up being a deal breaker, depending on the final cost of the existing music.

However, don't let these facts persuade you that using existing music is entirely out of the question. Recordings of the original music of bands and musical groups in your area are excellent sources of music. If you aren't connected with your local music scene and the musicians in it, find a local critic, club owner, or music fanatic who can introduce you to the right people and the right sound for your movie. It's a win-win situation for everyone. The artists get some excellent exposure for themselves and the music they've already recorded, and your movie's soundtrack moves up a couple notches. It doesn't cost the musicians or you anything, and you both might share some profits down the line.

Finding a composer
As with the other professionals and soon-to-be professionals you'll gather to help make your movie, finding your version of James Newton Howard or John Williams may take equal amounts of perseverance and luck.

In our case, we got lucky. We stumbled upon the Hope Diamond in the rough. When our composer joined us for our first film, he had never scored a movie, but he did possess an encyclopedic knowledge of music and a burning desire to compose for features — a winning combination. He has since moved out of our budget range, which is Hollywood's gain but our loss.

As with the other people on your team, you need to look for a composer who is passionate about her or his role and committed to your movie. By this late point in your production, it's possible that you've been contacted by composers eager to ply their trade on your project. During our productions, we received inquiries from both coasts and many places in between from composers who were willing to work on feature projects, even one as low-budget as ours.

If you haven't received any inquiries by the time you've begun editing, then it's time to start beating the bushes. Some of the best sources are industrial composers in your area or the nearest large city. These are composers who create jingles and write music for commercials and industrial films and videos. They are working professionals who understand the process, have a lot of the connections that will help get the music produced, and who are already doing what you need, albeit on a smaller scale.

It's possible that one of these industrial composers will leap at the chance to do a dramatic music score for a movie that doesn't star bug spray or bathroom tissue. Of course, the only way to find out is to track them down

221

and ask them. Once they learn what your budget is, some will lose interest. Be persistent. Make a list of the best composers in your area and go down it until you find a composer who connects with you and your movie. Every time you're turned down, be sure to ask if they know of someone who might be interested, a new composer, a promising assistant, or an unknown waiting to blossom. As with every other facet of this production, the more experienced people you can get, the better the end result will be. However, enthusiasm and talent can make up for inexperience, a lesson we've learned many times.

Besides tracking down industrial composers and networking through the grapevine of your film community, you can look to local schools and universities. Schools with a music arts program can be an excellent resource not only for finding your composer, but also musicians to perform the music and maybe even recording engineers. And don't forget: Both students and teachers are potential candidates.

What to give your composer

Composing for movies is a very precise art. In order for your composer to create a finished score that fits your movie like a glove, you'll need to provide an accurate copy of your movie. By "accurate," we mean that the picture should be locked, with no further changes. Once your composer has started scoring the movie, let him or her know if you make any changes. Even trimming a few frames from a scene can throw off a music cue, so it's essential to provide a new tape of any sequence that you've changed once the composer has started.

You can give the composer a copy of the whole movie or just segments of it as you finish them. The composer doesn't necessarily need the sound effects, but all of the dialogue is essential. The composer needs to know exactly when characters are and aren't talking to get the right timing for the music. A time code burn-in on the video is ideal. However, if your composer's equipment is set up to receive and lock to audio SMPTE time code, and if you can get access to a video recorder that does this without breaking the bank, it's worth the extra step and the money.

Working with your composer

Just as you've done with the writer, the actors, the editor, and all the other creative people who've brought their skills to your movie, it's essential that you give your composer some latitude in creating the score. It's best not to dictate musical instructions or give the composer a temporary score filled with existing music and ask them to duplicate what they hear. This isn't a good use of their time or their talent.

The first step you'll go through with your composer is the spotting session. This is where you sit down and watch the movie, pointing out where you feel the music should go. Why is this called a spotting session? We don't know. It might be because you're trying to "spot" the best place to put the music, but that's a guess. However, it's an important and fun part of the process.

Before the spotting session, watch the movie on your own a couple of times. By this point you've seen it a million times, but now you're looking at it strictly from the standpoint of its musical needs. Take notes as you think about when, where, and why you want music. What do you want the music to do? What should it accomplish?

A good preparation for this part of postproduction is watching other movies. Figure out why and where they have music, and see the effect it can have on scenes. Listen to movies, and watch scenes with the sound off to figure out what role the music is playing. If you have a DVD player, rent some DVDs that allow you to turn off the dialogue and sound effects on a movie and just listen to the music while you watch the picture. This can be an education in itself. Then you'll be ready to sit down with your composer and go through your movie scene by scene and sequence by sequence.

Steve Martin has been quoted as saying, "Talking about music is like dancing about architecture." It's true; talking about music can be tough, particularly if you don't have the vocabulary to do it. You may be tempted to give your composer very precise directions ("I want violins to come in here, and then a single clarinet over this part"), but unless you have a master's degree in music, you're really talking the wrong language.

A better approach is to talk about the emotions you're looking for in each scene ("I want some tension here," "The mood needs to be lighter in this scene," or "We need a jolt right now"). It's the composer's job to translate those emotions into music, and they'll know the best way to create what the scene needs.

That doesn't mean you can't play examples for them. We always played music for our composers that had the mood, spirit, or orchestration that we

223

were thinking of for certain parts of our projects. They never duplicated what we played for them, but instead used it as a form of research for the score they were producing.

You can also create a temporary music track with existing music. A temporary score is a fine tool for your editor to cut against, and it will give your composer a strong sense of the mood you're after. The drawback is that you'll get used to the temporary score, and you may want the composer to duplicate it instead of reinterpreting it. That's the situation composer Alex North found himself in after Stanley Kubrick fell in love with the temporary score full of classical music he'd put on *2001: A Space Odyssey*. North's finished score was set aside and never used because Kubrick was unwilling to let go of his temporary score. Of course, since you can't afford to pay for the existing music on a temporary score, this won't be a big problem for you.

The final output to tape
It's going to take some careful file management to get your 90 minutes of movie in and out of your digital editing system. There are three limitations that you'll have to work around.

First, most computers have a limit on the size of an individual file that you can capture or digitize. For the iMac DV computer we've included in the budget, it's two gigabytes (Gb), which is ten minutes of digital video. Other systems and capture cards may limit you to one Gb.

Second, to hold and play back a 90-minute movie, you'll need 20 Gb of hard-drive space in addition to the space you need just for your editing software. The system we've specified has a 13Gb hard drive. We didn't include the extra cost for the additional 7Gb in the budget because there are cheaper ways to get the same result, and because nonlinear edit systems don't always play long projects without glitches. It will save you money and frustration to output in segments that are ten minutes long or less. In the category of keeping your options open, if a distributor wants to transfer your digital movie to 35mm film for a theatrical release, ten-minute (1000-foot) reels are the standard size used in 35mm postproduction.

And third, the camera you'll be buying and using as your input and output deck will likely use mini-DV tapes which can only hold 60 minutes of video, so you'll need to rent a recording deck that takes the full-size (180-minute) DV tapes.

Though you'll be editing in segments about ten minutes long, you'll be recording them out to DV tape so you can review them while you edit other segments. This is also a backup copy of your edit work. To see how segments flow together, you can copy them from your camcorder to a two-hour VHS tape. While you will have to discard your digitized video clips to regain hard-drive space as you move on to later segments, you'll have enough hard-drive space to save your project files with your edit instructions. Also, save a batch-capture list so you can redigitize the clips if you want to re-edit later. If you decide to redigitize from these tape segments, be aware that sometimes you may get a one- or two-frame shift in the sound synchronization. It's easily corrected by shifting the audio track. Take the time to carefully read your software manual, and test these procedures before you start editing to make sure they work properly. You don't want to find out that you missed something after you've edited your entire 90-minute movie.

When you're all done editing, rent a DV recording deck that takes full-size DV tapes. Recapture each of your ten-minute edited segments — a couple at time — and then use your editing software's "export to tape" or "edit to tape" control to specify the in point and preroll time for recording each segment to tape, starting at the last frame of the previous segment. Whether you're preparing for a film or video release, it's probably obvious that the breaks between these ten-minute segments should be cuts or fades to black. They also should not have sound crossing the section break. Again, read the software manual's instructions, and test this procedure with your camera before you go out and rent the DV deck.

Along with the DV deck, rent a lower-cost S-VHS deck so you can make two back-up copies of your movie on two-hour S-VHS tapes. These are also masters for making low-cost VHS preview copies or dubs for self-distribution. (Some consumer S-VHS decks are now below $200. You may want to buy one if you're self-distributing.) Get the S-VHS and DV decks on a weekend rental that you pick up Friday afternoon and return Monday morning. After you get the master assembled — which will probably take a day — plan to sleep only in 90-minute blocks of time (set your alarm clock), because you'll have more than 30 hours of dubbing to do to create your S-VHS masters and 20 VHS preview dubs. If you can borrow some extra VHS recorders from friends, you can either make more dubs or sleep more. You can make your VHS preview dubs from either the S-VHS deck or DV deck or both.

This last step is a bit tedious and complicated, but the good news is that you'll be at the end of postproduction when you do it.

Keeping in touch

The postproduction process we've just outlined can take from three months to three years, depending on your degree of patience and the depth of your pockets. While you may be quite busy working on the movie during this time, many of the people who worked on earlier phases of the project may begin to think that you and the movie have dropped off the face of the earth. Nowadays, with TV docudramas turning up on television only weeks after the actual event, most people don't realize how long it can take to complete a feature, particularly a feature that's darn near out of cash.

In order to keep your ever-growing list of supporters updated on the progress of your movie, we recommend creating a regular or irregular newsletter. It doesn't need to be elaborate. It's enough to give a one-page recap of the production's current status, the upcoming steps in the process, and maybe news about what's going on in the lives of the cast and crew.

This can even take the form of a Web site devoted to the project, on which you can post periodic updates of your progress. For *Grown Men*, we created a photo site so that that cast and crew members could view and download the shots from the most recent shoots. Other projects have used regular e-mailings to keep the troops informed. And, of course, there's always the old standby: a snailmail form letter.

These are all simple ways to keep in touch, and they allow the people who've donated their time and talents to follow the moviemaking process to its inevitable (and occasionally interminable) conclusion.

DISTRIBUTION
(Meet the New Boss, Same as the Old Boss)

Ah, how times have changed.

In the old days, there used to be only one kind of distribution. You'd sign over the rights to your movie to some (occasionally slimy) individual or company, who would in turn market and sell your movie to various venues (theatrical, home video, cable, and broadcast) around the world. Maybe you got some money. In most cases you didn't.

It was a good, solid system. They made money. You didn't. That was the lot of the independent producer.

Then came the Internet... and everything changed.

Or did it?

Well, there certainly are a lot more venues for independent movies now because of the increased interest in the Internet. More marketing opportunities. More sites that will post your movie to anyone who has the time and inclination to download it. And some of them will even pay you for the privilege.

And some won't.

Yes, releasing your movie on the Internet is a very cool venture, but not one that's necessarily going to put some of your hard-spent coins back in your pocket.

Our feeling on the role of the Internet in the distribution of your movie is that it's just one element in your distribution plan. You can use the Internet to market your movie to distributors who have the clout (and the checkbooks) to get your movie to a wider, paying audience. The Internet is a means to an end.

We recognize that we may be parting ways with some of you at this juncture. You may be thrilled to have finally finished your movie, and you may want nothing more than to have it posted on a Web site and downloaded by a curious few. That's fine. You've made the journey; you completed your dream.

227

The Internet may be the future of movie distribution. Or it may just be another chapter in the long story of distributors making money while independent producers don't. It's a similar story to the early boom of home video. The rules for this new distribution stream are being written and rewritten even as we write this book, and we don't claim to have all the answers. However, even for those of you who merely want to get your movie onto the Internet and leave it at that, there are some valuable lessons to be learned by looking at the more traditional methods of distribution.

We also suspect that many of you want to push on toward more traditional distribution of your movie. The following pages are designed to give you a notion of what to expect on this, the last leg of your journey.

First, it's time for a little painful reality.

The reality is that most independent movies never find distribution — and when we say distribution, we're talking about a system that gets your movie to an audience and gives you a cut of the profits. Some statistics suggest that only about 10% of the feature-length movies made every year ever find any sort of outlet. That means 90% of all the ultra-low-budget, low-budget, medium-budget, and occasionally even high-budget movies never see the light of day. And with additional productions coming from the new wave of digital moviemakers, these numbers may be even higher.

Of course, there are those rare few that break through, reach an audience, receive acclaim, and pave the way for the moviemaker's next project. But for every one of those success stories, there are another nine (or more) stories with less-happy endings.

The road to independent-movie success is strewn with movies that got this far and then petered out. What went wrong with these movies? Did their makers simply lose momentum? Were the finished movies unmarketable? Or did the distributors refuse to take a risk and let these movies die before they ever really had a chance to live?

Yes. Yes. And yes. Plus a thousand other reasons.

Distribution is its own special level of hell, different from the raising-money level of hell, the production level of hell, and the rough-cut level of hell.

The primary cause of this torment is that when you start looking for a distributor, your movie changes from being a personal expression into a mere product, which will be marketed and sold alongside Crest and Spam.

But unlike those well-known brand names, your product is the one and only, a prototype without an audience. Of course, this problem is not unique to independent movies. This is true of all movies, and that's why distributors love movies with presold elements, such as big-name actors, a well-known director, a screenplay based on a famous book, or nearly any title that's followed by Roman numerals. Your movie will likely have none of these elements, which will make it more difficult as you wend your way through the distribution obstacle course.

The one thing your movie *can* have that will make it attractive to distributors is a great story. An involving story. A surprising story. In talking to distributors about what they look for in movies, we heard again and again that the more excited they are about your story, the less concerned they are about big names and big production values. In short, you don't need to blow up buildings, but you do need a story that explodes onto the screen with characters who engage the audience.

So if you're reading this chapter before you've dived into production, double your efforts on your script, and make sure it's the very best it can be. There's usually a long time between when you write your script and when you start knocking on doors to find a distributor, but your early efforts on perfecting the script will pay off when it's time to try to sell your finished movie.

The distribution stream
For years and years, most dramatic movies followed a similar path through the various levels of the distribution system. The Internet and Web-based distribution may change all that once broad-band becomes common and distributors figure out how to make money on the process.

For now, the typical path for a movie is a theatrical release in mainstream or art-house theaters, followed by an appearance on one or more of the pay-per-view systems and airline in-flight movies. Once these venues have been exhausted, the movie moves onto the pay-TV channels (that is, premium cable channels such as HBO and Showtime). At about that same time, the movie will show up on video store shelves. Next, it's on to the basic cable networks, network television, and finally syndicated TV. (There have also been some interesting forays into electronic-cinema distribution by LucasFilm and Pixar, but these remain in the test stages and follow pretty standard theatrical distribution models. However, it's a development worth watching.)

A movie can jump into this distribution stream at any point. For example, many low-budget independent movies never get a theatrical release or even make it to pay-per-view. Instead they start their distribution life on cable channels or go directly to video stores. On very rare occasions a movie may swim upstream; that is, it starts on home video or cable and then moves to a theatrical release. Notable examples are *Red Rock West* and *The Last Seduction*, both directed by John Dahl and made for theatrical release but debuted on cable before moving into the theaters. In most cases, though, wherever you dive in is your starting point, and it's all downstream from there.

When should you approach distributors?

There are two answers to this question: As soon as your movie is perfect, and when it's completely done. Whichever comes first.

Showing your movie before it's entirely finished is not a wise move because distribution people are notoriously literal-minded. They see what is, not what might be. As a result, it can seriously hurt your movie's chances to screen it for them in rough cut or unmixed form.

Showing a rough cut with a partially mixed soundtrack to an audience to gauge their reaction is one thing. Showing the same, unfinished movie to distributors is entirely another. No matter how many caveats you issue before the screening, once the lights go down or they press "play" on the VCR, your movie will be judged as a finished product and not for its potential. And once a distributor has looked at a movie and passed on it, very few will reconsider the same movie later. The demands on their time are just too great.

How to find distributors, how to be found

Before you can start tracking down distributors, you need to decide what sort of distributor you want; that is, at what point in the distribution stream are you going to dive in?

To do that, you have to step back and take a cold, analytical look at your movie — not the movie you set out to make, not the movie you hoped to make, but the movie that you've actually produced. It's no small task to divorce yourself from your movie and look at it completely objectively. This may not even be entirely possible, but you do have to look at the movie realistically to determine where it is likely to fit into the distribution stream. Otherwise, you will waste a good deal of money and time barking up the wrong distributors.

Of course, everyone wants their movie to receive a big, splashy theatrical release with 1,200 prints opening simultaneously in multiplexes throughout the country. While this is a nice wish, it's not a particularly realistic goal. Even if your movie is released theatrically — a darned big " if " — it's more likely to be rolled out with a small number of prints, territory by territory. So you need to establish some realistic, attainable goals.

After looking at your movie realistically, you may conclude that it's not theatrical material. Instead, it may be better suited for cable television or home video, and you may wish to concentrate on those venues. Or you may realize that your movie has little commercial potential and is better suited to the festival circuit. Or, as we mentioned earlier, you may decide that your movie is best suited to living on the Web, available to anyone who wants to take the time to download it. There's nothing wrong with recognizing your movie's limitations. It's a whole lot cheaper (and less demoralizing) to realize this before you spend tons of time and money looking for the wrong kind of distributor.

There's no great trick to finding distributors; most of them actively want to be found because they need a constant flow of new product to keep their doors open. Almost all distributors will look at your movie, because they're afraid they might miss The Next Big Thing if they don't. Imagine yourself as one of the distributors who passed on *The Blair Witch Project* at the Sundance Film Festival, and you can see why the distribution business is run on paranoia and fear.

So finding them is no great trick. As we mentioned back in the chapter on preproduction, you can list your movie in the trade papers, *Variety* and *The Hollywood Reporter*, at any point during production or postproduction. These listings run weekly and are a primary source for distributors looking for new movies. As soon as your listing appears you'll start to get calls and letters from the more aggressive distributors, anxious to view your movie.

Besides the trade papers, there are five tried-and-true methods of getting your work in front of distributors: film markets, festivals, the direct approach, Web site promotion, and getting someone else to do it.

Film markets

A film market is like a supermarket for movies. Buyers come, squeeze the melons, read the ingredients, and try to find the freshest, ripest produce in the store.

Sometimes a market is attached to a film festival, like Cannes; sometimes it's a free-standing event, like the American Film Market. For an ultra-low-budget feature, there currently is no better venue than the Independent Feature Film Market (IFFM), put on each fall by the East coast branch of the Independent Feature Project. It's overcrowded, overbooked, and exhausting. But a handful of movies have been "discovered" at the IFFM, so it's worth investigating.

As of this writing, the market is divided into four categories: feature-length movies (including documentaries), short movies, works in progress, and scripts. This wide array of product is one of the reasons the event is so overcrowded and exhausting. Housed in the Angelika Film Center in New York City, the market runs for seven days, screening movies from 9 a.m. to 5 p.m. in all of the Center's six theaters. Throughout the day, the lobbies are packed with moviemakers trying to corner buyers. The buyers, meanwhile, are racing from theater to theater, trying to find The Next Big Thing. It's a zoo, but most of the buyers are actual buyers, and the reality is that some movies do get discovered, bought, and distributed based on their showing at the IFFM.

Several words of advice before you go to the IFFM (or any movie market, for that matter):

- Be sure you need to go. It can be an expensive proposition, particularly if you don't live in the city where the market is held. With our usual low-budget approach and free lodging, we still managed to spend around $3,000 at the IFFM on entry fees, plane tickets, and promotional items, money we're not convinced was well-spent. For that reason, we didn't include a visit to this market in our sample budget. So check out other options before making this trek.

232

• Track down attendees from previous years, and get tips from them about how to attack the market. For the IFFM, check with your local IFP office for names of people from your area who have attended. Recent attendees can give you an idea of what promotional tricks seemed to work, who was buying, and what to do (and not to do) to get your movie noticed.

• Target the buyers you think would be right for your movie and work on getting them to your screening. Don't spread yourself and your resources too thin by trying to get all the buyers to attend. Peruse past market catalogs to get an idea of who buys what.

If you do decide to attend a market, consider the following advice:

• When you're at the market, attend as many screenings as you can. Talk to the other moviemakers, compare notes, trade horror stories about production, and invite them to your screening. To get the best reaction possible for your movie, you'll want to pack the house with as many sympathetic bodies as you can, and for the most part, other moviemakers are a very supportive group.

• Keep a firm handle on your expectations. Walking away from a market with several offers would be nice, but you may end up with nothing but memories. As you look through materials from previous years, compare the number of movies that have any name recognition to those that don't ring any bells at all. You'll see that the majority of movies are in the latter category.

• Don't sign anything without talking to a reputable entertainment attorney first.

• Finally, try to have some fun. A movie market can be a very intense environment, buzzing with hundreds of people who all have a lot on the line. So relax. See some movies. Meet some people. And try to enjoy yourself a bit. A good time may be all you get from a movie market.

Festivals

One benefit of the IFFM is that it is attended by many of the big movie festivals, including Sundance, and it's a good way to spark their interest in your movie and start some buzz about it.

If you're only looking for awards, then it makes sense to blitz all the festivals. If you're looking for a buyer, then you're better off selecting the events at which your movie is likely to be seen by the right people. Check with a festival's promoters and moviemakers who entered in previous years to see how much buying takes place at the event.

While there are hundreds of movie festivals throughout the world, only a handful are regularly attended by buyers, among these are the Toronto Film Festival, the Sundance Film Festival, the Miami Film Festival, the Berlin Film Festival, and the Cannes International Film Festival.

Currently, the hottest festival ticket is the Sundance Film Festival. Everyone wants to attend, and everyone wants to have their movie entered, accepted, screened, and then sold to the highest bidder. It's happened to many other ultra-low-budget movies, and there's no reason why it can't happen to yours. All you need to do is get accepted. But that's the tricky part.

As with any popular festival, you'll have a better chance of getting in if you submit your movie well before the deadline. Sending in your movie at the last minute — in order to give yourself as much time as possible to make final tweaks — will bury your movie in the crush of eleventh-hour entries, and you may disappear without a trace. So get yourself organized, and get your entry in early.

The direct approach
The third approach to finding a distributor is the most direct. Find the distributors you feel are right for your movie, contact them directly, and send them a cassette copy of your movie for review.

Not so surprisingly, this approach — like all the methods we've outlined — has an up side and a down side. The up side is that it's generally faster and cheaper than pouring money into prints, cassettes, publicity and entry fees for markets and festivals. The down side is that there's nothing like screening your movie for distributors in a theater with an actual audience. Watching the same movie in a five-by-six cubicle on a 12-inch screen under fluorescent lights is hardly an ideal viewing situation. Particularly when you realize that many distributors watch tapes with one eye on the clock and one finger hovering above the fast-forward button.

It's also important to remember that distributors are people (Really. We've heard this to be true.), and that they all share the very common human trait of not wanting to be the first person to dive into the pool. They want someone else to test the water for them. With that in mind, it's best if you can provide them with reassuring information that makes it okay for them to like — and want to distribute — your movie. The best tools are great reviews and awards from a variety of festivals. It may take you a year or so to accumulate this paper trail, but it's time well spent if it says to a distributor "come on in, the water's fine."

Researching distributors is the key to successfully using the direct approach. Don't waste your time and theirs by sending your movie to distributors who are not suited for your project.

- Look through back issues of *Variety* and *The Hollywood Reporter* to learn who is distributing what. Each publication puts out special issues several times a year, right before the Cannes Market, the MIFED market (an international audiovisual market in Milan, Italy*), and the American Film Market, with ads from all the key distributors touting their movies.

- If you're looking for a particular venue (such as a theatrical release), make sure the distributors you approach are in that business.

- Learn what types of movie they release, and then approach the distributors that specialize in the same genre as your movie. If you're approaching a cable channel directly, make sure you've watched that channel and understand the kinds of movies they buy. The same is true of home-video buyers.

- If you're targeting basic cable channels (such as Lifetime, USA Network, the Sci-Fi Channel) and broadcast channels, keep in mind that they present movies in two-hour blocks. This means your movie needs to be between 90 and 92 minutes long (the other 28 to 30 minutes are devoted to commercials). Sending them a 120-minute movie tells them that you don't understand their business.

- Many basic cable channels have standards-and-practices departments (a fancy word for censors) just like the broadcast channels. Consider this if

---

* That's *Mostra Internazionale dei Film e Documentari* for you purists and Sophia Loren fans.

your movie's content requires any serious cleaning up before it can be aired. A four-letter word here and there can be cut out, but wall-to-wall swearing, explicit nudity or sex, or over-the-top violence are not what they're buying.

After you've picked the distributors who are most likely to be interested in your movie, send each of them a short inquiry letter. Briefly describe your movie and include photocopies of any reviews you've received from premieres, screenings, or festivals. Don't send a preview cassette until they ask for it. It's a waste of your limited money to give cassettes to people who haven't asked to watch them.

It may seem to verge on paranoia, but for your preview video cassettes it's a good idea to have "For Preview Only" superimposed on the picture throughout your movie. Usually this text is semi-transparent and placed across the bottom third of the screen so it doesn't obscure too much of your movie. Piracy, especially illegal video-cassette duplication, continues to be a big problem throughout the industry, and there's no reason you should make it easier for the thieves.

After you've sent out the preview cassettes, be patient. In most cases, you'll be approaching small companies with small acquisition staffs. One person may be in charge of doing all the screening, all the negotiations, filling out the paperwork, and helping out with other projects. But you should check in on a monthly basis or whenever they say to call back next. A polite, brief nudge every so often keeps your cassette from becoming part of the bottom sediments on the desk.

Web site promotion
Regardless of your stand on the merits of *The Blair Witch Project*, the movie proved the value of a strong Web site. As a marketing tool, it turned out to be the movie's secret weapon.

You can put that power behind your movie and get the attention of distributors at the same time. A well-designed and well-executed Web site that promotes your movie doesn't need to be expensive to be effective. It just needs a clear point of view, interesting graphics, and enough information to whet the viewers' appetites and make them want to see more.

The site can take a lot of different forms, from an ongoing diary chronicling the making of your movie to a polished promotional vehicle that clearly introduces your movie to the Web audience. Photos, sound files, a trailer... all these elements are a great way to introduce the world (and distributors) to your movie.

As with your movie, it's best to wait until your site is finished before you send out invites for visitors. A distributor is unlikely to visit to an incomplete Web site more than once.

You can also save yourself the hassle of creating your own site by placing a trailer or short from your movie on one of the many independent-movie sites. While these sites can't do all your promotional work for you, they can help get your movie to a wider audience, and they may, in years to come, join festivals as the first stopping place for new movies.

We've included a list of some of these independent-movie Web sites in the appendix.

Getting someone else to do it

Up to this point, making your movie has been pretty much a do-it-yourself affair. However, finding a distributor is a time-consuming process, requiring you to become a promoter, a salesperson, and a negotiator. You may simply not want to do this. Maybe you want to focus on your next project or recover from this one. In that case, you need to find someone else to help you sell your movie.

The people who help moviemakers sell their movies go by many names: sales representative or rep, sales agent, producer's representative, and others. Often these are people who've spent some years in the distribution business and are now out on their own. Some are people who have spent time selling their own projects. Most work out of their homes using only a phone, fax, e-mail, their good judgment, and their industry connections to make their living. The best ones are very aggressive and knowledgeable about the business (however, don't ever confuse aggressiveness with knowledge).

As with all professions, some reps are better than others. To find the ones who do the best job of selling, talk to the buyers. Place a couple calls to key theatrical distributors, buyers at cable networks, or large home-video distributors and find out whom they know and — more importantly — whom they trust.

Sales reps generally work on commission. Some have set rates that they use regardless of the project; others slide their commission scale, depending on how much or how little work they think they'll need to do to sell your movie. If they like your movie (or even if they hate it but think they can sell it), they'll want the right to sell the movie in all the territories they cover, and they will want to be able to sell these rights for periods of up to 20 years. As with all contracts that you sign during the distribution process, you should have an experienced entertainment attorney look over any sales-rep agreement before you sign it.

The budget question
One question you may be asked by many potential distributors is "What was your budget?" Even after the success of ultra-low-budget movies such as *The Blair Witch Project*, *Clerks*, and *El Mariachi*, there are still some distributors who feel that a movie can't be worth their time if it cost less than a decent European vacation. Of course, the viewing public doesn't really care about a movie's budget. They may be curious about a movie that's being advertised as a dirt-cheap production, but if the story doesn't grab them, then the budget won't either. So when a distributor asks the question, you can do one of four things: You can lie outright; you can tell an alternate truth; you can skirt the issue; or you can tell the complete truth.

Lying
This is a bad idea. It always trips you up somewhere down the line, and it puts you on that slippery slope to becoming yet another Hollywood lowlife. If you insist on lying ("Our budget? A million three, plus deferrals."), keep in mind that most distributors are pretty smart. They've looked at hundreds of movies and perhaps have produced a few of their own. They know what it costs to make a movie. So if you lie, you'd better stay within the bounds of reality.

An alternate truth
You can tell an alternate version of the truth by figuring out what your movie would have cost if you had actually paid everyone. Then, when you're asked the budget questions, you can say, "A quarter of million, including deferrals," and you'll be telling the truth. Sort of.

Skirting the issue
We're big fans of skirting the issue by turning the question around and asking, "What do you think the budget was?" With *Beyond Bob*, only one distributor

came close (guessing "around $50,000, with lots of deferrals"). As we've bragged before, one knowledgeable person even went as high as $900,000, which was obviously way off and which also made our day. This approach can also be educational because it will give you an objective assessment of your production values.

The truth

Telling the unguarded truth about your budget will have more impact if you skirt the issue first and let the distributor guess. The person who guessed $50,000 felt good about himself when we told him the actual cash budget had been under $30,000; he was also impressed by what we were able to achieve for that budget. The person who guessed $900,000 was enormously impressed with us when we revealed our true costs. In both cases, we got the maximum benefit out of telling the truth.

The big fear about the truth is that it will come back to haunt you, particularly in the form of a low offer from the interested distributor. Don't be afraid; simply stand your ground. The production budget of a movie has no bearing on its market value; witness *The Blair Witch Project* and *Waterworld* as the two sides of that coin.

At this point in the process, your movie is worth whatever the market will bear.

The deal & other details

Once a distributor makes an offer, you need to do two things: Check them out some more, and if they pass the inspection, hire professional legal talent. We can't overstate this enough: Don't accept any offers or sign any contracts without the aid of an experienced entertainment attorney. Distributors buy movies all the time, week in and week out. They write the contracts. On the other hand, this will probably be the first time for you. Who do you suppose has the advantage in this situation? Don't take any chances. Get yourself some expert advice.

Your local Independent Feature Project will have the names of lawyers who are both experienced in entertainment law and sympathetic to your cause. Some work for free or on a sliding scale. Others may accept a deferral or perhaps a credit in the movie in exchange for their services.

But before you get to that stage, you need to investigate the distributor a little further. You need to find out how they've dealt with other moviemakers in the past. Ask for the names of people they're currently doing business with who can vouch for their business practices. Call everyone on the list and question them in detail about the deal they got, the results they've achieved, and their overall impression of the company.

Then disregard everything you've heard and dig deeper.

Find out what other movies they've released and track down those moviemakers — the ones who didn't make the reference list. Ask them the same questions.

We followed this approach with one distributor and didn't even need to get off the reference list. We sent a letter to one of the moviemakers, and she phoned us a few days later. She was out of town at a retreat miles away from a phone. But when she got our letter, she drove into town and called us immediately to warn us away from the distributor. Needless to say, we didn't sign with that company, and a few months later they disappeared off the face of the earth.

Just as every movie and every distributor are different, so too is every deal. What's a standard contract item in one medium is something you may need to fight for in another. Here are some of the things that are the same and different in each venue:

- It costs money to distribute a movie. In the case of a theatrical release, it can cost a lot of money. With low-budget independent movies, it's not uncommon for a distributor to spend two or three times the movie's production budget on prints and advertising (P&A). It cost hundreds of thousands of dollars to get the ultra-low-budget *The Blair Witch Project* in shape for its theatrical release. The sound mix alone for *Clerks* was twice the movie's production budget. A home-video release also requires considerable capital for advertising, tape duplication, and packaging.

That's why distributors resist paying a cash advance for a movie and frequently offer the producer a smaller percentage of the movie's profits, such as a 60-40 split or less. Of course, profits don't happen until they make back their costs, which could take a long, long time. For distributors who are sharing percentages of profits with you (such as theatrical and home video), find out in advance what expenses are going against the revenues. If all the distribution costs are being subtracted (including distribution-staff salaries) you'll probably never see profits. A better deal is one that gives you a percentage of the revenues. In either case, ask for quarterly reporting and payments. They may try to negotiate an annual reporting structure, which basically allows them to keep your money longer. Don't let them do that.

• Large distributors, such as those run by the studios, have lots of ways of burying losses and cross-collateralizing their movies. A small distributor can't afford to simply break even on a movie; each movie must make back its costs plus some more. It only takes two or three bombs to put a small distributor out of business.

In order to protect their investment, both large and small theatrical distributors are probably going to want to hang on to all the other rights as well, including home video, cable, and anything else they can think of. Their argument will be that the theatrical release of the movie is the locomotive that pulls the rest of the train, publicizing the movie for cable and home-video release. They may want to be able to make cable and home-video sales to offset any losses from a theatrical release.

So if you're planning to splinter your rights (sell theatrical rights to one distributor while retaining other rights to sell elsewhere), you may be in for a big fight with your theatrical distributor. If you insist on doing this, you'll be in a better position if you go into the negotiations with these ancillary rights (like home video and cable) already sold. Even then, the absence of these rights may break your deal with a theatrical distributor.

Depending on the movie and the distributor, you may have an easier time holding onto the rights for things like a soundtrack album, book publishing, or merchandising, although you'll probably fight tooth and nail over all that stuff as well.

• For lump-sum deals, such as a contract with a cable network, the distributor or buyer may try to spread out payments as much as possible. For example, you may ask for the first payment to be due upon delivery of the movie. They may counter by making the first payment due on the first air date. If they lock up your movie with a contract and have no required air date, you could sit around for the duration of the contract and never see payment. Stand your ground and make them pay for the right to tie up your movie. They can be pretty tough about this, but it's just another technique for holding onto your money a little longer.

• If a basic cable network wants your movie, they're probably going to want it exclusively, and they're going to want it for a long time. A five-year exclusive contract is not uncommon. Their reasoning is that in order to stay in business, they have to be able to offer product that viewers can't find anywhere else. Otherwise, they'll be swallowed up in the mass of cable channels and eventually disappear. So find which network is right for your movie, and don't expect to accumulate sales across the cable dial.

• As more and more cable channels are added, the prices paid for movies go down, not up. Sure, there are more buyers of movies, but as each network is added, the ratings (market share) go down for everyone because there are more of them dividing up the same audience. As the ratings go down, the budgets shrink proportionally, and the pieces of the pie keep getting cut smaller and smaller. The positive aspect of this growth of cable channels is that more channels need more product, particularly exclusive product. Although they won't necessarily be paying as much for the movies they buy, it should increase your chances of making a cable sale.

What you'll need to provide
Again, the specific requirements of what each distributor needs will change, depending on the company and their venue. But some things are true across the board.

• Many distributors are going to want Errors-and-Omissions (E&O) insurance to ensure you have ownership or use rights to all elements of your movie (as we discussed in the chapter on business). Who pays for this insurance is a negotiable point. With their access to blanket policies, distributors are in a better position to put up the money, but since that adds to their overhead, they're often resistant to doing it. However, in many cases the deal can't proceed until it's resolved, so if they really want your movie, they'll cover this cost.

- Foreign distributors (theatrical, home video, cable, and broadcast television) may need for you to provide a music-and-effects (M&E) track for your movie. This is a special mix of your soundtrack which includes all the sound effects and music, but none of the dialogue. (That's why we told you to put all the dialogue on separate tracks and to create one sound-effects track that replicates any sound effects that were intermingled with the dialogue.) Using this M&E track, the foreign distributor can create foreign-language versions of your movie for each country in their territory.

  In addition to the M&E track, the foreign distributor will also need a continuity script. This is a word-for-word transcript of your finished movie, which will be the basis for the foreign-language translation.

- Publicity stills and PR material. This will vary from venue to venue. As we mentioned in the chapter on production, theatrical distributors desperately need quality production stills to promote your movie in newspapers and magazines. And they have to be smart stills — photos that really capture the tone and mood of the movie, not snapshots of actors and crew mugging for the camera (unless that really captures the tone and mood of your movie). Not having these professional stills will make your movie less attractive to buyers, because they'll need to do more work to promote it.

  Home-video buyers also need stills for video-box art, but these photos generally need to be more stylized, with slick, well-lit images and a lot of attention paid to hair and makeup. Spend some time in a video store, and look at a lot of different boxes to get an idea of the types of photos used to sell movies in this venue. If your time and budget allow, schedule a photo shoot for right after you've finished with principal photography (before the actors, costumes, and locations disappear) to shoot some high-quality images. This will make your movie more attractive to the home-video market, where the artwork on the box is often more important than the movie inside.

  Cable television has less need for photos, because they usually promote movies using on-air promotions (which are short trailers of footage from the movie) and the synopsis that is printed in the cable guide.

• Incidentally, don't expect to have much say about the creative campaign your distributor puts together for your movie. Most will listen to your thoughts, but it's not a contractual right that they're likely to give to you. It would mean that if you don't like their campaign, you could hold up the release of the movie. In their defense, most moviemakers are not equipped to put together an effective trailer or a powerful poster. That's what distributors are good at doing, so don't be surprised when you're left out of this loop.

• Some distributors (and movie markets and festivals) may ask you for a press kit on your movie. This is written information about your movie — the story, the cast, the crew, the production history, and reviews — that will be given to the press for promotional purposes. Publicity photos are also included. You may also use elements of the press kit to entice distributors to look at your movie and to promote any local premiere that you do for your movie. In short, it's a selling tool and should be approached as such.

If you've created a Web site for your movie, many of the materials may already be in place for your press kit. If you're creating a press kit, you'll have many of the materials for your Web site. It's just a matter of moving them from one medium to another.

Every press kit has a few basic elements:

1) *Cast List* — This is a list of your principal cast members, along with the names of the characters they play in the movie. In a movie such as yours, which will be populated with unknowns, this is how movie critics will know who plays which character. This is also where the critics will go to find out how to spell the actors' names, so proofread it twice, and then get someone else to proof it, and then proof it one more time yourself.

2) *Production-Team List* — Same as above, this time featuring everyone behind the camera: producer, director, writer, director of photography, editor, composer, and so on.

3) *Story Synopsis* — This is a one- or two-page synopsis of the key elements of your story. Some moviemakers prefer to tell the whole story in the synopsis; others use it to set up the story and leave the reader hanging,

so as not to give away the movie's ending. This second approach is a better selling tool. It entices the reader to want to watch the movie, and if the reader is a potential distributor, that's a good thing.

4) *Production Notes* — This is something of a catch-all where you can high-light the biographies of your key players and present interesting anecdotes about your movie. Although every part of your press kit should be professionally written, the production notes segment needs to shine. The better it is, the more likely newspaper writers are to simply retype it and print it as is, which is exactly what you want them to do. (Newspaper entertainment writers are notoriously willing to let someone else do their work, except for those few who review books about movie production. Those writers are the best in the business.)

Keep in mind that all this promotional material — which will help with your local premiere and may pique the interest of a distributor — may be tossed out and rewritten by your distributor if your movie gets picked up. Or, if you've done a really stellar job on it, they may follow the example of the newspaper writer and simply retype it on their letterhead.

Self-distribution & self-flagellation: how to tell them apart
Despite your best efforts, you may not find a home for your movie with any of the big or small fish swimming in the distribution stream. You may have been turned down flat at all venues, or you may have received some offers that offered more harm than good. Whatever the reason, you may now feel like the proud owner of a fairly expensive paperweight.

Don't despair. You're not dead yet.

Self-distribution is a viable alternative for you and your movie. On the positive side, it allows you to control how and where your movie is shown, and it eliminates that pesky middleman who seems to come out ahead on most deals. On the negative side, you have to commit to distribution in the same way you committed to production, recognizing that this is nearly a full-time job, requiring as much faith and stamina as the production process did.

One of the reasons that traditional distributors insist on Errors and Omissions insurance is that they don't want to get sued. If you cut out the middleman and release your movie yourself, you will be solely responsible if your movie defames, libels, infringes, violates, spindles, bends, folds, mutilates, and on and on. In short, since you can't afford the insurance, you need to make doubly sure that you haven't trampled anyone else's rights while making your movie.

The most likely markets for self-distribution are theatrical, home video, and the Internet. Before you dive into any of them, consider the following:

Theatrical
- Theatrical distribution is the most risky of the three, because it generally requires more capital: renting a theater, renting video-projection equipment (or spending more to make a 35mm blow-up print), and buying advertising. None of this comes cheaply, so try to think of ways to cut costs. For example, rather than four-walling (renting the entire theater and keeping all the hoped-for profits), strike a deal with a local theater owner. Split the house and let him keep all the concessions, which is where the theater makes all of its money anyway. However, you'll have to persuade the theater owner that you can draw in an audience before he or she will be willing to make that deal. If your movie falls in the cult category, you can offer to make it a midnight movie on weekends so it doesn't cut into the theater's prime time.

- Use articles and reviews in the local media as your advertising. Don't stop with the major newspaper; do some legwork, and make sure you get mentioned in the alternative press, in neighborhood papers, on local radio, cable and broadcast television shows, anywhere! A press release written in news style will often be picked up by neighborhood newspapers, which are well-read by their audience. This sort of publicity is cheap and will pay off with paid admissions at the door.

- Don't blow the bank on elaborate posters with expensive photography and graphics unless the theater is located in a high traffic area where the poster will serve as advertising. Otherwise, go with a simple, elegant (meaning cheap) poster that lets people know they've made it to the right theater.

Home video
Home video is cheaper to break into than theatrical, although not necessarily easier. You can rent space in a movie theater; you can't necessarily buy your

way into a video store — unless you want to own the entire store. More and more, video stores are only looking for the "A" titles (big name movies with big name stars) and the "B" titles (exploitation and action pictures with semi-big name stars). This often leaves the "C" titles (small, independent movies with no name stars) out in the cold.

There are some things you can do, however, to get your movies into video stores on a local, regional and even national basis:

- Generate interest in your movie, so that store owners will see a value in buying your movie. Stage a local premiere and get as much publicity as you can. Then approach local chains and dealers about buying copies of your tape, using the publicity and reviews as supporting arguments to prove there is a demand for your movie.

- If cast and crew members are from out of town, send video copies of the movie (and any reviews you've already gotten) to their local papers to generate publicity. Then use that publicity to persuade video-store owners in that area to stock your movie. By the same token, if you shot in any towns outside of your own, be sure to generate some publicity in those towns as well, and then start hitting on those local video-store owners.

- Work with your area's film commission to persuade all the video chains in the your state to create displays in their stores of movies that were made in your state — both the big-buck Hollywood movies that have passed through the state and the locally produced movies such as yours.

- Create a great, eye-catching box. To find out what sorts of designs work, walk through a few video stores, and see what catches your eye. If you're not a graphic designer, don't pretend to be one. You've done a lot for your movie so far, but don't feel that you have to do absolutely everything. Find yourself a graphic designer to create the right look for your video box. Get a friend of a friend or a promising student at a local art school, or call ad agencies in your area and see if they can recommend someone looking for the experience. You need to make your box look great, and you may need a professional to do that. Also, try to get them to do it for resume experience with you covering the production costs.

• You'll also need great photos. If you didn't shoot them before, shoot them now. On both of our movies, we ended up shooting photography for the video box long after the movies had wrapped. It can be a hassle to get the actors back together. If they have moved on, you'll have to use your imagination. In the case of *Resident Alien*, one of our key actors had moved to Los Angeles, so we used a stand-in wearing the large alien "bug head" we had created for the movie, which was actually a more eye-catching approach!

Staged publicity photos from Resident Alien *and* Beyond Bob.

• Keep your price point low. If you're charging $70 for your tape and a store owner knows she can get two "A" titles or four "B" titles for the same price, what do you think she's going buy? To keep your price low, use the same methods you used during production. Never pay full price for anything, cut deals at every turn, and use your networking skills to get the most bang for your buck.

For example, for less than 400 copies, it's usually cheaper to create an insert cover (artwork that slides into a clear plastic sleeve that surrounds a plastic video case) than a paperboard cover. And to keep your overhead down, make only one copy of your full-color cover and then color photocopy it. This will cost about the same as four-color printing for quantities up to about 500, but you don't have to spend the money until you get the orders. Make sure your designer knows that you might do this in order to ensure that the design is compatible with photocopying technology. Some colors and designs copy better than others.

If you've got a good quality printer for your computer, you can buy some high-quality photo-grade paper, and print the covers yourself. Just make sure the designer creates a file format you can print from.

• Contact all the libraries in your state. Many buy videos and will be interested in locally produced movies, particularly if those movies have garnered some local publicity.

• Be persistent. Be very persistent. This is a hard way to make sales, one to a dozen at a time. You'd probably make more money flipping burgers for the hours you'll invest, but then you'd miss all the glamour of show business.

Internet

As of this writing, there are at least a dozen Internet sites devoted to showing independently produced shorts, and a few are even offering features. Already several moviemakers are selling their videos using previews on the Internet. As broadband and streaming video become more available, more sites will appear, and more importantly, more people will be hitting these sites and watching these movies.

As the cable industry and the Internet become more linked, it's increasingly likely that people will turn to the Web for entertainment just as they now turn to broadcast and cable channels. Even if you can't sell your movie, making it available on the Internet may be a good way to promote your crew, your cast, and yourself. It could be a good stepping-stone for the careers of everyone in your movies.

It's a great time to be an independent moviemaker. With your digital movie just sitting in your computer, you will be well-positioned to ride this new digital wave.

There are a couple of things to watch out for, however.

• As with any other form of distribution, you need to be vigilant about protecting your rights. The technology for getting your movie to the masses may be in place before the mechanisms for recouping your investment have been built. It may be okay if *no one* makes money off your movie, but it's hardly fair if *someone* (like a distributor or Web site provider) does and you don't have a piece of it. As with any other distributor, make sure you don't sign anything or commit to anything without the proper legal advice.

- Be very careful that you understand the terms of your agreement with the Web site provider. Most will want exclusive rights to show your movie, and they may want those rights for a good long time. If you're using the Web exposure to move your movie up the food chain, you may be trapped in that Web when a bigger distributor shows interest in your movie and you can't sell it to them because you've signed away the exclusive rights.

🎥🎥🎥

We're not giving away any secrets when we say that distribution is perhaps the toughest part of this entire process, primarily because most of the control is out of your hands for the first time. However, you are not without some advantages. The biggest is that, from the financial point of view, you don't have to do a lot of business to be successful.

A producer with a movie that has a $500,000 or million-dollar budget has to earn back a lot of money just to break even. You don't have that problem. You don't have to make a killing to pay back your investors, your child's college fund, or your retirement savings.

By the same token, your movie can be attractive to buyers simply because it doesn't cost a lot; you don't need to demand big advances and large percentages in order to be profitable.

The final advantage you have is one of patience. Depending on how you raised your money and who you raised it from, you probably won't have high-rolling investors breathing down your neck. They won't be insisting that you unload your movie as quickly as possible to get them a return on their money. You can afford to be selective and patient as you look for the right distributor. This is good because you may need to be patient. Perhaps *very* patient.

AFTERWORD

Well, we've reached the end of the book together, and now we must part ways. You've got a movie to make, and we've got to get back to making ours.

We hope you've found this book as informative as we have. It's been a great experience for us to be writing this book while we've made our way through the long production process of creating our own digital feature, *Grown Men*. It's been really fascinating to take the things we learned while making two ultra-low-budget films, *Resident Alien* and *Beyond Bob*, and discover how that information works (or doesn't work) in the digital realm.

When we wrote *Persistence of Vision*, the film edition of this book, back in 1995, Michael Wiese gave us a bit of prescient advice: "Writing a book will change your lives in ways you can never imagine." He was right.

One of the best changes is that we've met some wonderful moviemakers since the publication of that earlier edition — women and men with some amazing visions and the tenacity to bring those visions to life. They remind us of the thrill that comes from creating a fictional world and its inhabitants in the 90-minute cosmos of a movie. It's why we keep pouring our extra time and extra dimes into small movies. The exhilaration of creation outweighs the comfort of common sense. We give little heed to the fact that there may be only a small audience for our work. It doesn't matter. We make movies because we have to.

If this is your passion, then we hope this book has helped fuel it. We wish you the best success... which, of course, is to have fun doing it.

Remember that you aren't alone. Be persistent with your vision. And keep us posted on your progress.

John Gaspard
Dale Newton
www.graniteproductions.org

ENLARGED APPENDIX

(Not a useless appendage with inflammation along your digestive tract. Instead a useful appendant of information to digest along with this tract.)

Sample script layout

RESIDENT ALIEN

An Original Screenplay

by

Dale Newton

14. EXT. ROOFTOP - NIGHT

Cal is on the flat roof of the apartment building. A clamp-on work light casts a pool of illumination around him. Stars fill the night sky behind him. The apparatus seen earlier is now sitting on an overturned milk crate, and Cal is perched on a folding chair next to it. He has the control panel open and he's using a volt meter to test the wiring.

> LESLIE
> (o.s.)
> You can't hide from me! I hear you up there
> every night.

Cal looks over to the side of the roof where a permanent ladder is attached and then turns back to his work. From the ladder, there is the sound of irregular shoe steps on metal, accompanied by huffing and puffing.

> LESLIE
> (slurring)
> Hey! Stop shaking the ladder.

Cal finishes his tests and closes the panel. He flips a switch and it glows to life with various colored lights reflecting off his face.

15. INT. SPACECRAFT - SPACE

Another control panel with odd, fluid shapes and buttons suddenly begins to flash wildly. An unearthly wail of a siren is heard with intermittent bursts of sound. The entire room begins to shudder.

16. EXT. ROOFTOP - NIGHT

Leslie slowly appears at the top of the ladder, weaving slightly. She's obviously spent the afternoon getting cozy with her whiskey bottle.

> LESLIE
> My plug's still tubbed.

Sample forms

Call Sheet

Date _____

Production Title _____

Location and Address	Scene Numbers

Cast Member & Role	Makeup Call Time	Set Call Time	Remarks

Extras	Makeup Call Time	Set Call Time	Remarks

Notices of Changes or Future Schedule

GROUP RELEASE   Date _____

In exchange for screen credit under the names listed below, each of the undersigned grants [PRODUCTION CO.] the right, but not the obligation, to use her or his name, voice, likeness or any simulation thereof, or any film or photographs taken by [PRODUCTION CO.] of each of the undersigned individually or with others in connection with this production, tentatively titled

_____

These usage rights are given forever and throughout the world, and include, but are not limited to, the production, distribution, advertising and exploitation of this motion picture by any means whatsoever by the [PRODUCTION CO.].

Name (Print)	Signature	Address

CAST AND CREW RELEASE

I accept all of the conditions and provisions of the following release form covering my work on the production which is tentatively titled

_____

and which is being produced by [PRODUCTION CO.].

Ownership

I assign to [PRODUCTION CO.] the ownership and all rights to use, exhibit, distribute, assign, license, and otherwise exploit the products of my work on the production. I also waive any and all claims to copyright, patent, or other ownership of my work products on the production.

I agree to keep confidential all written, creative, technical and financial detail of the production unless requested by [PRODUCTION CO.] to disclose such information.

I agree to participate in publicity for the production.

Liability

I indemnify [PRODUCTION CO.], the owners of any locations used, and the owners of any uninsured rental equipment against any claims and demands of personal injury, damage to property, and death resulting from my work on the production.

I understand that I am responsible for all necessary personal injury, death, and liability insurances, and am responsible for any damage caused by my actions and by my personal property used during my work on the production.

I accept full responsibility for all personal risks during my work on the production.

Compensation

I am volunteering my services for the production. I understand that I will receive credit under the following name in the screen credits of the completed production:

Name for Screen Credits _____

Signatures

_____
Name [print]   Signature   date

_____
Address

Social Security # _____ - _____ - _____

LOCATION RELEASE

I hereby grant permission to [PRODUCTION CO.] to enter and use my property located at

_____for the

purpose of photographing and recording scenes (interior and exterior) to be used in the motion picture tentatively titled

_____

Use of Property
I give permission for [PRODUCTION CO.] to bring personnel, equipment, props, temporary sets, and any other necessary materials and supplies onto this property for this purpose.

Ownership Rights
I give [PRODUCTION CO.] or any person or company it licenses, the right to use, exhibit, distribute, advertise or otherwise exploit worldwide forever any scenes photographed and recorded on this property in connection with this motion picture.

Care of Property
[PRODUCTION CO.] agrees to use reasonable care to prevent damage to this property and to remove any and all materials placed on the property in connection with this production. The property will be restored as nearly as possible to its original condition, excepting ordinary wear and tear.

Liability
During the photographing and recording on this property, [PRODUCTION CO.] agrees to indemnify and hold the property owner harmless from any claims and demands of any members of the cast or crew of the production arising from personal injuries or death suffered while working on this property.

Authority to Enter Agreement
I hereby state that I have full right and authority to enter into this agreement concerning the property described above and that the permission of no other person, company or corporation is necessary in order for [PRODUCTION CO.] to enjoy full rights to use this property. I also indemnify and hold harmless [PRODUCTION CO.] from all losses, costs, liability, damages, or other claims that arise out of any false statements or representations made by me in this agreement.

Signatures
Approved and accepted by

_____

Printed name of property owner or authorized representative

_____

Signature of property owner or authorized representative

Date _____

Shot log

Tape # _____   Date _____

Project _____ Videographer _____

Locations _____

Time Code	Scene	Take	Description / Remarks / Sound

Equipment rental list

Camera
• Tripod with fluid head

Sound
• Sound mixer
• Batteries for mixer
• Headphones
• Shotgun microphone
• Windscreen
• Shock mount
• Fish pole
• 200' mike cable (4 @ 50')

Lighting
• 4 1000-watt lights with barndoors (Arriflex or Lowel DP)
• Light stands
• 4 extra lamps
• 38" Flexfill reflector (white/silver)
• 2 1000-, 1500-, and 2000-watt Lowel softlights with barndoors
• Softlight stands
• 4 extra lamps

Expendable Supplies to Purchase
• 1 roll 2" gray gaffer tape
• 1 roll 2" black gaffer tape
• 1 roll 2" white gaffer tape
• 4' x 3' spun (105 Roscolux tough spun — 1 stop)
• 10'x 58" daylight to 3200K correction gel (3401 RoscoSun 85)
• 4'x 3' 3200K to daylight correction gel (3202 Rosco Full Blue CTB)

Postproduction
• Desktop microphone for sound effects, foley and dialogue looping
• DV record deck that uses full-size DV tapes
• S-VHS deck

Sample menus for weekend film shoots

We fed a production company that ranged in size from 12 to 20 cast and crew for $125 each weekend of shooting, which included six meals and a snack. We fed everyone well for less than $1.50 per meal by purchasing supplies on sale and at bulk-food and warehouse stores whenever possible. We bought very little prepared food, and we had the help of friends and relatives preparing and serving it. Our menus were planned around the foods that we could purchase within our budget.

Below are sample menus for one weekend of production.

Friday evening
Snack
- Cucumber sandwiches on cocktail bread slices
- Peanut-butter cookies
- Pink lemonade, soft drinks

Saturday
Breakfast
- Lemon bread and banana bread with butter
- Apple juice, coffee, milk, hot cocoa

Lunch
- Hamburger chili over sliced baked potato
- Raw vegetables (carrots, broccoli, cauliflower) and dill dip
- Chocolate-chip cookies
- Soft drinks, milk

Dinner
- Grilled bratwurst on buns
- Potato chips
- Lettuce salad and dressing
- Apples
- Brownies
- Soft drinks, milk

Sunday
Breakfast
- Egg and sausage baked casserole
- Orange juice, coffee, milk, hot cocoa

Lunch
- Submarine sandwich on French loaf (Swiss and cheddar cheese, turkey, ham, pastrami, lettuce, onion, tomato, mayonnaise)
- Oranges
- Cranberry juice, soft drinks, milk

Dinner
- Lasagna
- French bread with garlic butter
- Raw vegetables (green peppers, radishes, celery, mushrooms)
- Ice cream
- Apple cider, soft drinks, milk

Condiments and supplies for meals
- Catsup
- Mustard
- Salt
- Pepper
- Instant cocoa
- Tea bags
- Coffee bags
- Sugar
- Instant creamer
- Paper plates
- Paper cups or borrowed ceramic mugs
- Utensils
- Paper towels
- Coffee urn for hot water

Press kit: sample synopsis

"Resident Alien" — The Story

Resident Alien, a new science fiction-comedy feature film from Granite Productions, Ltd., is the story of a UFO crash that changes the lives of two down-on-their-luck people in a small Midwestern town.

Cal Gilbert (PATRICK COYLE), a former Ph.D. candidate in astrophysics, now runs a motel as a low-rent apartment building. He spends his evenings on the roof, scanning the night skies for a discovery that will reestablish his credibility within the scientific community.

His only tenant, Leslie Winter (NESBA CRENSHAW) is newly divorced, out of work, and at the end of her rope. Her dreams of world travel have gotten her out of Fargo, North Dakota and dumped her — without hope or cash — in Stillwater, Minnesota.

One night, after Leslie has climbed up on the roof to harangue Cal about her apartment's plumbing problems, they both witness — and are nearly incinerated by — a crashing UFO.

With this too-close encounter, Cal and Leslie embark on a journey of mystery and adventure, during which they become entangled with an enigmatic, but friendly, stranger (MARK PATRICK GLEASON); a wily, small-town sheriff (JOHN MUNGER); an unscrupulous UFO investigator (RICHARD GIBBONS); an Air Force cover-up; and an eye-opening rendezvous on a dark country road.

Resident Alien mixes comedy, science fiction and romance to create a memorable story about the dangers and complications that occur when you wish on a star — and your dreams come true.

Press kit: sample credit list

"Resident Alien" Credit List

CAST
Patrick Coyle	Cal Gilbert
Nesba Crenshaw	Leslie Winter
Mark Patrick Gleason	Allen
Richard Gibbons	Professor Davis
John Munger	Sheriff Jack Martin
Janet Mitchko	Joyce (social worker)
Nancy Gormley	Leslie's Mother
Michael Paul Levin	Deputy Gary Ort
Craig McNamara	Bunsen
Tom Monn	Verner
Amelia Barnes	Tish
Eve Black	Naom
Marvel Newton	Addie Wagner

CREW
Dale Newton	Writer-Producer
John Gaspard	Director
Kathy Erickson	Production Manager
Scott Lee Dose	Director of Photography
Steve Knudsen	Assistant Camera
Bryan Carey	Sound Mixer
Rick Selin	Sound Mixer
Dan Martinson	Sound Mixer
Paul David	Lighting Gaffer
Debbie Simmons	Clothing Designer
Minnefex	Special Effects Design & Production
(Mike Berglund and Dave Weiberg)	
Dale Newton	Second Unit Director
Dave Reynolds	Music
John Gaspard	Editor
Kathleen Laughlin	Consulting Editor
Kelly Kersting	Editing Assistance
Kathy Hedberg	Editing Assistance
Jeff Vlaming	Special Effects Art Direction

"Reach For A Star" (Theme from "Resident Alien")
Written & Produced by Dave Reynolds
Sung By Ruth MacKenzie

Press kit: sample production notes

"Resident Alien" Production Notes

Making a low-budget movie is like riding a roller coaster without a seat belt — it's loaded with fun, excitement, terror, and you're never sure if you can hold on until the end. At least that's the way director John Gaspard and writer-producer Dale Newton describe their experience shooting *Resident Alien*, a science fiction-comedy feature film.

"There were many points when the work behind us and ahead of us looked overwhelming, and we asked ourselves, 'Why do we want to do this?'" Gaspard said. "And then we'd grin ear-to-ear, because the answer was obvious: We were having the time of our lives."

The production was full of new challenges for the pair from Minnesota who founded Granite Productions, Ltd. to make feature films in the Midwest. But by combining their skills, they were able to guide the project to a smooth completion.

"We both had experience in different parts of the process," Gaspard said. "I had directed or produced five other feature-length projects on Super 8mm and video, while Dale was experienced with special effects and the technical considerations of 16mm. Plus we're both screenwriters, so we started with a strong screenplay and collaborated to turn it into a film."

The film chronicles how a UFO crash changes the lives of Cal (Patrick Coyle) and Leslie (Nesba Crenshaw), two down-on-their-luck residents of a small Midwestern town. Comedy, romance, and intrigue are provided by an enigmatic stranger (Mark Patrick Gleason); an unscrupulous UFO investigator (Richard Gibbons); a wily small-town sheriff (John Munger); and other characters (Amelia Barnes, Eve Black, Nancy Gormley, Michael Paul Levin, Craig McNamara, Janet Mitchko, Tom Monn, Marvel Newton) who help and hinder Cal and Leslie's pursuit of their dreams.

"It's appropriate that the film's main characters are striving to achieve impossible goals. That pretty much describes the making of this movie," Newton said.

- more -

Other resources

The following lists are not comprehensive; they are only a starting point in your search for the services and supplies that you need. These listings do not imply any endorsement by the authors. Buyer beware.

Independent Feature Project offices

Independent Feature Project
East
104 West 29th Street
12th Floor
New York, NY 10001
Phone: (212) 465-8200
Fax: (212) 465-8525
E-mail: ifpny@ifp.org
www.ifp.org

Independent Feature Project
Midwest
1803 W. Byron
Suite 1E
Chicago, IL 60613
Phone: (773) 281-5177
Fax: (773) 281-5178
www.ifp.org

Independent Feature Project
North
401 North Third Street, Suite 450
Minneapolis, MN 55401
Phone: (612) 338-0871
Fax: (612) 338-4747
E-mail: info@ifpnorth.org
www.ifp.org

Independent Feature Project
South
210 Second Street
Miami Beach, FL 33139
Phone: (305) 538-8242
www.ifp.org

Independent Feature Project
West
1964 Westwood Boulevard
Suite 205
Los Angeles, CA 90025
Phone: (310) 475-4379
Fax: (310) 441-5676
E-mail:
dearifpwest@earthlink.net
www.ifp.org

Web sites
(Please note that this list only scratches the surface and that it was out-of-date the instant we typed it. However, many of the sites mentioned offer links to other, newer sites.)

Features and Shorts

Always Independent Films
www.alwaysif.com

AtomFilms
www.atomfilms.com

Ifilm
www.ifilm.com

The Sync
www.thesync.com

WireBreak Entertainment
www.wirebreak.com

Yahoo! Broadcast
www.broadcast.com/broadband/
movies_and_film

Film.com
www.film.com

Pop.com
www.pop.com

Bijou Cafe
www.bijoucafe.com

Undergroundfilm.com
www.undergroundfilm.com

ShortBUZZ
www.shortbuzz.com

SCREEN 47
www.screen47.com

Educational Sites

Cinema
www.learner.org/exhibits/
cinema

The Complete Eejits Guide To Filmmaking
www.exposure.co.uk/eejit

Cyber Film School
www.cyberfilmschool.com

The Film Maker's Home Pages
www.filmmaker.com

Film Secrets
www.rivalquest.com

Next Wave Films
www.nextwavefilms.com

Film Festival Resources

www.filmfestivals.com

www.film.com/reviews/rev_ff

www.moviemaker.com/festival/
index.html

www.eurofilmfest.org

www.filmland.com/festivals/
index.html

dir.yahoo.com/entertainment/
movies_and_film/film_festivals

www.insidefilm.com

Film Commissions

www.hollywoodnetwork.com/hn/
producing/usfcs.html

www.entertainet.com/
film_com/filmcom_htm

Movie Scripts Online

www.dailyscript.com

www.script-o-rama.com

www.movie-page.com/
movie_scripts.htm

www.geocities.com/nashville/2237
/script1.htm

www.screentalk.org/gallery.htm

Educational resources

The American Film Institute
2021 North Western Avenue
Los Angeles, CA 90027
Phone: (323) 856-7600
Fax: (323) 467-4578
www.afionline.org

Association of Independent Video
and Filmmakers
304 Hudson Street
New York, NY 10013
Phone: (212) 807-1400
Fax: (212) 463-8519
E-mail: info@aivf.org
wwwaivf.org

Film Arts Foundation
346 Ninth Street
San Francisco, CA 94103
Phone: (415) 552-8760
Fax: (415) 552-0882
www.filmarts.org

Dov S-S Simens
Hollywood Film Institute
Phone: (800) 366-3456
www.hollywoodu.com

Sundance Institute
225 Santa Monica Boulevard
8th Floor
Santa Monica, CA 90401
Phone: (310) 394-4662
Fax: (310) 394-8353
www.sundance.org

Tape-to-film transfers

(There are many vendors supplying this service. This one is included because its Web site offers a lot of good preproduction information if you are planning to make a film print of your digital movie.)

DVFilm
2819 Foster Lane, Suite F150
Austin, TX 78757
Voice and Fax: (512) 459-0502
Cell phone: (512) 497-2271
www.dvfilm.com

Videotape suppliers

New Tape

The Tape Company
Corporate Headquarters
325-A West Lake Street
Elmhurst, IL 60126
Phone: (800) 851-3113
Fax: (630) 758-0930
with offices in
Atlanta, GA
Irvine, CA
Pittsburgh, PA
Cincinnati, OH
Kansas City, MO
Philadelphia, PA
Columbus, OH
Miami, FL
San Francisco, CA
Dallas, TX
Minneapolis, MN
Seattle, WA
Detroit, MI
New York, NY
Plano, TX (Telesales only)
Hollywood, CA
Orlando, FL

Recycled Videotape

Coarc Video
P.O. Box 2
Route 217
Mellenville, NY 12544
Phone: (800) 888-4451

Evaluated Videotape

Carpel Video
429 E. Patrick Street
Frederick, MD 21701
Phone: (800) 238-4300
Fax: (301) 694-9510
www.carpelvideo.com

Where to buy movie scripts

Script City
8033 Sunset Boulevard
Suite 1500
Hollywood, CA 90046
Phone: (800) 676-2522
www.scriptcity.net

Hollywood Book City
6627 Hollywood Boulevard
Hollywood, CA 90028
Phone: (323) 466-2525
Fax: (323) 962-6742
www.hollywoodbookcity.com

Publications

The Hollywood Reporter
5055 Wilshire Boulevard
Los Angeles, CA 90036
Phone: (323) 525-2000
www.hollywoodreporter.com

Variety
5700 Wilshire Boulevard,
Suite 120
Los Angeles, CA 90036
Phone: (323) 857-6600
www.variety.com

Free magazines for production professionals
(Remember, you're a producer now.)

AV Video Multimedia Producer
P.O. Box 3034
Northbrook, IL 60065-3034
Fax: (847) 291-4816
www.avvideo.com

DV Magazine
P.O. Box 1212
Skokie, IL 60076-8212
Fax: (847) 647-5972

Millimeter
P.O. Box 1170
Skokie, IL 60076-8170
Fax: (847) 647-7543
www.millimeter.com

Video Systems
P.O. Box 12912
Overland Park, KS 66282-2912
Fax: (913) 967-1903
www.videosystems.com

Videography
P.O. Box 0513
Baldwin, NY 11510-0513
Fax: (212) 378-2159

Copyright and script registration

U.S. Copyright Office
Library of Congress
101 Independence Ave. S.E.
Washington, DC 20559-6000
www.loc.gov/copyright/

Writers Guild of America,
West
Registration Department
7000 West Third St.
Los Angeles, CA 90048
Telephone (323) 782-4500
Fax: (323) 782-4803
www.wga.org/manuals/
registration.html

Photo processing

PhotoWorks
Elliot Bay at Pier 89
1260 16th Avenue West
Seattle, WA 98119-3401
Phone: (800) 746-8696
www.PhotoWorks.com

Skrudland Photo
5311 Fleming Court
Austin, TX 78744-1197
Phone: (512) 444-0958

Walgreen's Photo Centers
Call (800) 925-4733 for location.
*(In blind tests judged by professional
photographers, their photo processing
ranked better than that of many high-
priced professional labs.)*

Incorporating in Delaware

State of Delaware
Division of Corporations
P.O. Box 898
Dover, DE 19903
Phone: (302) 739-3073
www.state.de.us

Corporate-stock rules

Security and Exchange
Commission
(See "Small Business Information")
www.sec.gov

Business tax forms

Internal Revenue Service
www.irs.treas.gov
*(Business and nonprofit forms and
publications along with some wacky
IRS humor)*

BIBLIOGRAPHY

While we don't recommend blowing your budget on a new library, we also recognize that this one book is by no means the final word. Most of the following books can be found at the library or can be read while standing in the stacks at your favorite book store.

Abbott, L. B. *Special Effects: Wire, Tape and Rubber Band Style.* Hollywood: The ASC Press, 1984.

Bayer, William. *Breaking Through, Selling Out, Dropping Dead And Other Notes On Filmmaking.* New York: Limelight Editions, 1971, 1989.

Blake, Larry. *Film Sound Today: An Anthology of Articles From Recording Engineers and Producers.* Reveille Press, 1984.

Bobker, Lee R. *Elements of Film.* New York: Harcourt Brace Jovanovich, Inc., 1974.

Brady, John. *The Craft of the Screenwriter.* New York: Simon and Schuster, 1981.

Buchanan, Mark A., and Thomas, David John. *Simplified Business Incorporation: A Self-Help Manual — Minnesota Procedure.* St. Cloud, Minn.: Small Business Development Center, St. Cloud State University.

Chamness, Danford. *The Hollywood Guide to Film Budgeting and Script Breakdown for Low Budget Features.* Los Angeles: The Stanley J. Brooks Company, 1988.

Clark, Frank P. *Special Effects in Motion Pictures.* Hollywood: Society of Motion Picture and Television Engineers.

Corman, Roger, with Jerome, Jim. *How I Made A Hundred Movies In Hollywood And Never Lost A Dime.* New York: Random House, 1990.

Detmers, Fred H., ed. *American Cinematographers Manual*. Hollywood: The ASC Press, 1986.

Beacham, Frank. *American Cinematographer Video Manual — 2nd Edition*. Hollywood: The ASC Press, 1994.

Eisen, Peter J. *Accounting*. New York: Barron's Educational Series, Inc., 1985.

Engel, Joel. *Screenwriters on Screenwriting*. Hyperion, 1995.

Field, Syd. *Screenplay: The Foundations of Screenwriting*. New York: Dell Publishing Co., Inc., 1979, 1982.

Field, Syd. *The Screenwriter's Workbook*. New York: Dell Publishing Co., Inc., 1984.

Froug, William. *The New Screenwriter Looks At The New Screenwriter*. Los Angeles: Silman-James Press, 1992.

Gaspard, John, and Newton, Dale. *Persistence of Vision: An Impractical Guide to Producing a Feature Film for Under $30,000*. Los Angeles: Michael Wiese Productions, 1996.

Gelmis, Joseph. *The Film Director As Superstar*. New York: Doubleday, 1970.

Glimcher, Sumner, and Johnson, Warren. *Movie Making: A Guide to Film Production*. New York: Simon & Schuster, Inc., Pocket Books, 1975.

Goldman, William. *Adventures In The Screen Trade*. New York: Warner Books, 1983.

Goldman, William. *William Goldman: Five Screenplays*. Applause Books, 1994.

Goldner, Orville, and Turner, George E. *The Making of King Kong*. New York: Ballantine Books, 1976.

Goodell, Gregory. *Independent Feature Film Production*. New York: St. Martin's Press, 1982.

Grodin, Charles. *It Would Be So Nice If You Weren't Here*. Vintage Books, A Division of Random House, Inc., 1989.

Hamilton, Peter, and Rosen, David. *Off-Hollywood: The Making and Marketing of Independent Films*. New York: Grove Weidenfeld, 1990.

Hunter, Lew. *Lew Hunter's Screenwriting 434*. New York: Perigee Books, Putnam Publishing Group, 1993.

Hurst, Walter E., and Hale, William Storm. *Motion Picture Distribution: Business or Racket?* Hollywood: Seven Arts Press, 1975, 1977.

Kael, Pauline, Mankiewicz, Herman J., and Welles, Orson. *The Citizen Kane Book*. New York: Bantam Books, 1971.

Karlin, Fred. *Listening To Movies — The Film Lover's Guide To Film Music*. Schirmer Books, 1994.

Karlin, Fred, and Wright, Rayburn. *On The Track — A Guide To Contemporary Film Scoring*. Schirmer Books, 1990.

Katz, Steven D. *Film Directing Shot By Shot*. Los Angeles: Michael Wiese Productions, 1991.

Katz, Steven D. *Film Directing Cinematic Motion*. Los Angeles: Michael Wiese Productions, 1998.

Litwak, Mark. *Deal Making In The Film And Television Industry*. Los Angeles: Silman-James Press, 1994.

Litwak, Mark. *Contracts In The Film And Television Industry*. Los Angeles: Silman-James Press, 1995.

Lumet, Sidney. *Making Movies*. Alfred A. Knopf, 1995.

Lyons, Donald. *Independent Visions*. New York: Ballantine Books, 1994.

Pintoff, Ernest. *Directing 101.* Los Angeles: Michael Wiese Productions, 1999.

Rosenblum, Ralph, and Karen, Robert. *When The Shooting Stops... The Cutting Begins.* New York: Penguin Books, 1979.

Sautter, Carl. *How To Sell Your Screenplay: The Real Rules Of Film And Television.* New York: New Chapter Press, 1988.

Schanzer, Karl, and Wright, Thomas Lee. *American Screenwriters: The Insiders' Look At The Art, The Craft, And The Business of Writing Movies.* New York: Avon Books, 1993.

Schmidt, Rick. *Feature Filmmaking At Used Car Prices.* New York: Penguin Books, 1988.

Sherman, Eric. *Directing The Film: Film Directors On Their Art.* Boston: Little, Brown and Company, 1976.

Seger, Linda. *Making A Good Script Great.* New York: Dodd, Mead & Company, 1987.

Vogler, Christopher. *The Writer's Journey.* Los Angeles: Michael Wiese Productions, 1993.

Warshawski, Morrie. *Shaking The Money Tree.* Los Angeles: Michael Wiese Productions, 1992.

Weston, Judith. *Directing Actors — Creating Memorable Performances for Film and Television.* Los Angeles: Michael Wiese Productions, 1996.

Wiese, Michael. *Film & Video Financing.* Los Angeles: Michael Wiese Productions, 1989.

Wiese, Michael. *Film & Video Marketing.* Los Angeles: Michael Wiese Productions, 1988.

Wiese, Michael. *The Independent Film & Videomakers Guide.* Los Angeles: Michael Wiese Productions, revised 1990.

Wiese, Michael. *Producer to Producer*. Los Angeles: Michael Wiese Productions, 1993.

Wiese, Michael, and Simon, Deke. *Film & Video Budgets*. Los Angeles: Michael Wiese Productions, 1995, revised 2000.

Wolff, Jurgen, and Cox, Kerry. *Top Secrets: Screenwriting*. Los Angeles: Lone Eagle Publishing Company, 1993.

FILMOGRAPHY

This is a list of the movies mentioned or alluded to in this book.

11 Harrowhouse. Twentieth Century-Fox, 1974.

2001: A Space Odyssey. Warner Bros., 1968.

Annie Hall. MGM/UA, 1977.

Betrayal. Twentieth Century-Fox, 1983.

Beyond Bob. Granite Productions, Ltd., 1995.

The Birds. Universal, 1963.

The Blair Witch Project. Artisan Entertainment, 1999.

Carnal Knowledge. MGM/UA, 1971.

Casablanca. Warner Bros., 1943.

Citizen Kane. R.K.O. Radio Pictures, Inc., 1941.

Clerks. Miramax, 1994.

Dr. Strangelove. Warner Bros., 1964.

El Mariachi. Columbia/Tristar, 1993.

Ernest Goes To Camp. Buena Vista, 1987.

Four Weddings and a Funeral. MGM/UA, 1994.

Glory. Columbia/Tristar, 1989.

Gone With the Wind. Warner Bros., 1939.

The Graduate. MGM/UA, 1967.

Grown Men. Granite Productions, Unlimited, 2001.

Guess Who's Coming To Dinner? Columbia/Tristar, 1967.

It's A Mad, Mad, Mad, Mad World. MGM/UA, 1963.

King Kong. R.K.O. Radio Pictures, Inc., 1933.

The Last Seduction. USA Films, 1994.

Legends Of The Fall. Columbia/Tristar, 1995.

Little Murders. Twentieth Century-Fox, 1971.

Living In Oblivion. Columbia/Tristar, 1995.

The Matrix. Warner Bros., 1999.

The Night They Raided Minsky's. MGM/UA, 1968.

The Passenger. Warner Bros., 1975.

Plan 10 From Outer Space. LEO Home Video, 1994.

The Player. New Line Cinema, 1992.

Postcards From The Edge. Columbia/Tristar, 1990.

Pulp Fiction. Miramax, 1994.

Red Rock West. Columbia/Tristar, 1994.

Resident Alien. Granite Productions, Ltd., 1991.

Resident Alien (a.k.a. *Resident Alien: Quentin Crisp in America*). Films Around The World, 1991.

Run, Lola, Run. Columbia/Tristar, 1999.

Schindler's List. Universal, 1993.

The Sound Of Music. Twentieth Century-Fox, 1965.

Star Wars. Twentieth Century-Fox, 1977.

Star Wars: The Phantom Menace. Twentieth Century-Fox, 1999.

Stranger Than Paradise. MGM/UA, 1984.

A Thousand Clowns. MGM/UA, 1965.

Touch Of Evil. Universal, 1958.

Toy Story. Pixar, 1995.

The Truman Show. Paramount, 1998.

Waterworld. Universal, 1995.

Windhorse. New Yorker Films, 1998.

The Wizard Of Oz. MGM, 1939.

ABOUT THE AUTHORS

When it comes to producing successful movies on a shoe-string, John Gaspard and Dale Newton know of what they speak.

Together they created *Grown Men*, a completely digital feature, as well as *Resident Alien* and *Beyond Bob*, two critically acclaimed ultra-low-budget feature films.

Dale Newton wrote and produced *Resident Alien*, produced *Beyond Bob*, and was executive producer on *Grown Men*. He's an award-winning writer of numerous screenplays and scripts. He's also received awards for his work producing and directing films, videos, and audiovisual projects, which he has done for more than 20 years. An early goal in life was to avoid working as an accountant or business manager. Sadly, producing three feature movies has dashed both those dreams.

Besides *Grown Men*, *Resident Alien*, and *Beyond Bob*, John Gaspard has also directed, written, or produced four other features. John got into filmmaking when he heard it was the fastest route to fame, riches, and meeting intriguing women. It was only after doing it for 20 years that he realized he'd been misinformed. His writing credits include American Public Radio's *Good Evening* and *First House On The Right* programs, along with episodes of the popular European comic-western television series *Lucky Luke*, starring Terence Hill.

Authors Dale Newton (left) and John Gaspard making decisions on the set of their digital feature movie, Grown Men.
(Photo courtesy of Granite Productions, Unlimited.)

YOU'VE READ THE BOOK ...
NOW SEE THE MOVIES!

To find out more about our three ultra-low-budget features, "Resident Alien," "Beyond Bob," and our digital feature, "Grown Men," please visit our web site at: **www.graniteproductions.org**

Each feature was produced using techniques outlined in this book.

"Resident Alien" mixes comedy, science fiction, and romance to create a memorable story about the dangers and complications that occur when you wish on a star -- and your dreams come true.

"Beyond Bob" is an award-winning comedy from the other side. It's a story of love and friendship, of passion from beyond the grave, and of a love that was made in heaven ... and was just too darned important to stay there.

"Grown Men" is a comic-drama with four interlocking stories about love, romance, sex and friendship.

Granite Productions, Unlimited
P.O. Box 852
Stillwater, MN 55082
www.graniteproductions.org

DIGITAL MOVIEMAKING
A BUTT-KICKING, PIXEL-TWISTING VISION OF THE DIGITAL FUTURE AND HOW TO MAKE YOUR NEXT MOVIE ON YOUR CREDIT CARD

BY SCOTT BILLUPS

NEW!

You've got the script. You've got the vision. Now all you need is a deal to get your film made. But what if the powers-that-be say no? Do you have to give up your dream? Not any more. The digital revolution has made it cheaper and more possible than ever before for people to shoot and edit their own professional-quality films. This book will show you how to grab the bull by the horns and make your dream a reality.

Written for both experienced film and video directors who are new to the digital format and up-and-comers new to filmmaking in general, video guru Scott Billups' guide takes you through the brave new world of digital

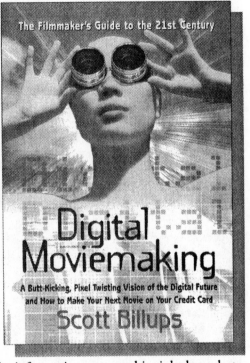

The Filmmaker's Guide to the 21st Century

Digital Moviemaking

A Butt-Kicking, Pixel Twisting Vision of the Digital Future and How to Make Your Next Movie on Your Credit Card

Scott Billups

moviemaking. All the nuts-and-bolts information you need is right here, but technophobes need not fret. Billups explains in clear, concise, plain English what all these new terms and tools mean, and why it's not as hard as you think. He'll show you how to choose the technology that best fits your needs (and budget!) and how to get the maximum effect out of your equipment. Learn about different formats, effects tools, and cameras, as well as issues and challenges unique to shooting digitally.

ORDER # 2RLS
$26.95
ISBN: 0-941188-30-2

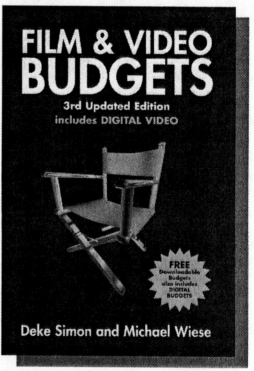

The Independent Film and Videomaker's Guide

—2nd Edition
Expanded & Updated

Michael Wiese

This is the new, completely expanded and revised edition with all the information you need from fundraising through distribution. A practical and comprehensive book that will help filmmakers save time and money and inspire them to create successful projects.

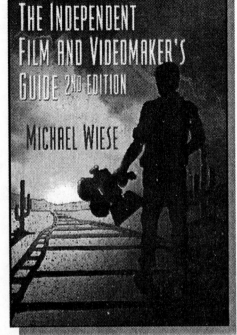

Contents include:

- writing a business plan
- developing your ideas into concepts, treatments and scripts
- directing, producing, market research
- distribution markets (theatrical, home videos, television, international)
- financing your film
- how to do presentations, writing a prospectus
- Plus an appendix filled with film cash flow projections, sample contracts, valuable contact addresses, and much more.

Using the principles outlined in this book, Wiese recently co-directed a 20 minute short film titled "Field of Fish," and is currently developing an independent feature film, *Must Be Love*, to be filmed in England. Additionally, Wiese is national spokesperson for Kodak's Emerging Filmmakers Program. He has conducted his workshops on independent filmmaking in England, Germany, Finland, Indonesia, Ireland, Canada, Australia and throughout the US. Contact Wiese at mw@mwp.com.

"The prospectus/business plan (section) of this new edition is alone worth the price of the book."
Release Print, Dec/Jan 1999

"Required reading for anyone serious about making pictures. I recommend

Wiese's book not as a source, but THE source for information regarding independent film and video producing."
Sam L. Grogg
Dean, AFI Center for Advanced Film and Television Studies

"A significant contribution to the literature on independent film production. A "must-read" for anyone seriously interested in independent film."
John Mason
Director of Kodak Worldwide Emerging Filmmaker Program

$29.95, ISBN 0-941188-57-4
500 pages, illustrations, 6 x 9
Order # 37RLS

Film Directing: Shot by Shot

Visualizing from Concept to Screen

Steven D. Katz

An instant classic since its debut in 1991, "Film Directing: Shot by Shot" and its famous blue cover is one of the most well-known books on directing in the business, and is a favorite of professional directors as an on-set quick reference guide. This international bestseller is packed with visual techniques for filmmakers and screenwriters to expand their stylistic knowledge.

Contains in-depth information on shot composition, staging sequences, previsualization, depth of frame, camera techniques, and much more.

Contains over 750 storyboards and illustrations, including never before published storyboards from Steven Spielberg's *Empire of the Sun*, Orson Welles' *Citizen Kane*, and Alfred Hitchcock's *The Birds*.

Over 100,000 Sold!

film directing
shot by shot
visualizing from concept to screen

by steven d. katz

> "(To become a director) you have to teach yourself what makes movies good and what makes them bad. John Singleton has been my mentor...he's the one who told me what movies to watch and to read the book Shot by Shot."

Ice Cube, Rap artist, actor and filmmaker
Quoted in *The New York Times*, April 16, 1998

Doubleday Stage & Screen Book Club Selection
Movie Entertainment Book Club Selection

$27.95, ISBN: 0-941188-10-8
370 pages, 7 x 10, 750+ illus.
Order # 7RLS

Both Katz books only $44

Setting Up Your Shots:

Great Camera Moves Every Filmmaker Should Know

Jeremy Vineyard

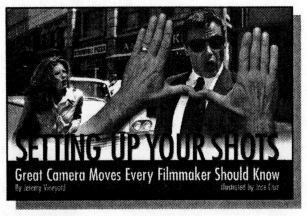

Whether you need to learn the difference between a jump cut and a match cut or you're a working filmmaker looking for visual ideas on how to best communicate the stories you want to tell, *Setting Up Your Shots* is an encyclopedia of camera moves and cinematic storytelling techniques that directors of all levels will find useful.

Written in clear, non-technical language and laid out in a nonlinear format with self-contained chapters for easy reference, this book provides detailed descriptions of more than 100 camera setups, angles and techniques, using examples from over 140 popular films. An excellent primer for beginning filmmakers, as well as a handy quick-reference guide for experienced directors.

Contains 150 references to the great shots of your favorite films, including *2001: A Space Odyssey, Blue Velvet, Citizen Kane, The Matrix, She's Gotta Have It, The Usual Suspects* and *Vertigo.*

> *"Perfect for any film enthusiast looking for the secrets behind creating film...it is a great addition to the collection of students and film pros alike."*
> **Ross Otterman**
> *Directed By* Magazine

JEREMY VINEYARD is a Los Angeles-based writer, director and software engineer. He has just completed post-production on *The Meridian Project*, a sci-fi short film he wrote and directed. He is also working on an epic fantasy graphic novel series called Paraxis™, which you can learn more about by visiting **www.paraxis.com**.

Doubleday Stage and Screen Selection

$19.95, ISBN 0-941188-73-6
135 pages, 11 x 7, horizontal wide screen format
Order # 8RLS

THE WRITER'S JOURNEY
2nd Edition
Mythic Structure for Writers

Christopher Vogler

See why this book has become an international best-seller and a true classic. First published in 1992, *The Writer's Journey* explores the powerful relationship between mythology and storytelling in a clear, concise style that's made it required reading for movie executives, screenwriters, scholars, and fans of pop culture all over the world.

Both fiction and nonfiction writers will discover a set of useful myth-inspired storytelling paradigms (i.e., "The Hero's Journey") and step-by-step guidelines to plot and character development. Based on the work of Joseph Campbell, *The Writer's Journey* is a must for all writers interested in further developing their craft.

THE WRITER'S JOURNEY
2ND EDITION
MYTHIC STRUCTURE FOR WRITERS

CHRISTOPHER VOGLER

The updated and revised 2nd Edition provides new insights, observations, and film references from Vogler's ongoing work on mythology's influence on stories, movies, and man himself.

Christopher Vogler, a top Hollywood story consultant and development executive, has worked on such high-grossing feature films as The Lion King *and* The Thin Red Line *and conducts writing workshops around the globe.*

$24.95
Order # 98RLS
ISBN: 0-941188-70-1

Directing Actors

Creating Memorable Performances for Film & Television

Judith Weston

The most crucial relationship on a movie set is between the director responsible for the telling of a story and the actors entrusted with bringing that story's characters to life. Good communication between actor and director can mean the difference between a great film and a missed opportunity.

Directing Actors is a method for establishing creative, collaborative relationships between actors and directors that takes the reader on a journey through the complexities of the creative process itself. Using simple, practical tools that both directors and actors can use immediately, this book shows you how to get the most out of rehearsals, troubleshoot poor performances, and give directions that are clear, succinct and easy to follow.

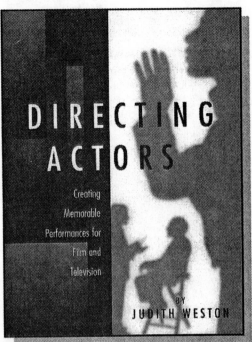

"This is everything a director should know about working with actors."
Steven Charles Jaffe, Executive Producer, *Ghost*; producer, *Star Trek VI, Strange Days*

"I think that if Judith's book were mandatory reading for all directors, the quality of the director-actor process would be transformed, and better drama would result."
John Patterson, Director, *The Sopranos, The Practice, Law and Order, Hill Street Blues, Rockford Files*

"Judith's course is probably the single best thing you could do for yourself as a director. I was able to use the techniques the very next day on the set. Judith has made a difference in my career."
Brian Roberts, Director, *Everybody Loves Raymond, The Drew Carey Show, King of Queens, The Hughleys*

Doubleday Stage & Screen Book Club Selection

JUDITH WESTON draws on 20 years of experience as an actress and teacher of acting. With her seminars, workshops and private consultations, she has helped thousands of actors refine their craft and nearly as many directors clarify their directing and casting choices.

$26.95, ISBN 0-941118-24-8
300 pages, 6 x 9
Order # 4RLS

ORDER FORM

MICHAEL WIESE PRODUCTIONS
11288 VENTURA BLVD., # 621
STUDIO CITY, CA 91604
E-MAIL: MWPSALES@MWP.COM
WEB SITE: WWW.MWP.COM

WRITE OR FAX FOR A FREE CATALOG

PLEASE SEND ME THE FOLLOWING BOOKS:

TITLE	ORDER NUMBER (#RLS _____)	AMOUNT
	SHIPPING	
	CALIFORNIA TAX (8.00%)	
	TOTAL ENCLOSED	

PLEASE MAKE CHECK OR MONEY ORDER PAYABLE TO:

MICHAEL WIESE PRODUCTIONS

(CHECK ONE) ____ MASTERCARD ____VISA ____AMEX

CREDIT CARD NUMBER _____

EXPIRATION DATE _____

CARDHOLDER'S NAME _____

CARDHOLDER'S SIGNATURE _____

SHIP TO:

NAME _____

ADDRESS _____

CITY _____ STATE _____ ZIP _____

COUNTRY _____ TELEPHONE _____

Printed in the United States
60929LVS00003B/10